Also available from Northwest Parent Publishing, Inc.:

MONTHLY NEWSMAGAZINES FOR PARENTS
Eastside Parent
Portland Parent
Puget Sound Parent
Seattle's Child
Snohomish County Parent

BOOKS
Going Places: Family Getaways in the Pacific Northwest
Out and About Seattle with Kids

OUT AND ABOUT

PORTLAND

WITH KIDS

The Ultimate Family Guide for Fun and Learning

BY ELIZABETH HARTZELL DeSIMONE

RESEARCH ASSISTANT:
MARILYN SOULAS

FIRST EDITION

FROM THE PUBLISHERS OF

PORTLAND
Parent

ACKNOWLEDGEMENTS

To research assistant Marilyn Soulas,
who gave more than she thought possible.
To proofreader/fact-checker Anina Bennett,
who now knows what to do with children,
should she ever decide to have some.
To my friends, if I still have any.
To my children, who learned the meaning of "sacrifice."
And to Sam, who knows why.

Northwest Parent Publishing, Inc.
2107 Elliott Avenue, Suite 303
Seattle, Washington 98121 U.S.A.
(206) 441-0191

IBSN: 0-9614626-7-1

Layout and Design: John Rusnak

TABLE OF CONTENTS

HOW TO USE THIS BOOK:

The listings in *Out and About Portland with Kids* were current at press time, but I urge you to confirm locations, hours, and prices of selected destinations.

Tips (otherwise known as "best-kept secrets and unsolicited advice") are included with many entries to help you plan the most rewarding adventures.

The Quick Index, beginning on page 228, offers outing suggestions that meet specific needs.

Four icons appear regularly throughout:

Offers classes and/or workshops for children

Offers birthday-party packages

Offers field trips for schools or large groups

Features facilities that are accessible to persons in wheelchairs

INTRODUCTION

I moved 3,000 miles on a hunch. In 1990, my husband, toddler twins, and I settled in Portland because we had a good feeling about the place: big enough to be exciting, yet small enough to be accessible; busy enough to offer career challenges, yet calm enough to leave parents with time for their children. Portland appeared to be capable of satisfying our professional and personal needs.

As the editor of *Portland Parent*, the region's pre-eminent monthly newsmagazine for parents, I've spent six years confirming what my sixth sense long ago knew to be true: Portland is a city that works for families. My three children, husband, and I have romped, tramped, and camped; hiked and biked; dined and (occasionally) whined our way around town. We've visited museums, attended plays and concerts, hosted birthday parties, and gone sightseeing. The day the word "outing" met with the same crestfallen expression my children use for "spinach," I knew I had enough data for a book.

As the region's definitive guidebook for parents, *Out and About Portland with Kids* is more candid than comprehensive. But I didn't feel confident relying solely on personal experience. I sifted through our office files of event listings, articles about kids' programs and facilities, and news about current plans and projects that will affect local youths. I interviewed children, teachers, parents, grandparents, aunts, and uncles, to gather ideas from a wide segment of the community. Then I weeded out the mediocre, checked and re-checked the rest, and focused on the best.

I trust *Out and About Portland with Kids* will prove to be as indispensable to adventurous families as Kleenex and Band-aids.

—Elizabeth Hartzell DeSimone
May 1997

Chapter 1

EXPLORING DOWNTOWN

The best way to experience downtown Portland is on foot. Grasp your child's hand in yours, keep him against your right flank (sheltered from traffic) and slow to his speed. He'll sense immediately by your revised pace that this isn't errand-running, this is something special.

Make a pact: He'll forgo pebbles, dropped coins, and cracks in the sidewalk, and you'll forgo window-shopping. Now, look at the statues, fountains, and buildings (many boast intricate architectural features). You've never seen Portland like this before. This is a treasure hunt.

Portland's shorter city blocks lend themselves to walkers—and to shorter legs—but even the best hikers grow weary and need a rest. A downtown walking tour can be especially ambitious, and even more fun, if you arrange to return to the car by public transportation.

Tri-Met

Tri-Met manages Portland's public transit system, which consists of Tri-Met buses, MAX (Metropolitan Area Express) light rail, and vintage trolleys. Within a 300-block section of downtown called Fareless Square, passengers ride Tri-Met buses and light-rail cars for free (trolleys are always free). The square is bordered on the west and south by Interstate 405, on the north by Irving St., and on the east by the Willamette River.

For travel beyond Fareless Square, the basic fee is $1.05; longer rides cost $1.35. Youths age 7-18 pay 80¢, and as many as three children age 6 and under are permitted to ride free with each fare-paying adult. Day passes are available for $3.25.

Place exact change or a ticket in the farebox when boarding the bus. MAX tickets may be purchased and validated using the vending machines at each station. Tri-Met tickets and schedules are available weekdays at Tri-Met's two offices: Pioneer Courthouse Square (SW 6th Ave. & Yamhill); and 4012 SE 17th Ave. Tickets can also be purchased at local Safeway, Albertsons, and Cub Foods stores, and at some Wells Fargo banks. For more information, call the Tri-Met hotline: 238-RIDE.

Most of Tri-Met's 87 bus lines loop through the downtown transit mall on SW 5th and 6th avenues. Shelters line the broad, brick sidewalks of these byways, and auto traffic is minimized and even eliminated along certain sections of the mall.

The MAX light-rail route travels 15 miles east from downtown to Gresham. Trains run every 15 minutes, more often during rush hour. Construction is currently under way to extend light-rail service 18 miles west to Beaverton and Hillsboro, with an estimated completion date of September 1998. For recorded schedule information, call 22-TRAIN.

MAX is only Portland's latest public-transportation innovation. At the turn of the century, electric trolleys offered regular service throughout downtown and into the West Hills. In November 1991, four working replicas of the original Council Crest cars were introduced along a light-rail route that links the downtown shopping district with Lloyd Center on the east side. Free rides are offered 9:30 am-3 pm weekdays, and 10 am-6 pm weekends. Board the trolley along SW Morrison, Yamhill, or 1st Ave., and continue to Holladay Park (NE 11th Ave. & Multnomah). A round trip takes about 40 minutes (May-December, every half-hour daily; March-April, every half-hour weekends only; service suspended January-February). For more information, call 22-TOOTS.

Parking

You can no longer count on finding a parking space when you

need it in the downtown core. But when you do get lucky, be prepared with lots of quarters. On weekdays and Saturdays, 8 am-6 pm, 25¢ will buy you 17 1/2 minutes (that's 90¢ an hour) at a parking meter. Parking is free at night and on Sundays and holidays.

Even parking garages fill up with some regularity these days. The city's most affordable short-term parking is found at any of the seven Smart Park locations downtown (look for their circular, red-and-white signs). Expect to pay 75¢ an hour for the first four hours ($1 an hour at the Portland Building) and about $3 for each additional hour. After 6 pm there is a flat rate of $1.50 for the entire evening, or $3 for all day on weekends ($2.50 in the garage at SW 1st Ave. & Jefferson).

If you're shopping downtown, ask the merchants you patronize about the FreePark program. Nearly 200 participating merchants, including some restaurants and offices (look for FreePark decals), validate the parking tickets of customers who make purchases of $15 or more. Each stamp is good for two hours of free parking at any downtown lot or garage. The merchants pick up the tab. ■

A n inscription on the city's oldest artwork, Old Town's Skidmore Fountain, erected in 1888, reads: "Good citizens are the riches of a city." In Portland, "good" citizens have turned the city into riches.

The Percent for Public Art ordinances, established in the city of Portland and Multnomah County in 1980, require that 1 percent of major capital construction budgets be earmarked for public art. From a mammoth, hammered-copper statue to computerized water fountains to trompe l'oeil (fool-the-eye) murals—there's something curious around virtually every downtown corner.

A Portland trademark almost as recognizable as the rose, the **Benson Bubblers** that punctuate the downtown streetscape have come to symbolize Portland's free-flowing hospitality. In response to his workers' claims that they frequented the saloons in town

The Skidmore Fountain was designed in 1888 to refresh horses, dogs, and people.

because there was no fresh drinking water, teetotaling lumber baron Simon Benson donated $10,000 in 1912 to outfit the city with 20 drinking fountains. The bronze, four-bowl design is that of A.E. Doyle, architect of the Multnomah County Library, Meier & Frank, and U.S. National Bank buildings (see below). There are now 49 Benson Bubblers in Portland. During the drought of 1992, the city installed push buttons for use during periods of water shortage.

When the **Skidmore Fountain** (SW 1st Ave. & Ankeny) was built, its placement marked the center of town. Made of bronze using funds designated for this purpose in druggist Stephen Skidmore's will, the fountain is now a centerpiece of **Saturday Market**, Portland's beloved weekend street fair. More than 200 craft and food vendors cluster under the west end of the Burnside Bridge 10 months of the year (March-December; Saturday, 10 am-5 pm; Sunday, 11 am-4:30 pm; 222-6072) to sell their hand-made wares and homemade treats. Much of what you see, smell, hear,

Named for a generous benefactor, Benson Bubblers dot the streetscape downtown.

and taste is new and unfamiliar; you can travel the world without straying from the makeshift tents.

Keep tabs on the kids, who will inevitably scatter—one in pursuit of a balloon artist, another beguiled by a display of wooden toys, the third hungry for an ice cream cone. It's easy to lose sight of them amid the crowds and warren of booths.

In 1890, Portland's Chinatown was the nation's second largest. Today the neighborhood north of Burnside is rather shabby and not particularly hospitable to families, but it's fun to examine the great **Chinatown Gate** (NW 4th Ave. & Burnside) up close. Dedicated in 1986 to commemorate Portland's Chinese citizens, this authentic design features two fearsome bronze lions, five tiered roofs, and 64 dragons.

Designed in 1917 by architect A.E. Doyle (see Benson Bubblers),

the neoclassical **U.S. National Bank** building (SW Broadway & Stark), with its soaring Corinthian columns, looks like a bank should—imposing, elegant, and above all, permanent. The entrance on 6th Ave. is decorated with glazed, turn-of-the-century terra cotta coins.

TIPS

Think you're lost? Need a public restroom? Portland Guides to the rescue! Sponsored by the Association for Portland Progress, the volunteer guides are trained to offer assistance to downtown visitors. You can't miss them: They dress in kelly-green jackets with identifying APP patches.

This colorful, authentic gate commemorates Portland's Chinese citizens.

Affectionately referred to as the city's "living room," **Pioneer Courthouse Square** (SW Broadway & Yamhill) is another example of forward-thinking civic planning. Once a parking lot, the grand public space is now host to planned cultural events (concerts and festivals) and impromptu gatherings. Brown-bagging executives sprawl on its steps at noon, teens congregate to play hacky-sack, mothers bring their toddlers to romp, and commuters line up for the ride home.

To fund the square's construction in 1984, more than 63,000 personalized bricks were sold. Read the names under your feet. Who

"Allow Me" is but one of many public artworks on permanent display in Pioneer Courthouse Square.

can find "Wm. Shakespeare," "Sherlock Holmes," "Frodo Baggins," and "Bruce Springsteen"? Then hunt for the echo chamber.

Let the kids discover and explore the whimsical artwork in the square: "Allow Me," a life-size bronze gentleman with umbrella; "Mile Post"; and terra cotta columns that pay homage to the city's architectural roots (to name a few). Plan your visit to coincide with lunch hour, and you'll be treated to an electronic fanfare by the "Weather Machine" in the northwest corner. See the wrought-iron gate and fence? It once graced the Portland Hotel, which was built in 1890 on this spot. The elegant hotel played host to eight U.S. presidents and Portland's high society until 1951.

Opened in 1875, **Pioneer**

Courthouse (SW 6th Ave. & Yamhill, 326-2115) is the oldest U.S. courthouse on the West Coast. Still in use today, by the U.S. Court of Appeals and the U.S. Post Office, the building is open to the public on weekdays, 8 am-5 pm.

Take the elevator to the third floor, then continue up the stairs to the glass-enclosed cupola for a view of the city and mountains beyond. (If the door's locked, ask a security officer for assistance.) The rippling of the aged glass, and the historic photographs up here, put it all in perspective.

Flanking the courthouse on SW Yamhill and Morrison is a series of concrete pools decorated with native animals and birds cast in bronze—seals, bears, ducks, otters. Let the kids perch on a deer and pet a beaver.

Few children can resist "Animals in Pools," which flanks Pioneer Courthouse.

TIPS

Atwater's Restaurant, 30 floors up in Portland's tallest building, the U.S. Bank Tower (111 SW 5th Ave., 275–3600), boasts the best view in town. Call ahead to schedule a visit before 3 pm, when Atwater's is operated as a private club, or come after 3 pm, when the restaurant is open to the public. If you're lucky, the auditorium on the 41st floor will be vacant, and you'll be treated to a 360–degree panorama.

Portland has been called unsophisticated, provincial, sleepy—even backward. There was even a time, in 1974, when the governor razed a freeway to build ... a park! **Tom McCall Waterfront Park**, which stretches for 22 blocks along the west shore of the Willamette, stands as a testament to progressive visions of civic development.

A riverside greenway first conceived in 1904 by the Olmsted brothers, Boston's landscaping gurus, the park is a focal point for fair-weather recreation and festivities. It's fun to bike or rollerblade by the harbor and along the promenade, but if you walk, you're more likely to enjoy the scenery.

Begin at the Steel Bridge. **Friendship Circle**, erected in 1990, commemorates Portland's 30-year association with sister city Sapporo, Japan. A collaboration between sculptor Lee Kelly and composer Michael Stirling, the stainless-steel sculpture resonates with sounds that are reminiscent of the flutes and drums of Japan.

A maze of image and word pathways etched in granite paving stones, **The Story Garden** (just south of the Burnside Bridge) was commissioned in 1993 in response to citizens' requests for a children's playground in Waterfront Park. It sits on a site that was previously rife with drug use and late-night carousing, and now elicits life-affirming conversation. Move from slab to slab as you would on a game board, and create a story. Play King of the Hill on the massive granite throne. Or share your responses to the tough questions, e.g., "What is your sadness?" or "Why is there evil?".

Blink and you'll miss it. That's **Mill Ends Park** (SW Front Ave. & Taylor), the world's smallest. It used

"Friendship Circle" marks the beginning—or is it the end?—of Tom McCall Waterfront Park.

REGIONAL ARTS AND CULTURE COUNSEL

TIPS

"Essential Forces" makes "Salmon Street Springs" look like a romp through the backyard sprinklers. Constructed as a gift to the city by multibillionaire Paul Allen, and sited at the main entrance to his new east-side arena—the Rose Garden (1 Center Ct.)—this impressive computerized fountain features 500 water jets and two towers that emit geyser-force blasts of water and gusting flames. Come in summer dressed for water play and slathered with sunscreen (there isn't much shade in the plaza), and bring a blanket to spread out on the unforgiving pavement.

Parking in Rose Quarter garages is free for 30 minutes. After that, it pays to duck into one of the plaza restaurants for refreshments and a validation stamp, which buys you an additional 2 1/2 hours of free parking. Of course, you may be drawn into the restaurants for a more immediate pur-

Dragon boat

pose: They have the plaza's only restrooms.

The lobby areas of the nearby Oregon Convention Center (777 NE Martin Luther King Jr. Blvd.) showcase commissioned paintings, glasswork, and artistic tiling. Of more interest to children are the full-size dragon boat suspended from the ceiling, and the Foucault Pendulum, which demonstrates the Earth's rotation. Look outside for a set of temple bells donated by sister cities in Japan and South Korea, and for a decaying, segmented Douglas fir stump. Arranged horizontally to emulate a fallen classical column,

Temple bell

the "host" trunk is kept moist by an irrigation system to foster new growth.

PHOTOS: REGIONAL ARTS AND CULTURE COUNSEL

to be a pothole below the office window of *Oregonian* journalist Dick Fagan, until he planted it with flowers. Visit, so you can say you did, but use caution at this busy intersection.

On a sunny afternoon come prepared, because no amount of pleading will keep your kids dry at **Salmon Street Springs** (SW Front Ave. & Salmon). Best to dress them in swimsuits and stuff a few towels

"The Story Garden" gameboard raises intriguing questions.

in your backpack. The 185 water jets are programmed by computer to keep the frolickers on their toes. Just when they've adjusted to the fountain's rhythms, they change, and the kids are drenched (and grinning).

Children like to wade, splash, and play in the **Ira Keller Fountain** (SW 3rd Ave. & Market), opposite Civic Auditorium. Named after an advocate of urban renewal, the naturalistic brooks, terraces, and cascading waterfalls are suggestive of the Northwest landscape. Walk several blocks to the south to visit the **Lovejoy Fountain** (SW 3rd Ave. &

The Ira Keller Fountain brings the sights and sounds of the wilderness to the downtown core.

Hall), another cascade. Ask the kids to comment on the two fountains' similarities and differences. Which is most realistic? Which do they prefer, and why?

Terry Schrunk Plaza (SW 3rd Ave. & Jefferson) boasts an echo chamber (How does it compare to the one in Pioneer Courthouse Square?), a small-size replica of the Liberty Bell, and shrapnel from the Oklahoma City bombing.

The **Plaza Blocks** (SW 3rd Ave. from Madison to Salmon), comprising Chapman and Lownsdale squares, are separated by Main Street, which curves around a mas-

This defiant bull-elk statue commands a place of importance, right in the middle of Main Street.

sive bull-elk statue that was given to the city in 1900 by a former mayor. Elk from the West Hills are said to have grazed here before the parks were dedicated in 1852. The squares, which attracted orators and milling crowds of citizens, were segregated into ladies' (Chapman) and gentlemen's (Lownsdale) "gathering places" in the 1920s to encourage decorous behavior.

TIPS

Downtown Portland's dining options run the gamut from fast–food frenzy to gourmet grand, from healthful Mexican to eclectic Continental. If you and your children are especially adventurous, consider trying one of the popular bento places, which serve Japanese–inspired skewers of grilled meats and vegetables atop mounds of sticky rice.

Cascades, the Pioneer Place shopping–mall food court (SW 5th Ave. & Taylor), is arguably the best bet for families. Its attractive setting, with cascading waterfalls and seating on several levels, showcases more than a dozen separate concessionaires who sell pizza, sandwiches, salads, gyros, corn dogs, ice cream—everything but the kitchen sink. Popular with the business crowd on weekdays at noon, the atrium gets very noisy. Come before or after the lunch–hour rush, or on weekends.

These downtown restaurants offer kids' menus and mostly conventional fare:

- **Harborside Restaurant,**
  0309 SW Montgomery, 220-1865
- **Macheezmo Mouse,**
  723 SW Salmon, 228-3491
- **Mayas Taqueria,**
  1000 SW Morrison, 226-1946
- **McDonald's,**
  1035 SW 6th Ave., 295-1234
- **Newport Bay RiverPlace,**
  0425 SW Montgomery, 227-3474
- **Pizzicato,**
  705 SW Alder, 226-1007
- **Stanford's Restaurant & Bar,**
  1831 SW River Dr., 241-5051

Michael Graves' controversial **Portland Building** (SW 5th Ave. & Madison) represents the nation's first major postmodern structure. What do your children think of it? Do they like the colors, the adornments? How is it different from and/or similar to some of its historic neighbors?

Stand in the shadow of "Portlandia," which looms out over the entrance, and look up. A jolly green-ing giant modeled after Lady Commerce, she is the nation's second largest hammered-copper statue (her trident alone is longer than a Tri-Met bus). Who can name the largest? (Hint: She's in New York City.)

From Portland State University at the south (Jackson St.) to Salmon St. at the north, the 12 grassy, shaded **Park Blocks** that form downtown's cultural core are punctuated by sculptures and benches. Look for statues of Abraham Lincoln and

REGIONAL ARTS AND CULTURE COUNSEL

"Portlandia" crouches on a ledge above the entrance to the Portland Building.

TIPS

For a new perspective on "Portlandia," enter the Portland Building and climb to the second-floor atrium. Here the Metropolitan Center for Public Art (open weekdays only) showcases a full-size plaster cast of the statue's head, in addition to photographs taken during her arrival via barge. Another vantage point can be had from the Standard Plaza building across the street. Take the escalator to the enclosed landing area for an unobstructed view.

REGIONAL ARTS AND CULTURE COUNSEL

This trompe l'oeil mural, one of several, was commissioned by the Oregon Historical Society in 1989.

Theodore Roosevelt, and for "In the Shadow of the Elm" (Clay St.), a granite pavement sculpture constructed in 1984. One of Benson's original bubblers stands at SW Park and Salmon. Who can spot "Salmon on Salmon"? (Hint: It's at the corner of SW Salmon St. & 9th Ave.) Continue north to the Studio Building (SW 9th Ave. & Taylor),

REGIONAL ARTS AND CULTURE COUNSEL

"In the Shadow of the Elm" is a subtle granite inlay at Park Ave. and Clay St.

whose frieze features the busts of famous composers.

Commissioned by the Oregon Historical Society in 1989, Richard Haas' **Oregon History Murals** use a trompe l'oeil technique. Adorning the Sovereign Hotel, the west (SW Park & Madison) and south (SW Broadway & Jefferson) murals depict historic personalities, panoramas, and architectural details. Where does three-dimensional reality give way to two-dimensional art?

TIPS

Nike Town (SW Broadway & Salmon), the local shoemaker's first adventure in retailing, is similarly disorienting. Designed to resemble a two-story street scene, with balconies and catwalks, the store features eight "pods," each devoted to a specific sport's requisite gear and footwear. Kids have fun picking out the architectural "oddities" and ogling the tropical fish, but it's easy to lose them in the tangle of merchandise and tourists.

Resources

The office of the Portland Oregon Visitors Association (World Trade Center #2, SW Salmon off Front Ave., 275-9750) is stocked with dozens of free maps, travel brochures, and event calendars for Portland and its environs. Trained volunteers are available at the front desk to answer questions. Hours: Mon-Fri, 9 am-5 pm; Sat, 10 am-4 pm; Sun, 10 am-2 pm.

The Regional Arts and Culture Council (309 SW 6th Ave., Suite 100, 823-5111) has developed *Public Art Walking Tour*, a 65-page guide to the city's art collection. Most recently revised in 1992, the booklet divides downtown and Lloyd Center districts into eight zones. Numbered works of art are located on zone maps and briefly described. Drop by RACC offices for a free copy of the guide.

Portland Development Commission (1900 SW 4th Ave., Suite 100), in cooperation with the Historic Preservation League of Oregon, created three walking-tour brochures in 1988. Still in circulation, each pamphlet emphasizes an architecturally historic downtown district: Yamhill, Skidmore/Old Town, and Glazed Terra Cotta (commercial core). The map guides are available at PDC offices for 50¢ apiece. For details, call 823-3200.

Powell's Books also publishes a free walking map of downtown with numbered highlights and descriptive information. Outlined on a simple fold-out leaflet, the complete tour is 7 miles long, so families are advised to design an abridged version. Pick up a map at any Powell's store, or call 228-4651 for more information.

Use the text of the *City Kids Fun Book* as inspiration for a downtown scavenger hunt. Published by the Association for Portland Progress, the colorful, "hip," 14-page booklet features a map, games, trivia tidbits, and historical information that focus on five downtown neighborhoods. It's available for free at area locations—including Portland Art Museum, Pioneer Place, Pioneer Courthouse Square, Saturday Market, The Children's Museum, OMSI, and Washington Park Zoo—or by calling 224-8684. ■

TIPS

When in Salem, get a free copy of *A Walking Tour: State of Oregon Capitol Grounds* at the Capitol information desk. The brochure highlights the plantings, fountains, and monuments on the mall. For little kids, there's a sculptural metal play structure called "The Parade of Animals." Older kids will appreciate the Peace Plaza (Commercial St., between City Hall & the public library). Decorated with colorful symbolic banners, the centerpiece is a concrete wall that features remarks on the subject of peace by renowned international figures and local citizens.

W here were you in third grade? Here in Portland that's the year schoolchildren study civics, learn about cities, and explore their hometown. Classrooms sign up en masse with local tour operators to trudge the streets and pick up tidbits about the history and architecture of the sights many of us take for granted.

You don't have to be 9 years old to get something out of a guided walking tour, however. Families are welcome, though advance reservations are required. Tour guides are generally amenable to designing a tour to fit your special interests and requirements. Most guides cover lots of territory in upwards of two hours of fast walking and talking. So, if your children are younger than 5 years old, consider their attention spans and stamina before booking a tour.

Peter's Walking Tours
665-2558
Season: Year-round
Fees: $10/adult; free/child 12 years & under; $20/family

An elementary-school reading instructor, Peter Chausse knows how to captivate the attention of children. He stuffs his pockets with magnets, paper, and crayons before a tour, then passes out the materials when the time comes to test the properties of the cast-iron Franz Building (SW 1st Ave. & Yamhill) and make rubbings of the intriguing phrases in "Streetwise" (SW 3rd Ave. & Yamhill). His entertaining, 2 1/2-hour downtown walks highlight art, architecture, urban parks, fountains,

and local history.

Call at least a day ahead to reserve. Tours are offered on weekday afternoons and weekends.

Portland Bridge Walk
Portland Parks & Recreation
823-5132
Season: Spring, summer, & fall
Fees: $16/adult; $10/child 14 years & under

Sharon Wood wrote the book on Portland bridges. She can quickly rattle off the three main bridge types (arch, suspension, beam), the three main moveable bridge types (vertical lift, bascule, swing), and local examples of each. Her Portland Bridge Walk is offered monthly in season for Portland Parks & Recreation, and made possible by the city's compressed layout: Portland has eight notable bridges in close proximity to one another.

Children are welcome on the 3 1/2-hour outings, and Wood, who has lots of experience hosting school groups, can fashion a tour to meet the needs of her guests. Participants view and discuss the eight bridges, walk across two, learn how the city works, and play games to simulate a bridge's balancing act. Reservations are suggested.

Urban Tour Group
227-5780
Season: Year-round
Fees: $25/group of 1-5 people; $5/each additional person

A nonprofit, volunteer organization with 85 trained guides and 26 years of experience leading free downtown walking tours for school groups, the Urban Tour Group also offers guided tours to the public. Call two weeks ahead to schedule a tour. Weekdays are preferable to weekends, when accessibility to many buildings is limited. ■

Chapter 2
KID CULTURE

The signs are universal and predictable: Feet wiggle with anticipation inches above the floor, bottoms bob in the plush seats, and necks crane anxiously for a clear view around the hairdo in front. Then the curtain rises, and there's a squeal of delight, a sigh of satisfaction.

You've given your child a gift. Though he may not thank you outright, he will hum a tune that captured his senses, he will make a drawing inspired by another, he will tote home a library book to show you the story he remembers, he will point out the Big Dipper on a clear night, and he will ask to go again.

And then you know you've done a good thing; you've opened a secret door and tiptoed down a hidden pathway. New, unusual, intimidating, enlightening—culture is all these things. Follow the yellow brick road.

continued ➡

TICKET DISCOUNTS

Arts experiences should be a treat, but they need not be expensive. Thanks to Young Audiences of Oregon and Southwest Washington, a branch of a national nonprofit organization devoted to making the arts accessible to children, families can now afford to take advantage of some of the region's cultural riches.

The Young Audiences Family Arts Card is as good as gold. Buy one ticket and get a child ticket free to as many as 60 special events throughout the year. Participating local arts groups include the Oregon Symphony, Children's Museum, Northwest Childrens Theatre, Oregon History Center, Tears of Joy Theatre, and Oregon Ballet Theatre. Applications are available at metro-area schools and libraries, or by calling 224-1412 or 360-693-1829.

Students and seniors have a few discount options of their own. For $8, students can attend Portland Opera dress rehearsals at the Civic Auditorium. Call the opera (241-1802) a month ahead to receive a ticket application form, then arrive early for the best seats. Educators are also entitled to participate; their tickets cost $10 each.

The Oregon Symphony sells $5 student tickets to Monday-evening classical concerts; these can be purchased up to one week in advance. And an hour before showtime on Mondays, Tuesdays, and Wednesdays, students and seniors can buy unsold tickets to any classical concert for half-price from the box office (719 SW Alder St., 228-4294).

Young Adult Specials are offered on select dates to each show in the U.S. Bank Broadway Series. These discounted tickets (usually $2 off face value) are available at the Portland Center for the Performing Arts box office (1111 SW Broadway) to youths 18 years and younger who present student identification. For details, call 224-7384.

TICKET AGENTS

Fastixx: 224-8499
Ticketmaster: 224-4400, 790-ARTS

American Advertising Museum
50 SW 2nd Ave., Portland 97204
226-0000
Hours: Wed-Sat, 11 am-5 pm;
Sun, noon-5 pm
Admission: $3/adult; $1.50/senior,
child 12 years & under
Annual family membership: $75

Though many parents endeavor
to shield their children from advertising, it permeates society and has
a vital, enlightening history of its
own. All this becomes frightfully
clear at the American Advertising
Museum. Since opening in 1986, the
museum has amassed the industry's
most comprehensive collection of
advertising and business artifacts.
The quarters may be tight, but the
shows are remarkably engaging.

Best for children from age 10,
the displays highlight, through print
and broadcast advertising, nearly 300
years of social history and trends.
Exhibits in the front gallery change
every three months. Recent shows
have included "Dream Girls: Images
of Women in Advertising (1890s-
1990s)" and "Animation Celebration,"
which highlights the claymation
creations of local hero Will Vinton.

Carnegie Center Children's Museum
606 John Adams St.,
Oregon City 97045
557-9199
Hours: Mon-Fri, 9 am-7 pm; Sat,
10 am-6 pm; Sun, 1-5 pm
Admission: $2/child

Annual family membership: $50

This Oregon City building, sited
on a flat square block beside a small
playground, was the public library
for 82 years before its recent rebirth
as a community center. Upstairs is
an art gallery. Downstairs, the daylight basement has been outfitted
for exploratory play.

The kid sister to Portland's
Children's Museum (see below), the
Carnegie Center is equipped with
pint-size versions of a grocery store,
diner, hospital, post office, and credit
union. Young visitors vie for a turn in
the wheelchair, at the typewriter, and
on the motorcycle (it's stationary).

When the kids (or the parents)
wear down, gather around the children's table in the upstairs coffee
shop for juice and cookies.

Children's Museum & Children's Cultural Center
3037 SW 2nd Ave., Portland 97201
823-2227
Hours: 9 am-5 pm daily; Cultural
Center hours vary
Admission: $3.50/adult, child over 1
year
Annual family membership: $48

Housed since 1950 in what was
once a dormitory for nurses, the
three-story Children's Museum has
an intimate, lived-in quality that's
inherently inviting to young kids.
Quickly they disperse to explore a
huge bubble machine, a tangle of
train tracks, a tyke-size grocery

The basement-level clayshop at Children's Museum is free with admission; pay a little extra to have pieces glazed and fired.

store, and doctor's examining room. Here the child is boss; nothing's off-limits. The basement-level Clayshop hosts drop-in activities and special workshop sessions on select days.

Across Lair Hill Park is the museum's second building, now a

TIPS

The Children's Museum and Children's Cultural Center sit at opposite ends of Lair Hill Park. With its vast lawn, big trees, and play-ground equipment, the park is a nice place in which to picnic and frolic before or after visiting the museum. In summer the Children's Museum hosts special cultural events in the park. Call in May for a schedule.

Children's Cultural Center with rotating "let's pretend" exhibits of varied cultures. In 1996 the center opened "Living Legends," an exploration of the artifacts and lifestyles of Northwest Native Americans today and in the past. Visitors can camp out in a tepee, beat a ceremonial drum, and create petroglyphs.

Clackamas County Museum of History

211 Tumwater Dr., Oregon City 97045
655-5574
Hours: Mon-Fri, 10 am-4 pm; Sat-Sun, 1-5 pm
Admission: $3/adult; $2/senior; $1.50/child 6-12 years; $7.50/family

Built in 1990, the Clackamas County Museum of History, a striking contemporary structure on the bluffs above Willamette Falls, provides a thorough overview of the inhabitants of Clackamas County from prehistory to the present day. Arrowheads and stone tools are artifacts from early settlements. A covered wagon sits packed and ready for adventure. The shelves of a replica pharmacy are stacked with hundreds of tiny, colorful bottles. And display cases reveal the tools used by practitioners of various trades. Children are asked not to touch these and other artifacts—many of which are not under glass. But their curious fingers are likely to wander, so plan to provide some supervision.

Admission to the museum includes a visit to the Stevens-Crawford Museum *(see Restored Houses).*

End of the Oregon Trail Interpretive Center

1726 Washington St.,
Oregon City 97045
657-9336
Hours: Winter; Mon-Sat, 9 am-5 pm;
Sun, 11 am-5 pm. Summer; Mon-
Sat, 9 am-6 pm; Sun, 10 am-5 pm.
Admission: $4.50/adult;
$2.50/senior, child 5-12 years;
free/child 4 years & under

From I-205, you can't miss it:
three Paul Bunyan-size covered
wagons in conference on Abernethy
Green. This is the End of the
Oregon Trail Interpretive Center—
not quite museum, not quite theater.
The live, 60-minute presentation
inside helps enlighten visitors as to
the history, heritage, and spirit of
the immigrants who arrived here via
wagon train in the mid-19th century.

Enter first the barnlike
Provisioner's Depot, and take a seat
among crude barrels, flour sacks,
and earthenware jugs to hear a "trail
guide" describe the shopping trips
and other preparations that preceded the 2,000-mile trek. Move next to
the Cascades Theatre for a multime-
dia dramatization of the journey,
which blends 100-year-old photo-
graphic images with 20th-century
film footage and surround sound,
lighting, and special effects. Complete the visit in the gallery, with its
small collection of artifacts, including a Barlow Road toll book, clothing, tools, and household items
used by early settlers.

Fort Vancouver

1501 E. Evergreen Blvd.,
Vancouver, WA 98661
800-832-3599, 360-696-7655
Hours: Winter; 9 am-4 pm daily.
Summer; 9 am-5 pm daily.
Special re-enactments: May, July,
August, October, & December
Admission: $2/adult; $4/family;
free/senior, child 16 years & under

The hub of regional activity dur-

Three larger-than-life covered wagons mark the site of the End of the Oregon Trail Interpretive Center.

GARY POUSH/ZUMA

TIPS

Guided shows at the End of the Trail Center begin every 45 minutes throughout the day in summer, and every hour during winter. When calling to make reservations, specify a preferred time, then arrive about 15 minutes early to pick up your tickets and settle into the theater.

The moving accounts and vivid images presented help comfortable folks of the technology age envision a harsh yet simple era. These concepts are abstract, however, and until your children have a firm grasp of history, it's best to leave them home.

Toddlers, particularly, will be frustrated by the "no-touch" rules and the lengthy, adult-style presentations. Furthermore, some children may be startled by the soundtrack's rifle blasts and thunderstorms.

If you do take young kids (and this center is an ideal pit stop for out-of-town guests), sit by an exit. If you need to make a quick escape, there's plenty to explore outside—Heritage Gardens and an amphitheater, site of the Oregon Trail Pageant each summer (see Theater).

ing its heyday in the early 19th century, Fort Vancouver is again standing tall, as reconstruction continues at a site once considered politically pivotal.

In a brash move to claim dominion over Oregon Country, a territory rich in furs, England established headquarters for its Hudson Bay Trading Company at Fort Vancouver in 1825 and enjoyed 20 years of prosperity. In 1846, following the mass migration of pioneers to the West, a division of Oregon Country relegated Fort Vancouver to American soil. So by 1860 the trading company had moved out, and within six years, fires and decay had destroyed what was once a bustling headquarters.

Much of the fort has since been reconstructed by the National Park Service. At the entrance is a period garden planted with the same vegetables and grains consumed at the fort. Enclosed in a stockade are a half-dozen buildings, including the chief factor's residence, a blacksmith's shop, bakery, trade shop, fur store, wash house, and kitchen.

Climb the three-story bastion to touch a cannon and spy on "enemies," handle beaver hats and pelts, watch blacksmithing and baking demonstrations. On-site archeologists are busy identifying and cataloging the thousands of objects (glass trade beads, ceramic shards, iron pieces, etc.) that have been uncovered in excavations here.

TIPS

Fort Vancouver would not have risen to regional prominence were it not for the organizational prowess and business acumen of Dr. John McLoughlin. After retiring as chief factor when the new boundary was drawn, McLoughlin settled in Oregon City. Take a guided tour of his residence to continue the history lesson (see Restored Houses).

Musicians disappear into "Karaoke for Kids," where they sing before a mirror using real equipment and a microphone. Actors stage a puppet show in "Children's Theatre." Daring adventurers descend into "Cave of Wonders" to uncover fluorescent minerals and special gems and rocks. Artists return from "The Artist Studio" proudly displaying their creations. Sleuths are invited to help solve "The Mystery of the Missing Diamond."

On the drawing board are plans to build, adjacent to the museum,

Gilbert House Children's Museum
116 Marion St. NE, Salem 97301
503-371-3631
Hours: Tues-Sat, 10 am-5 pm; Sun, noon-4 pm; open Mon, March-June, 10 am-5 pm
Admission: $4; $3/senior; free/child under 3 years; $3/after 3:30 pm, daily except Sun
Annual family membership: $50

Named for Salem native A.C. Gilbert—who founded The Gilbert Company and manufactured educational toys, including the Erector Set and American Flyer Trains—this museum occupies two historic Victorian houses on Salem's downtown riverfront. Opened in 1989 and expanded in 1992, the Gilbert House Children's Museum showcases a revolving selection of stimulating, interactive exhibits in the sciences, arts, and humanities.

TIPS

Some museums are designed for adults, who often drag their kids along. Others are designed for kids, who, through no fault of their own, are accompanied by their parents. If you're visiting the former—good luck. If you're visiting the latter, visit as a child.

Crawl on hands and knees, squeeze into nooks and crannies, get wet and dirty.

Slow down so your child can be the leader. If she wants to stay at the water table for two hours, let her.

Ask questions instead of giving answers. Unless your child needs your help, don't take over or explain what's happening. Let her play teacher.

an outdoor science center—a spacious playground with hands-on experiments and other activities. Such rapid growth at the Gilbert House can mean only one thing: This place is worth a trip to Salem.

Hart's Reptile World
11264 S. Macksburg Rd., Canby 97013
266-7236
Hours: 11 am-5 pm daily
Admission: $4; $3/child 3-6 years

At the end of a rutted road on the outskirts of Canby sits a battered shed. This is Hart's Reptile World, a menagerie of snakes, iguanas, geckos, lizards, turtles, tortoises, alligators, and crocodiles. Lovingly cared for by Mary Hart, a renowned West Coast reptile handler, these creatures (and their surroundings) may not be pretty, but they're pretty intriguing.

Far from a conventional museum, Hart's Reptile World is a slice of jungle, where the creatures look more comfortable than the people. Wilbur, the celebrity crocodile, has a pen full of memorabilia from his various media appearances. Sherman, a 355-pound tortoise, welcomes visitors into his enclosure. Many other inhabitants are likewise available for "petting." Cupboards along the walls harbor incubating snake eggs and other treasures; ask for a peek, but beware the escaped mouse or wandering iguana.

The largest alligator, who tips the scales at 450 pounds, was retrieved by Hart from a stretch of California highway during a midnight rescue mission several years ago.

TIPS

Feeding time at Hart's Reptile World is not for the squeamish. Smaller snakes are fed Saturdays at 3 pm, and larger snakes are fed Sundays at 3 pm. The alligators are fed Wednesdays and Saturdays at 3 pm.

Jeff Morris Fire Museum
55 SW Ash, Portland 97204
823-3700

This walk-by museum, adjacent to the Portland Fire Bureau building on SW Ash, is dedicated to the memory of Jeff Morris, a loyal firefighter who pioneered the bureau's safety-education program and died of cancer in 1974 at age 46. Signage describes the historic equipment inside, much of which tells its own story of the past—from hand-drawn handpumpers and ladder trucks (1860s-70s) to a horse-drawn steam-pumper from 1911.

The bell is perhaps the most poignant. Commissioned in 1873 following a tragic fire to which volunteer firefighters responded belatedly, the 4,000-pound alarm bell (it could be heard in Oregon City) arrived from New York in time to usher in a new, paid fire department.

John Inskeep Environmental Learning Center
19600 S. Molalla Ave.,
Oregon City 97045
657-6958 ext. 2351, 656-0155
Hours: 8 am-dusk daily
Haggart Observatory: Winter; Wed, Fri, & Sat (weather permitting), 7:30-11:30 pm. Summer; Wed, Fri, & Sat, 9-11:30 pm.
Admission: $2/person

   (except observatory)

Part museum, part park, this site on the Clackamas Community College campus wasn't always so inviting. In the early 1970s what is now home to a birds-of-prey exhibit, native wetlands nursery, small exhibit hall, and observatory was an abandoned industrial complex. Restored by volunteers, the 8-acre John Inskeep Environmental Learning Center stands as a model for cooperative projects of this kind.

Plan a daytime visit to enjoy the gravel trails that meander beside Newell Creek. Examine the owls, falcons, hawks, and eagles. Inspect the buildings, made almost entirely of salvaged and recycled materials.

Then return at night to view the stars. A 40-foot tower, Haggart Memorial Astronomical Observatory houses a 26-inch reflecting telescope. Staffed by volunteer astronomers, stargazing parties are open to the public year-round.

Kidd's Toy Museum
Parts Distributing Inc.
1300 & 1327 SE Grand Ave.,
Portland 97214
233-7807
Hours: Mon-Fri, 8 am-5:30 pm; Sat, 8 am-1 pm

Frank Kidd is serious about toys—especially mechanical banks, of which he owns hundreds. Unfortunately, one has to be just as serious as Kidd is to enjoy his "museum." Arrayed behind glass on floor-to-ceiling shelves that line the office of his auto-parts distributorship and an upstairs hideaway are all manner of mechanical banks, many in multiple.

As Kidd tells it, he didn't particularly like toys as a child, but began collecting for fun more than 30 years ago. When his hobby mushroomed into an investment, Kidd established the museum for tax purposes.

By spring 1997, Kidd plans to have opened a larger exhibit space in a third office annex across the street.

Metro Washington Park Zoo
4001 SW Canyon Rd.,
Portland 97221
226-ROAR, 226-1561
Hours: Winter, 9:30 am-4 pm daily; spring/fall, 9:30 am-5 pm daily; summer, 9:30 am-6 pm daily; grounds are open for an hour after entry gates close
Admission: $5.50/adult; $4/senior; $3.50/child 3-11 years; $1-$2.50/train. Free admission 2nd Tues of month, 3 pm-closing
Annual family membership: $49, $74

When you live in a community lucky enough to have such a wonderful zoo, you find yourself making

MICHAEL DURHAM

Exhibits at the Kongo Ranger Station depict life in the jungles of Africa.

some rather unsavory friends—like fruit bats, for instance, naked mole rats, pythons, and arctic wolves. Their habits become familiar, and you talk about them around the dinner table as you would a favorite uncle. To many Portlanders, the Metro Washington Park Zoo is family.

Set amid the forest and rolling lawns of Washington Park, the zoo has managed to maintain its own parklike identity, with attractive landscaping, bubbling brooks, a vast amphitheater centerpiece, and intimate alcoves with benches for resting. Indeed, like the nation's best "natural-style" parks, the zoo invites visitors to wander, to discover; even regulars stumble upon unfamiliar paths and new pieces of statuary. Also a botanical garden, the zoo has identification plaques on many of its trees. Ask at the entrance gate for a tree-tour brochure.

Lions, tigers, and bears ... Oh my! They are all here, and apparently quite happy in their capacious enclosures. The zoo boasts the world's most successful elephant-breeding program and has staked its reputation on its innovative toys. Admitting that the animals' enclosures fall far short of the challenging environments of the wild, the zoo has outfitted animal habitats with big plastic balls, styrofoam shapes, "blood balls" (balloons filled with frozen meat juices), and great, hanging tree trunks. It is believed that equipment of this kind, in addition to multilevel climbing structures and sprinklings of cinnamon, herbs, and other exotic scents, can help to keep the animals physically fit and mentally alert.

Zoos nowadays struggle to achieve a balance between emulating the animals' native habitats and appeasing members of the public who want to see the beasts up close. Peek into the shade of a great boulder or up onto a cantilevered

MICHAEL DURHAM

The Metro Washington Park Zoo offers a variety of opportunities to visit with creatures up-close.

MICHAEL DURHAM

Polar bears have ample space to explore—both indoors and out.

tree limb—that's where you're likely to find a sleeping cat or lazy bear.

Keepers (in blue denim shirts with name tags) and docents (in red polo shirts with name tags) wander the grounds, answering visitors' questions. In summer, keepers schedule special talks at select exhibits throughout the zoo. Check the handout map for subjects and times, and for the feeding schedule (the penguins receive a public feeding daily, year-round).

It's the unexpected that is most intriguing here. The quarter-mile Cascade Nature Trail, tucked into a back hillside, showcases native plants and animals: beavers, river otters, fish, and waterfowl. An indoor cafeteria overlooks the lush vegetation and colorful tropical birds of an enclosed aviary. In the Kongo Ranger Station, children clamor for a seat behind the wheel of a full-size jungle jeep. The train ride, with its three different locomotives, veers deeper into Washington Park along a wooded,

4-mile ravine route.

Founded in 1887 at the rear of a downtown pharmacy, the zoo is Oregon's leading paid attraction. And citizens intend to keep it that way. In fall 1996, voters overwhelmingly approved a bond measure to ensure the zoo achieves its objectives into the next century. On the drafting table: improved habitats for lions, bears, cougars, and beavers; a Family Farm petting zoo featuring native farm animals; and better access, a streamlined pathway system, and a new entry gate near the light-rail station.

(See Music for information about ZooTunes, a series of summer concerts for families; and Season by Season for details about other special events.)

TIPS

The Metro Washington Park Zoo is like Portland in microcosm: just big enough to be exciting, not so big as to be intimidating. A visit can expand or contract to fit your family's schedule and level of interest. And, just as the animals here need new and enticing play objects to keep them alert, so do regular visitors need to alter their patterns of experiencing the zoo.

Rather than taking in all the

continued ➡

exhibits every time, pick just a few. Pretend to be an animal behaviorist, and jot down your observations. Purchase a ZooTales key ($2) at the souvenir shop near the exit gates, then hunt down the talking boxes for tidbits and trivia. Or plan a backwards visit, starting with the Rain Forest, so your energy gives out at a different cage.

Break up the afternoon with a picnic lunch or snack (food from home is allowed, and you can rent a wagon to transport the cooler). Most people gravitate to the amphitheater at lunch time, where the kids can somersault and wrestle on the lawn. Another option is to set up on a bench along the Cascades Trail, a serene, forested corner back behind the big cats.

Visit in the early morning and in winter to see different animals at their best—and to avoid traffic snarls in the parking lot. If you can't resist the zoo on a sunny summer day, you'll be in good company, and chances are you'll have to park in the overflow lot (near the Hwy. 26 Sylvan exit). Have the driver drop an adult and children at the entrance gate first, then meet up with the group inside. The return trip to the overflow lot via shuttle bus is an almost welcome detour because the door-to-door service cuts down on the walk.

There's no denying it, a trip to the zoo means a lot of walking. Take a stroller for the toddler (or rent one for $5; the plastic alligator model is fun but impractical). Otherwise you'll find yourself lugging a cranky child from Africa to the parking lot. The inconvenience inherent in the zoo layout, which dead-ends at the Rain Forest, will be rectified in summer 1997 by the renovation project. Until then, hail a ride from the Zoomer shuttle (75¢/person, each way), or plan to stop for a snack or train ride on the way out.

Mount Hood Community College Planetarium
26000 SE Stark St., Gresham 97030
667-7297
Public shows: October-May; Saturdays, once a month
Admission: $1/person

With its 30-foot hemispherical dome, comfortable seating for 70, special effects, and enhanced audio system, the Mount Hood Community College Planetarium puts on a star-studded show. Planetarium director Douglas McCarty, an astronomy instructor for more than 25 years, tailors the monthly public shows to his audience. Designed to appeal to children (McCarty welcomes questions), these programs use the current night sky as a springboard to discuss recent discoveries in astronomy and space science.

Old Aurora Colony Museum
2nd Ave. & Liberty St., Aurora 97002
678-5754
Hours: Tues-Sat, 10 am-4 pm;
Sun, noon-4 pm
Guided tours: Sat & Sun, 1 & 3 pm

In 1856 Dr. William Keil established a communal society on several hundred acres around a gristmill and sawmill in Oregon. Named for his daughter Aurora, for 27 years this colony attempted to live out a Christian experiment in brotherhood similar to those practiced by the Harmony, Amana, and Shaker communities in the eastern United States.

The only such settlement in the Pacific Northwest, the Aurora Colony left behind an old ox barn, two homes, a communal wash house, and a farm-machinery building. In spring and again in September, schoolchildren are invited to experiment with pioneer tasks, including cutting wood and spinning yarn.

Oregon History Center
1200 SW Park Ave., Portland 97205
222-1741
Hours: Tues-Sat, 10 am-5 pm;
Sun, noon-5 pm
Admission: $6/adult; $3/student;
$1.50/child 6-12 years; free/child
5 years & under, senior on Thurs
Annual family membership: $60

Operated in the heart of downtown by the Oregon Historical Society, the Oregon History Center is increasingly creating exhibits and special programming that cater to families. Planned to coincide with the city's 150th anniversary in 1996, "Portland!," a fitting introduction to Rose City history, is an ongoing display upstairs.

This $1.5 million show is the first

TIPS

ART, the Cultural Bus (Tri-Met bus *63), travels incognito. A brightly painted mural-on-wheels, it was designed in 1994 as a cooperative venture of the Northwest Business Committee for the Arts, Metropolitan Art Commission, Tri-Met, and Metro. The bus stops at SW Main and 4th Ave. once an hour, then follows a special route that encompasses many of the city's premier cultural venues: International Rose Test Garden, Japanese Garden, Lloyd Center mall, Metro Washington Park Zoo, Oregon Convention Center, Oregon History Center, OMSI, Portland Art Museum, Portland Center for the Performing Arts, Portland Oregon Visitors Association, Rose Quarter, and Tom McCall Waterfront Park.

For a route map and schedule, call Tri-Met: 238-RIDE. Fare: $1.05-$1.35/adult; 80¢/child 7-18 years; free/child under 7 years.

of a three-part educational project slated to include major installations that feature the history of the Willamette Valley and the Oregon Country. Take visiting grandparents, and you'll be surprised how quickly the kids disperse to explore on their own. *(See also Farms, Special Farms, Sauvie Island.)*

Oregon Maritime Center & Museum

113 SW Front Ave., Portland 97204
224-7724
Hours: Winter; Fri-Sun, 11 am-4 pm. Summer; Wed-Sun, 11 am-4 pm.
Admission: $4/adult; $3/senior; $2/child 8-17 years; $10/family

Located on the waterfront in a historic building, the Oregon Maritime Center & Museum features dozens of model ships—from the *Cutty Sark* and *Constitution* to vessels that plied the Willamette and Columbia rivers during Portland's early days as a leading seaport. These may be of limited interest to children, but there are other artifacts and hardware that will catch their eye.

Children enjoy inspecting the ships in bottles, hefting the Navy diving helmet and leaden boots, firing the miniature cannon, and working the propellor, sirens, and lights of a model Navy destroyer.

Admission includes a tour of the *Portland*, a restored sternwheel steam tugboat built in 1947 to help ships navigate the Willamette River.

Oregon Museum of Science and Industry (OMSI)

1945 SE Water Ave., Portland 97214
797-4000, 797-4600 (advance tickets)
Hours: Winter; Tues-Sun, 9:30 am-5:30 pm, Thurs until 8 pm.
Summer; Tues-Sun, 9:30 am-7 pm; Thurs until 8 pm.
Admission: $3.50-$12/adult; $3.50-$10/senior, child 4-13 years
Annual family membership: $55

Once as cramped and dingy as a mad scientist's basement laboratory, in its close quarters near the Washington Park Zoo, the new Oregon Museum of Science and Industry resides in a gleaming steel-and-glass structure whose sleek, polished interior is reflective of the scrubbed-clean environment preferred in this age of technology. The move hasn't been entirely smooth, however, and OMSI has been beset by financial woes. Which is a shame, because this ambitious state-of-the-art facility, with its commanding presence on the Willamette's eastern shore, has the makings of a great science museum.

All the crowd-pleasers are in place, from the Omnimax Theater, with its five-story, domed screen and pulsating sound system, to the Murdock Sky Theater's regular slate of planetarium shows; from the USS *Blueback*, a naval submarine in service for 30 years and now permanently docked in the river, to the twice-daily Laser Light Shows so popular with teens. *(See Active Play: Indoor Fun, Best for Teens.)*

Traveling blockbusters are de-

TIPS

If you're a Portland resident, or visit often, take a deep breath and appreciate the fact that you can visit OMSI at a leisurely pace. If you're a tourist, you may feel overwhelmed by the possibilities and frustrated by lack of time and energy. The size and scope of OMSI are overwhelming (imagine how small a toddler must feel in the cathedral-like lobby), so it's important to plan your visit accordingly.

Don't attempt to do too much. Little children are perfectly content to play with the pulleys, magnets, sand, and goo in the Discovery Space (children newborn–age 7 only, please). Older ones never tire of experimenting with the engineering stations in the Physical Science Exhibit Hall or riding in the wheelchairs in the "Breaking Down Barriers" exhibit.

Arrive during off-hours. Crowds are not always a problem, but to be sure you miss the rush, arrive early (by 9:30 am), or late in the afternoon. Avoid holiday weekends, particularly in inclement weather, and exhibit openings.

Pack snacks. OMSI exhibits are challenging and ambitious; even adults tend to flag after a few hours of deep concentration. Carry some munchies in a backpack and break for a picnic outside, where the kids can roll on the lawn and run along the riverside pathways. An attractive cafeteria with views out over the water serves light meals and snacks.

signed to appeal to a variety of audiences, with Richard Scarry's "Busytown" and "Backyard Monsters" aimed at children, and "Star Trek: Federation Science" aimed at parents.

OMSI's own engaging, interactive activities reach patrons on many levels. So it's almost enough to devote a visit to one of the permanent displays. Kids make a mad dash for anything electronic, which leaves the adults at peace to learn something. The Life Science Exhibit Hall explores human growth, fetal development, and the structure and function of the human body. The Earth Science Exhibit Hall focuses on geology, biology, and weather. The Information Science Exhibit Hall features computers, fax machines, satellite relays, and cellular phones. And the Physical Science Exhibit Hall includes an engineering design and testing facility in addition to a Chemistry Lab and Holography Lab.

TIPS

The Children's Museum and Gilbert House Children's Museum in Salem have separate playrooms equipped with infant and toddler toys, as well as restroom diaper-changing facilities. At the Gilbert House, nursing mothers can retreat to a private room equipped with comfortable chairs. OMSI's Discovery Space provides the best layout for parents who are trying to monitor the activities of preschoolers while also watching Baby. Separated from the ruckus by a low partition, the baby area here occupies a corner of the large, central classroom, so parents can oversee kids at many different stations simultaneously. A small, private room with a rocking chair is available for nursing mothers.

Pearson Air Museum

1115 E. 5th St., Vancouver, WA 98661
360-694-7026
Hours: Tues-Sun, 10 am-5 pm
Admission: $4/adult; $3/senior; $1.50/student, child 6 years & over; free/child 5 years & under; $10/family
Annual family membership: $35

Located at the nation's oldest operating airfield (it dates to 1905), the Pearson Air Museum is dedicated to preserving the field and its rich aviation heritage. View as many as a dozen fully restored planes that predate World War II, and visit the aircraft restoration center. Watch footage of the Soviet Trans-Polar Flight, which touched down at Pearson in 1937. And learn of the accomplished career of Lt. Alexander Pearson, for whom the airfield was named in 1925.

Under construction at press time, a new $3.6 million project has been designed to re-create a pre-World War II Army Air Corps airfield. Interactive exhibits for children, including a computer resource room, an 80-person theater, and two hangars, will open in May 1997.

Portland Art Museum

1219 SW Park Ave., Portland 97205
226-2811
Hours: Tues-Sun, 10 am-5 pm; Wed & 1st Thurs until 9 pm
Admission: $6/adult; $4.50/senior, student 16 years & over; $2.50/child
Museum Family Sunday: 1-5 pm, $6/adult; $4.50/senior, student; $1/child 3-15 years
Annual family membership: $60

Before the arrival in 1993 of Executive Director John E. Buchanan Jr., the Portland Art Museum was regarded by many as a diamond in the rough. The region's oldest and largest visual- and media-arts center, it was established in 1892 by seven successful Portland businessmen. Transplanted Northeasterners, they be-lieved in the power of art to create enlightened citizens. In the century since, the museum has amassed a substantial collection of more than 30,000

COURTESY OF PORTLAND ART MUSEUM

Museum Family Sundays at the Portland Art Museum feature hands-on activity stations.

ture, or Impressionism, for example. Local cultural groups, artists, and educators lead interactive activities, performances, and demonstrations that help make these esoteric exhibits more tangible and accessible to children. Tables are scattered in galleries throughout the museum, and kids virtually stumble upon new lessons: Learn calligraphy, watch a tea ceremony, build a sculpture from pipe cleaners and coat hangers, and make a mosaic picture using squares of colored construction paper. A few experiences like these, and children forget to complain about museums.

objects that span 35 centuries of Asian, European, and American art.

Allied with the Northwest Film Center, the city's most visible arts institution continues to play an important role in directing the region's cultural life. To that end, the Portland Art Museum has increasingly pursued collections that underscore the variety of artistic origins and expressions. For instance, its renowned collection of Native Ameri-can art features examples from nearly every cultural region of North America.

Nonetheless, if it weren't for its commitment to arts education, this museum, rather sterile and imposing, would not have much to recommend it to families. Museum Family Sundays, scheduled five to six times a year, are for kids. And legions of them come (with parents) to these free-for-all open houses.

Each event is designed to enhance the theme of a current installation—Japanese art, Rodin sculp-

TIPS

Museum Family Sundays are worth planning weekends around. Call ahead for a schedule of upcoming events (organizers try to have a year-round calendar ready in July), then be the first in line when doors open at 1 pm. Usually the hours between 2 pm and 3:30 pm are the most crowded. If you haven't visited all the activity stations by then, feel free to step outside for a snack and a walk, then return later in the afternoon when the place isn't so mobbed.

Portland Police Museum

Justice Center, 1111 SW 2nd Ave.,
16th floor, Portland 97204
823-0019
Hours: Mon-Thurs, 10 am-3 pm

Tucked away on an upper story
of the Justice Center are the three
small rooms and dozens of display
cases of the Portland Police
Museum, an operation run by volunteer members of the Portland Police
Historical Society. Children clamor to
sit atop the vintage Harley-Davidson
motorcycle and in its sidecar. Everything else is under glass: bulletproof
vests, firearms and other confiscated
weapons, drug paraphernalia, uni-
forms, badges, arrest logs, and historic photographs.

State of Oregon Sports Hall of Fame

321 SW Salmon, Portland 97208
227-7466
Hours: Tues-Sun, 10 am-3 pm
Admission: $2/adult; $1/child

As this book goes to press, the
State of Oregon Sports Hall of Fame
is getting a long-deserved facelift.
New interactive exhibits, three times
the space, and better visibility on
the street level of a downtown
building can only augment what is a
lovingly cataloged collection of local
sports memorabilia.

Each year the museum honors
a new slate of six inductees and
awards five scholarships to excep-
tional Oregon student athletes.

Washington County Museum

Portland Community College Rock
Creek Campus, 17677 NW
Springville Rd., Portland 97229
645-5353
Hours: Mon-Sat, 10 am-4:30 pm
Special events: May & September
Fees: $2/adult; $1/child 6-17 years;
free every Mon

This small museum and research
library features a rotating array of
exhibits that illuminate various periods of history in Washington County,
from the early Atfalati Indians to the
influx of today's high-technology
companies. Some examples:
"Crinolines to Miniskirts," an exami-
nation of a century of women's fash-
ions; "Open Wide," a look at early
modern dentistry; and "Our County
Collects," a changing selection of
private local collections.

In the works at press time is an
exhibit entitled "Discovering History," which explores the various
research techniques and materials
used by historians. This show will
be augmented by a Discovery Room
illuminating specific events in the
history of the region through the use
of artifacts, oral accounts, and repro-
ductions of photographs and maps.

Western Antique Powerland

*(See Active Play: Outdoor Fun,
Trains & Trolleys.)*

World Forestry Center

4033 SW Canyon Rd., Portland 97221
228-1367
Hours: Winter, 10 am-5 pm daily;

Visitors to the World Forestry Center can view a Pygmy family from Africa's Ituri Forest.

summer, 9 am-5 pm daily
Admission: $4/adult; $3/senior, child 6-18 years

Built in 1971 to replace the original 1905 Forest Parthenon, which had been destroyed by fire, the World Forestry Center is being refashioned as a $10 million, nine-month renovation project gets under way in fall 1998. The grand reopening in 1999 will unveil new thematic concepts and state-of-the-art interactive displays.

Current exhibits include "Old-Growth Forests: Treasure in Transition," "Tropical Rainforests: A Disappearing Treasure," and "The Burnett Collection of Petrified Wood." *(See also Farms, Special Farms, Magness Memorial Tree Farm.)*

Restored Houses

Fragile imported china, heirloom quilts, and young children don't mix. So think twice about subjecting a historic dwelling to your kids, and vice versa.

Some children are fascinated by glimpses of yesteryear, and will be on their best behavior in settings such as these. For them, restored houses provide private snapshots of family life at distinct periods in Oregon history.

■ The Hoover-Minthorn House Museum
115 S. River St., Newberg 97132
538-6629
Hours: March-November;
Wed-Sun, 1-4 pm.
December & February; Sat-Sun,
1-4 pm (closed in January).

Pittock Mansion, a stately restored home in northwest Portland, hosts a special holiday showcase each year in December.

Admission: $2/adult; $1.50/senior, student; 50¢/child 5-11 years

■ **McLoughlin House**
713 Center St.,
Oregon City 97045
Hours: Tues-Sat, 10 am-4 pm;
Sun, 1-4 pm (closed January)
Admission: $3/adult; $2.50/senior; $1.50/child 6-17 years
656-5146

■ **Pittock Mansion**
3229 NW Pittock Dr.,
Portland 97210
823-3624
Hours: Noon-4 pm daily
Admission: $4.25/adult; $3.75/senior; $2/child 6-18 years

■ **Rose Farm**
Holmes Lane (at Rilance Lane),
Oregon City 97045
656-5146
Hours: March-November;
Sun, 1-4 pm
Admission: $2/adult; $1/child

■ **The Stevens-Crawford Museum**
603 6th St., Oregon City 97045
655-2866
Hours: Tues-Fri, 10 am-4 pm;
Sat-Sun, 1-4 pm
Admission: $3/adult; $2/senior; $1.50/child 6-12 years; $7.50/family (includes admission to Clackamas County Museum of History)

Chamber Music Northwest

522 SW 5th Ave., Suite 725,
Portland 97204
294-6400, 223-3202
Dates: Mid-July; Sunday, 2 pm,
Catlin Gabel School. March; 1st
Thursday, 7 pm, The Old Church.
Tickets: $5-$9

For 26 years, Chamber Music
Northwest has been building a
national reputation on the strength
of its programming and informal,
intimate settings. The 25-concert
summer series at Catlin Gabel
School (8825 Barnes Rd.) is serious
business—and popular with metro-
area music-lovers.

*Chamber Music Northwest dedicates two
concerts a year to young audiences.*

Children younger than age 7 are
not admitted to evening performances. Instead they are offered a
special matinee (with refreshments
afterward) that's designed to serve as
a nonthreatening introduction to classical music. Last season's program
featured Prokofiev's *Peter and the
Wolf* and *The Fairy's Gift* by Seattle
composer-conductor Adam Stern.

CMN's winter family concert at
The Old Church (1422 SW Clay St.)
spotlights friendly musicians who
help explain their talents to children.
Previous visitors—who fill out their
week by performing in local school—
have included the Maia String Quartet
and Quintet of the Americas.

Oregon Symphony

711 SW Alder, Suite 200,
Portland 97205
228-1353, 228-4294
Season: September-June
Tickets: $8.50-$50; season
subscription available

The Oregon Symphony is committed to reaching diverse audiences
with a 10-month season of varied
music, including newly commissioned works, performances of works
dropped from active repertoires, and
works of contemporary composers
and U.S. composers. Under the lead-
ership of music director and conductor James DePriest, the orchestra,
which performs at the Schnitzer
Concert Hall (SW Broadway & Main),
has grown increasingly active in the
areas of education and outreach.

Its popular Kids Concerts series is
consistently rated among the city's
highest caliber children's musical
events. Featured in 1996-97 were

*Oregon Symphony's Kids Concerts series is a
crowd-pleaser.*

Imago Theatre (see Theater), Fred Penner, and a program consisting of *Carnival of the Animals* and *The Sorcerer's Apprentice.* Kept to about one hour in length, these fast-paced performances are designed to introduce children ages 3-10 to the instruments and sounds of the orchestra. Each of the three Sunday matinee concerts is performed twice, and seating is reserved.

Read the symphony's *Season Concert Schedule* more closely for other family offerings, such as the ever-popular annual Holiday Pops with Doc Severinsen and Kids Holiday Concert, in addition to periodic Special Events Concerts, such as the appearances in 1996-97 of Bobby McFerrin and The Magic Schoolbus.

Metropolitan Youth Symphony
P.O. Box 5254, Portland 97208
228-9125
Season: October-June
Tickets: $6-$27; season subscription available

Metropolitan Youth Symphony boasts more than 350 student musicians from kindergarten to college age in its four orchestras and two bands. Under the direction of principal conductor Lajos Balogh since 1974, MYS holds rehearsals every Saturday during the school year. Emphasis is placed on enjoyment through learning and satisfaction through accomplishment.

The annual performance schedule features three major concerts at the Schnitzer Concert Hall (SW

Broadway & Main), in December, March, and June, as well as several free concerts at local schools.

Portland Opera
1515 SW Morrison, Portland 97205
241-1802
Season: September-June
Tickets: $24-$100; season subscription available

Having adopted an "anything but stuffy" style in order to re-establish public enthusiasm for opera, Portland Opera consistently plays to sell-out audiences at Civic Auditorium (SW 3rd Ave. & Clay). Ranked as one of the nation's top 20 professional opera companies (out of 106), Portland Opera is a distinguished member of the metro area's arts community.

Its five-show season tends to blend traditional with innovative performances. In 1996-97, it daringly staged two all-new productions.

Ambitious education and outreach programs help expose school groups throughout the region to talented young opera and musical-theater professionals. Dress-rehearsal performances are reserved strictly for students and educators (see page 18), and demand for these discounted tickets attests to the success of Portland Opera's attempts to shed its highbrow image without compromising the integrity of its productions. *(See also Theater, Portland's Broadway Theater Season.)*

Portland Youth Philharmonic
1119 SW Park Ave., Portland 97205
223-5939
Season: November-May
Tickets: $5-$24

The Singing Christmas Tree pageant is an annual holiday tradition for many local families.

The nation's oldest youth orchestra, the Portland Youth Philharmonic was founded in 1924 and continues its long-standing tradition of commitment to excellence in musical education. Students age 9-22 audition for seats in the PYP, Preparatory Orchestra, and Young String Ensemble each season. About 200 are selected, and some choose to travel from as far as Eugene and Tillamook for rehearsals and performances.

PYP is far from a kiddie company. Its ambitious repertoire mirrors that of major professional orchestras, and it performs four concerts a year at Schnitzer Concert Hall (SW Broadway & Main), in addition to more informal recitals for local school groups.

Singing Christmas Tree
11040 SW Barbur Blvd., Suite 102, Portland 97219

557-TREE, 244-1344
Season: Late November-early December
Tickets: $8-$36

From its perch atop a 35-foot lighted and flocked Christmas "tree," a 260-member volunteer choir performs with a 60-piece orchestra and 50 children in one of the city's most popular and enduring holiday extravaganzas. Performed at Civic Audito-

Serious young musicians hone their skills with the Portland Youth Philharmonic.

rium (SW 3rd Ave. & Clay) beginning Thanksgiving weekend, the pageant "does" Christmas, by incorporating Santa and popular, commercial Christmas music with the Christ child and more traditional carols.

Waterfront Blues Festival

Tom McCall Waterfront Park, Front Ave., north of Hawthorne Bridge
282-0555
Dates: July 4th weekend, hours vary
Donation: $3 plus 2 cans of food

Surely it's sacrilegious to be caught smiling at a blues festival, but this four-day July 4th mega-jam has all the makings of a good time: two stages of world-class blues acts (Junior Wells, Charlie Musselwhite, Canned Heat, and Elvin Bishop, among others); a wide swath of lawn with ample room for dancing and tumbling; a view of the Willamette; a grand fireworks display on July 4; and food booths with enough variety to satisfy finicky as well as more sophisticated palates.

To top it all off, you can feel good about coming. Donations benefit the Oregon Food Bank, and volunteers at the gate typically collect more than 75,000 pounds of canned food.

ZooTunes

Metro Washington Park Zoo
4001 SW Canyon Rd.,
Portland 97221
226-ROAR
Dates: Mid-June-mid August;
5 Tuesdays, 7 pm

Tickets: $3.50-$5.50; free/child 2 years & under

Begun in 1994, this series of five outdoor family concerts supplements the ever-popular Wednesday/ Thursday concerts that have for years drawn hordes of picnickers to the zoo amphitheater after hours. Though the largely jazz-inflected program on Wednesdays and Thursdays has never discouraged parents from bringing their kids along—nor discouraged kids from jumpin' and jivin' down front—the ZooTunes lineup considers the musical tastes of children first.

No dancing dinosaurs here, however; concert promoters admit to a bias against cartoonish voices. Besides, they seek to attract to the shows parents who want to share with their children the "wholesome" folk music they grew up on. Tom Chapin, Riders in the Sky, and John McCutcheon have played Tuesday-night gigs.

MICHAEL DURHAM

ZooTunes concerts spotlight performers who delight parents and children alike.

MICHAEL DURHAM

Dancing is encouraged at the open-air ZooTunes affairs.

Summer Concert Series

A picnic at an outdoor summer concert has got to be as American as baseball, hot dogs, and apple pie. And if we're lucky, the sun shines just long enough in Portland for families to get their fill of all of the above.

In reality, the Rose City seems to have more than its fair share of concert series in the summer. Virtually every municipality with a patch of green lawn hosts one. Not that we're complaining. Events such as these have "family" written all over them. Yours won't be the only kids digging for ants and stepping on neighboring blankets.

Call your local city hall for details; the listing below is merely a sampling.

Peanut Butter & Jam Sessions. June-August; Tues & Thurs, noon-1 pm. Pioneer Courthouse Square, SW Broadway between Yamhill & Morrison. 223-1613.

Lunchbox Concerts. June-August; Wed, noon-1 pm. Oregon Square

TIPS

Parking for ZooTunes has not recently been a problem, but when you're planning your outing, consider that at 8:30 pm, little legs that walked blithely to the amphitheater may not make it all the way out. Arriving early isn't always the solution, however. Because the zoo admits summer visitors until 6 pm, the parking lot is often full into early evening. If you do come early, you can claim a prime piece of lawn after 4 pm, then enjoy the zoo until showtime.

Another way to avoid congestion is to purchase tickets in advance at the zoo office; ticket holders enter the zoo through a special gate that's never mobbed. (Note: Zoo members are not entitled to free admittance to ZooTunes.)

AfriCafe is open, and carts around the perimeter sell food and drinks as well, so you don't have to overburden yourself with coolers and picnic baskets (no alcohol, please).

Courtyard, NE Holladay between 7th & 9th. 233-4048.

Waterfront Concert Series. June-August; Wed, 6:30-8:30 pm. Rohr Park, Lake Oswego. 636-9673.

Concerts on the Commons. July-August; Fri, 6:30 pm. Tualatin Commons, 8345 SW Nyberg. 692-2000.

Summer Concert Series. July; Wed, noon-1 pm. Lewis & Clark College, behind Manor House, 0615 SW Palatine Hill Rd. 768-7297.

Music by Blue Lake. July-August; Thurs, 6:30-8:30 pm. 20500 NE Marine Dr., Troutdale. $3/parking; $3.50/adult; $1/teen; free/child 12 years & under. 797-1850.

Summer Jazz Concert Series. July-August; Fri, 11:30 am-1 pm. Beaverton Town Square, 11665 SW Beaverton-Hillsdale Hwy. 526-2288.

Forest Music Series. July-August; Sun, 2 pm. Tryon Creek State Park, 11321 SW Terwilliger Blvd. 636-4398.

Blue Heron Music Festival. July-August; Sun, 6-9 pm. Cathedral Park, N. Edison & Pittsburg. 289-5187. ■

L istening may be a dying art. It's hard to imagine today's "plugged-in" youth having the patience to sit still and concentrate on a radio storyhour. Which is precisely why it appeals—to parents. Below is a sampling of local kids programs.

Programmer Linda Stein and her 7-year-old daughter, Maya Rose, host "All Together Now," an hour-long segment devoted to children's music, stories, call-ins, and special young

guests. Tune in to KBOO-FM (90.7) on Sundays from 9-10 am.

"Rabbit Ears Radio," a nationally syndicated half-hour program in which celebrities take turns reading folktales, fairy tales, and other favorites, airs every Sunday evening at 7 pm on KOPB-FM (91.5).

KBPS-AM (1450), the mouthpiece of the Portland Public School District, broadcasts several programs for local kids and parents. Hosted by Benson High School announcers, "Kid Rhythm Radio" features children's music and news on weekdays from 1-3 pm. "Teen Sound" follows, with hipper music and pertinent announcements, from 3-5 pm.

Parents have two nationally syndicated programs to choose from on KBPS: "Sylvia Rimm on Parenting" and "The Parent's Journal," an award-winning series of interviews conducted by Bobbi Conner. Time slots vary; call 916-5828 for scheduling information.

Sue Shellenbarger, a Lake Oswego-based columnist for the *Wall Street Journal*, hosts "Work & Family," a live, nationally syndicated, call-in talk show. Each weekly segment examines a specific topic—such as childcare options, career stress and burnout, and eldercare. Shellenbarger interviews authorities in the field who can provide solutions, takes listener responses, and provides opinions and tips garnered from her professional reporting career and personal experience as a mother and stepmother. The "Work & Family" program airs on KEX-AM (1190) on Saturdays, 2-4 pm.■

The Children's Nutcracker
Beaverton Dance Center
12570 Farmington Rd.,
Beaverton 97005
644-6116
Season: 3 performances in
December
Tickets: $10/adult; $7.50/senior,
child under 6 years

Not to be confused with its
uptown cousin, this *Nutcracker* production has been lovingly choreo-
graphed by Joseph Wyatt, owner of
Beaverton Dance Center. Performed
annually at the Tigard High School
Auditorium (9000 SW Durham Rd.)
since its premiere in 1993, *The
Children's Nutcracker* is danced
entirely by students, ages 4-16,
who are selected by audition and
rehearse together for 3 1/2 months.

Jefferson Dancers
Jefferson High School Performing
Arts Dept., 5210 N. Kerby Ave.,
Portland 97217
916-5180
Season: April-early May
Tickets: $7-$13

Established in 1974, the Jefferson
Performing and Visual Arts Magnet
Progam was devised to improve
inner-city enrollment and student
motivation and self-esteem. Drawing
on a racially integrated student body
of nearly 500 high-schoolers, the program offers training in dance, theater,
music, television, and visual arts.

One of the Performing Arts
Center's unbridled success stories is
the Jefferson Dancers. An ensemble
composed of the department's most
advanced dance students, the
Jefferson Dancers tour the Northwest and western Canada each year,
returning to Portland in late spring
for a series of performances at the
Intermediate Theatre (1111 SW
Broadway).

Jefferson Dancers

Unlike most professional companies, this dance troupe maintains an
ambitious repertoire of works in all
dance styles—tap, ballet, jazz, modern, ethnic, and musical-theater
numbers—which makes their pot-
pourri productions all the more
exciting to children.

Oregon Ballet Theatre
1120 SW 10th Ave., Portland 97205
2-BALLET, 227-0977
Season: October-May
Tickets: $10-$85; season
subscription available

Established in 1989, Oregon
Ballet Theatre is the metro area's
flagship dance company. With an

Oregon Ballet Theatre's annual production of The Nutcracker is a highlight of Portland's dance season.

JOE WILHELM

annual season of four productions at the Civic Auditorium (SW 3rd Ave. & Clay) and Intermediate Theatre (1111 SW Broadway), this 25-member troupe is developing a uniquely American repertoire and a distinctly American style.

Artistic director James Canfield offered local families a magical holiday present in 1993 when his company unveiled an opulent new *Nutcracker*. Set in Czarist Russia and augmented by regal costumes and Fabergé-inspired scenery, this jewel of a production plays to full houses in December each year. Act I, with its pantomime party scene, is particularly beloved by young children. Act II showcases more traditional pas de deux.

In late August, OBT takes to the streets with a special three-week outdoor rehearsal program (10 am-4 pm daily). Housed on a tented stage behind the Arlene Schnitzer Concert Hall (SW Broadway & Main), "OBT Exposed!" premiered in 1995 to enthusiastic crowds and has since returned for an annual run. In full view of the public, company dancers go about their business, attending classes and rehearsals in preparation for the season opener. ■

TIPS

Oregon Ballet Theatre's *Nutcracker* is an opulent show, a vast improvement over the tired, dowdy productions many dance companies mount year after year. Think twice about taking young children, however, because this version—with all its pomp and circumstance—is 2 1/2 hours long. Kids younger than age 6 will likely lose interest after intermission, when the tutus take to the stage. Be forewarned, as well, that parents dress up and dress up their kids for *The Nutcracker*. Lace, velvet, bow ties, and blue blazers are de rigueur.

Broadway Rose Theatre Company

7925 SW Durham Rd., Tigard 97224
620-5262
Season: Summer
Tickets: $14/adult; $12/student,
senior; $8.50/child 12 years &
under; $5/children's show

The metro area's only professional summer-stock theater troupe, the Broadway Rose Theatre Company got its start in 1991, when a group of four experienced actors, directors, and designers began mounting professional—and affordable—productions at Tigard High School's 600-seat Deb Fennell Auditorium (9000 SW Durham Rd.). Its ambitious seven-week season consists of three main-stage shows and two children's musicals.

Chickadee Children's Theater

Cedar Hills Recreation Center,
11640 SW Park Way, Portland 97225
644-3855
Season: Winter & spring
Tickets: $1-$2

Under the aegis of the Tualatin Hills Park & Recreation District in Beaverton, Karolyn Pettingell Ainsworth's company was launched in 1993 to a receptive local audience. A teacher of puppetry and acting at the Cedar Hills Recreation Center for many years, and a former manager of a children's entertainment facility in Sacramento, Ainsworth writes and directs two plays at the center each year, in

December and June.

With a cadre of talented actors (both children and adults), a set designer, and other technical assistants, Chickadee Children's Theater plays to full houses. Works in progress: a musical about pirates and an adaptation of *Aesop's Fables*.

Children's Theater Series

Beaverton Community Center,
12350 SW 5th Ave.,
Beaverton 97005
526-2288
Season: October, weekends
Tickets: $1-$2

With invaluable assistance from a committed citizens' board of directors, the Beaverton Arts Commission, an agency of the City of Beaverton, has for four years raised the funds necessary to mount an increasingly diverse series of live theatrical events for children. In addition to nurturing future audiences of the arts, the series seeks to promote multicultural understanding and empathy in youths ages 3-10.

Performed in the newly expanded Beaverton Community Center, the four shows in the 1996 series featured *The Lion, the Witch & the Wardrobe* by Northwest Childrens Theater; *Music & Dance of the Philippines* by the Filipino-American Friendship Club Youth Dance Troupe; *Halloween Fun* by Young People's Theater Project; and *Coyote Steals Fire* by West Side Players. Face-painting and refreshments precede each show.

TIPS

The best children's-theater deal in town isn't even public knowledge. Local acting students from after-school and summer programs throughout the city typically culminate their coursework with a performance or two for family and friends.

Actually, anyone's welcome. Beyond providing free, informal entertainment, these shows are a good way to assess local theater-arts programs, should you be in the market for performance classes for your kids. Just call local theater schools (many are listed here) and ask for details regarding their end-of-term productions.

Do Jump! Movement Theater

Echo Theatre, 1515 SE 37th Ave., Portland 97214
231-1232
Season: October-June
Tickets: $10-$14

Under the direction of Robin Lane, a performance artist of the best kind, Do Jump!, founded in 1977, has outlasted all comparably sized local arts organizations. Yet what it does continues to defy description. "Cirque du Soleil meets Oregon Ballet Theatre" may have to suffice.

With a repertoire that consists of nearly 50 segments, the seven-member company is in the enviable position of being able to shuffle and reshuffle its programs to fill a nine-month season with elements of dance, acrobatics, physical comedy, aerial movement, and live original music.

The December holiday show features special appearances by Poptarts, student performers from the Do Jump! after-school program. Each Sunday show culminates in an all-ages, all-out juggle-in.

Built as a silent-movie house in 1910, the Echo Theatre has been outfitted with high-tech lighting and aerial work to serve as a community arts center and resident home for Do Jump!

Fairweather Theatre

Enchanted Forest
(See Active Play: Outdoor Fun, Amusements.)

Expect the unexpected at Do Jump! shows.

MIKE RENFROW

Hillsboro Actors Repertory Theater

230 E. Main St., Hillsboro 97124
693-7815
Season: Year-round
Tickets: $8-$12; season & family
subscriptions available

Launched in 1994 by the Sandstrom family, Hillsboro Actors Repertory Theater (HART) was recently purchased by a group of loyal season-ticket holders who intend to operate it as a nonprofit, semiprofessional suburban company. The audience probably won't notice the difference, as Kim Sandstrom continues to mount an ambitious year-round season that draws heavily on classic literature.

Families may choose from three or four productions a year. Recent favorites included *Belles on Their Toes*, *Pollyanna*, *Doctor Dolittle*, and *Hans Brinker or the Silver Skates*. Performed in a small, informal space at the rear of a shop that sells antiques, the shows are notable for their inspired use of tight quarters and amateur talent. (When making reservations, ask about special discounts for children.)

Imago Theatre

17 SE 8th Ave., Portland 97214
231-9581
Season: August-May
Tickets: $10-$15

Recognized as one of the nation's most innovative mask ensembles, Imago, like some of its vertiginous creations, continues to grow and evolve. Having established its reputation with the family favorite, *Frogs, Lizards, Orbs & Slinkys*, the 17-year-old company has since staged complex, even dark, adult dramas that

Imago Theater frogs

center on classic themes from literature by Dante and Sophocles, for example. Its performance space, completed in 1993, has spawned a second theater upstairs. And Imago is in the process of creating a new family show.

All said, it's hard to imagine anything upstaging good old *Frogs*, where amphibians with a sense of humor intermingle with ethereal globes and an overfed baby. The show still tours nationally and plays to an appreciative home crowd once a year.

Ladybug Theater has a long tradition of entertaining the region's youngest audiences.

Ladybug Theater

Oaks Amusement Park, SE
Spokane St., Portland 97202
232-2346

Season: November-May; special Halloween, Christmas, & spring break productions

Tickets: $2.50-$5; season subscription available

Originally housed at the Washington Park Zoo in a ladybug-shaped building (hence its name), this Portland theater institution has been performing for the region's youngest audiences for more than 30 years.

Don't let the rickety Oaks Park facility (Ladybug moved here in 1987) or the ragtag costumes fool you. There's nothing timeworn about this company. Ladybug's core of a half-dozen adult improvisational actors continues to refashion classic fairy tales and nursery rhymes into zany, original productions. Grimm's scary witches and abusive stepmothers land on the cutting-room floor to be replaced by silly dimwits and

their slapstick antics.

Committed to providing preschoolers with their first theater experiences, Ladybug has adopted

TIPS

Ladybug Theater is one of Portland's great entertainment bargains. When a Wednesday matinee costs $1.50 per person, there's little lost if you discover, half-way through, that your child's not yet ready to sit still for 45 minutes. And should that be the case, or should the baby grow fussy, you can almost bet you won't be the only parent sitting it out in the tiny lobby. Just try to make it to the finale, because after each show the cast members form a receiving line by the front door to greet the audience and answer questions. It's fun to inspect the costumes and make-up up close.

an informal, ad-lib style that invites audience input. Sometimes the cast is hard put to squelch the little cut-ups, but the show must go on!

For children from age 2 1/2, the troupe offers quickie Wednesday-morning productions. (Preschool groups are welcome on Thursdays.) Older children flock to the weekends' more elaborate shows, where they sit in a heap on the carpeted floor, as close to the action as possible.

Lakewood Theatre Company

Lakewood Center for the Arts, 368 S. State St., Lake Oswego 97034
635-3901
Children's season: Fall, winter (December), & spring
Tickets: $5-$9

Its primary emphasis may be on adult theater, with half a dozen productions scheduled annually, but the Lakewood Theatre Company is also dedicated to theater-arts education. In hosting an array of drama workshops for children and three children's theater productions each year, LTC continues to serve its suburban community with engaging arts experiences.

Each season's trio of kids' shows, mostly re-adaptations of fairy tales, feature young actors, many of whom are students in Lakewood classes. In partnership with Lake Oswego high schools, LTC also sponsors a holiday breakfast theater event for children in December.

Kinton Grange Players

19015 SW Scholls Ferry Rd., Beaverton 97007
848-6510
Season: Fall & spring
Tickets: Free

Founded in 1992 by Grange member Kathy Clair, this all-volunteer group produces two shows a year, in late November and before spring break, using schoolchildren exclusively. There is no cost for participating, and all interested children are included in the cast, though it is becoming increasingly difficult to find roles for everyone.

Parental involvement is required; adults make costumes, scenery, and props, and help out where needed. Some scripts are written by local playwrights (Clair herself has created more than a few), and have included *Arabian Nights* and *Snow White*.

Several hundred people typically come to see the performances in the wooden Grange Hall. Their donations help fund future productions.

Miracle Theatre Group/ Teatro Milagro

425 SE 6th Ave., Portland 97214
236-7253
Season: September-March
Tickets: $5-$8; Family Plan subscription available

Miracle Theatre Group, the Northwest's largest Hispanic arts institution, recently opened its own performance space (525 SE Stark), capping 11 years of touring, performing, and conducting workshops

Students from Ainsworth Elementary School participate in a Miracle Theater workshop.

in Hispanic theater arts and dance. Two separate companies, Miracle Theatre and Teatro Milagro, operate in tandem under the MTG banner.

Teatro Milagro, the family-oriented, touring branch of the organization, mounts bilingual musical plays that address the political, cultural, and social issues of Latin America. Based on myths, tales, and folklore, these high-energy productions showcase Milagro Bailadores, a multinational folkloric dance troupe that performs in traditional costumes, while providing cultural history from a bilingual script.

Two original musicals are created by Teatro Milagro each year, with performances scheduled in fall and early spring. Past shows have explored such issues as preserving the Brazilian rainforest, the U.S. embargo of Cuba, and the harmful effects of pesticides on farm workers. These works are suitable for schoolchildren.

Theatrical entertainment is also showcased at MTG festivals, where audiences are exposed to the celebratory customs of Mexico and other Latino lands. Best for families is Festival de Navidad (December).

Miracle Theatre presents more serious dramas by Hispanic playwrights, many of which are not appropriate for younger audiences.

Missoula Children's Theatre
200 N. Adams, Missoula, MT 59802
406-728-1911
Season: Year-round
Tickets: Prices vary

Each year this Montana-based band of traveling actor/directors crisscrosses the globe overseeing full-length productions starring legions of singing schoolchildren in more than 700 communities. Hired by a school, recreation department, church, or scout troop to put on a show, an MCT duo arrives on Monday to audition and cast 50 to

60 students. Tuesday through Friday afternoons are devoted to rehearsals and costume and set preparation. Saturday is the performance. And on Sunday the MCT team packs up and drives to the next town to do it all over again.

With 25 years spent directing shows in this fast-forward, soup-to-nuts fashion, MCT has developed quite a system. Thirteen productions—each one an original musical adaptation of a popular fairy tale—are in circulation annually among 21 teams of professional actors. Chosen for their backgrounds in the arts and education, these folks are very good at what they do.

MCT makes many visits to the Portland metro area during the school year and summer. Call your local school or recreation department to learn of a planned residency, or contact MCT directly to arrange for one. Cost of a week-long program (actors are boarded by sponsor families): $1,840.

In the past, the Musical Theatre Company showcased "Babes in Toyland" in December.

The Musical Theatre Company

1436 SW Montgomery,
Portland 97201
224-5411, 224-8730
Season: October-July
Tickets: $9-$29; season subscription available

Founded in 1983 as a branch of Portland's Bureau of Parks & Recreation City Arts program, The Musical Theatre Company has made a smooth and successful transition to independence in the wake of budget cutbacks in the early '90s.

In 1994, having established itself as a resident company at the Portland Center for the Performing Arts, this award-winning company added a fifth show to its season. A boon for families, *Babes in Toyland*, with its cast of Mother Goose characters, an evil private detective, and

TIPS

Sponsored by Parks & Recreation of Lake Oswego, Missoula Children's Theatre makes its most visible metro-area visit each summer in late June during the city's Festival of the Arts. Tickets to the show, performed in George Rogers Park on a tented stage, sell quickly. Call in advance: 636-9673.

TIPS

Just because we loved it as a child doesn't necessarily mean our own children will follow suit. Times have changed, and today's high-tech whiz kids aren't always beguiled by a chaste love story the way we were, so don't disappoint yourself by expecting them to sit still through a dated, full-length musical.

For a successful night of theater, do a little homework as a family beforehand. Rent the video and try to find an audiocassette of the soundtrack. Then share some stories about the good old days when you were a kid. This is a history lesson, after all.

Northwest Childrens Theater & School

Northwest Service Center, 1819 NW Everett St., Portland 97209
222-4480, 222-2190
Season: September-May
Tickets: $6-$15; season

subscription available

This nationally recognized company, in its present configuration for just four seasons, has lost no time in cornering the youth theater market with alternatives for all interests, age levels, and budgets. Operating from the Northwest Service Center, a former Christian Science Church, its three-tiered organization centers on entertainment, in the form of stage productions; education, in the form of acting classes and workshops; and enrichment, in the form of educational outreach and scholarship programs.

With a reputation for showcasing top-quality classic plays and original adaptations of children's literature (a

a platoon of toy soldiers, has been offered as a holiday theater treat.

TMTC specializes in the splashy epic musicals of which we never tire— *Oklahoma, The Music Man, A Chorus Line*— and splits its season between two performing spaces: the 900-seat Intermediate Theatre at Portland Center for the Performing Arts (1111 SW Broadway) and the Eastside Performance Center   (531 SE 14th Ave.).

Northwest Childrens Theater performed The Miracle Worker for older audiences.

recent season featured *To Kill a Mockingbird* and *The Secret Garden*, among others), NWCT is forever seeking new challenges. In 1995 it opened a second, more intimate stage in downtown Portland to appeal to younger audiences and to test-market experimental works. The Main Street Playhouse (904 SW Main) now hosts four productions each season (past hits included *Winnie-the-Pooh* and *Green Eggs & Ham*).

For season subscribers, NWCT offers a mix-and-match package of tickets to four or more productions at either stage.

Oregon Children's Theatre Company

600 SW 10th Ave., Suite 520, Portland 97205
228-9571
Season: Late November-early May

Tickets: $8-$16; season subscription available

Heading into its 10th year with

Little House on the Prarie, produced by Oregon Children's Theatre Company in 1997, was a big hit with schoolchildren.

DUANE MORRIS PHOTOGRAPHY

the 1997-98 season, Oregon Children's Theatre Company can feel proud of its contribution to arts education in the Northwest. A non-profit professional theater company and a resident of the Portland Center for the Performing Arts, OCTC presents two full-scale productions at the Civic Auditorium (SW 3rd Ave. & Clay) each season, and plays to more than 80,000 children, parents, and educators throughout Oregon and Washington.

TIPS

Though an afternoon at the theater is well spent if you and your child haven't read the book, the experience is all the richer when you have. So, before planning your family's theater outings, plan your storyhours; contact some of the companies listed here and ask to receive their season brochures. Northwest Childrens Theater and Oregon Children's Theatre, in particular, create award-winning plays that are drawn from the pages of award-winning children's literature. If you aren't familiar with the title, ask about the show's subject matter and target audience; some plays, such as *Bridge to Terabithia*, presented in 1994 by NWCT, are lost on (or overwhelming to) young children.

The selected scripts tend to be based on favorite children's books, such as *Stuart Little* and *A Wrinkle in Time*, so audiences not only benefit by experiencing live theater, but also by being exposed to great literature.

Oregon Trail Pageant

P.O. Box 68, Oregon City 97045
657-0988
Season: July-August
Tickets: $5-$12

After a 10-year run, *Oregon Fever*, Springfield playwright Dorothy Velasco's epic musical drama about immigration along the Oregon Trail, is retiring, to be replaced by an entirely new production. Scripted by Tom DeTitta, a Southern playwright especially skilled at creating shows that rely on oral accounts, the as-yet-unnamed pageant premieres in July 1998 on the grounds of the End of the Oregon Trail Interpretive Center (1725 Washington St., Oregon City). *(See also Exhibits & Museums.)*

DeTitta's drama emphasizes the cultural contrasts between pioneers and Native Americans, and the political, social, and commercial history of Oregon City. The accompanying musical score was written by local musician Marv Ross of The Trail Band.

The sights and sounds may be new, but the scope remains the same: 45 performers, including children (many of them amateurs), authentic covered wagons, and traditional clogging and fiddle music. Beginning at dusk and concluding in starlight, the show is most appropriate for children 7 and older.

© 1996, OWEN CAREY
The Oregon Trail Pageant is performed in the amphitheater at the End of the Oregon Trail Interpretive Center.

Portland Center for the Performing Arts

(See also Active Play: Indoor Fun, Behind the Scenes.)

PCPA entertains more than a million patrons a year at four theaters in town:

- **Arlene Schnitzer Concert Hall**
  SW Broadway & Main
  274-6564

  Italian Rococo Revival architecture and world's largest electronic organ. Resident companies include Oregon Symphony and Portland Youth Philharmonic.

- **New Theatre Building**
  1111 SW Broadway
  274-6566

  State-of-the-art facilities in award-winning, contemporary building. Two theaters: Intermediate Theatre, whose resident companies include Portland Center Stage; and Dolores Winningstad Theatre, whose resident companies include Tygres Heart Shakespeare Company and Tears of Joy Theatre.

- **Portland Civic Auditorium**
  SW 3rd Ave. & Clay
  274-6560

  Excellent acoustics and sightlines. Accommodates national touring shows. Resident companies include Portland Opera, Oregon Ballet Theatre, and Oregon Children's Theatre.

TIPS

Friends of the Performing Arts Center's Brown Bag Lunch Series features open rehearsals and selected highlights from resident companies' upcoming performances. A good way to preview a show or concert and the attention span of your youngster, the free hour-long events convene at PCPA venues at noon on occasional Wednesdays, October–June.

Recent events have included selections from Portland Youth Philharmonic's Fall Concert, an Oregon Symphony open rehearsal, musical highlights from Oregon Children's Theatre's *Little House on the Prairie*, and selections from Tears of Joy Theatre's *Fire on the Mountain*. For a schedule, call 274-6555.

Portland's Broadway Theater Season

Portland Opera, 1515 SW Morrison, Portland 97205
241-1407
Season: September-August
Tickets: $16-$62; season subscription available

Created in 1994 as a unique partnership between Portland Opera and Jujamcyn Theaters, this five-show series is already a local favorite, having played to 13,000 subscribers its first year. Booking top-quality touring productions, Portland's Broadway Theater Season showcases many of the musicals that make headlines in New York City. Some are suitable for children. Among recent visitors to Civic Auditorium (SW 3rd Ave. & Clay): *Beauty and the Beast, Grease!,* and *Joseph and the Amazing Technicolor Dreamcoat.*

TIPS

High schools are another good source of inexpensive entertainment. In spring, and sometimes also in time for the holidays, drama students put on end-of-term productions for families and friends. Musicals are usually the most suitable, and the most fun, for children. Call ahead for a schedule.

Shakespeare in the Parks
Portland area parks
321-0710
Season: July-August, weekends
Tickets: Free

For 26 years, a band of volunteer actors, writers, and artists who call themselves Portland Actors Ensemble has been organizing a minstrel-like summer Shakespeare series in metro-area parks. Sometimes traditionally Elizabethan, other times set in the Golden Age of Hollywood, the Wild West, or sometime in the near future, these plays are largely faithful to the Bard's text.

Each season brings a new title (*A Winter's Tale, The Merchant of Venice,* and *As You Like It* made the rounds in past years), which is then performed on consecutive weekend afternoons before repeating the following week in a different neighborhood park. Because the stage is designed to conform to its natural surroundings with minimal props and sets, each new location adds an unexpected twist to the proceedings. Audiences are encouraged to picnic on the grounds while watching the show.

For a schedule of performance locations and times, check *The Oregonian* A&E section on Fridays and *Willamette Week* beginning in late July. Final shows coincide with Labor Day weekend.

Student Matinee Series
Interstate Firehouse Cultural Center, 5340 N. Interstate Ave., Portland 97217
823-2000
Season: February, April, & May
Tickets: $4

Housed in a historic 1910 firehouse in North Portland, the nonprofit International Firehouse Cultural Center sponsors performing, literary-, and visual-arts events and programs that emphasize the cultural heritage and diverse ethnic traditions of area residents. Now in its 11th year, the Student Matinee Series consists of four theater productions that are designed primarily for school groups (the public is invited, provided there are enough seats available in the theater). Each production is performed four times, on weekdays.

Recent shows for older students have featured the work of Oregon Stage Company, IFCC's resident troupe, in *Driving Miss Daisy* and *Cobb*. Grade-school students have been treated to performances by Northwest Asian-American Theatre, shadow puppets, marionettes, and multicultural storytellers.

Tears of Joy Theatre
1109 E. 5th St., Vancouver 98661
248-0557, 360-695-3050
Season: November-April
Tickets: $8.50-$9.50; season subscription available

Was it prophetic that Tears of Joy should have its origins in an impromptu preschool performance about a courageous dragon? Surely this company, one of the nation's pre-eminent professional puppet troupes, is itself something of a brave beast. In operation since 1971, making do on the increasingly meager grants available to such endeavors, Tears of Joy continues to develop inspirational productions that enlighten audiences about distant peoples and far-off lands.

The puppets themselves, custom-built for each show, are other-worldly—big as sequoias or small as shrews. Visit with the puppeteers after the show to touch their creations and learn how they're manipulated. No doubt you'll be surprised at how versatile the performers are;

Toy Box
by Tears of
Joy Theatre

JUDI LYNNE BRADLEY

most take on multiple parts. Almost better than the puppets is the innovative use of simple materials and indigenous music in evoking a mood.

Typically, the company performs four shows a year at the Columbia Arts Center in Vancouver (400 W. Evergreen Blvd.) and also at the Portland Center for the Performing Arts' Winningstad Theatre (1111 SW Broadway). Arrive early to peruse the display of photographs, mementos, and artifacts profiling the culture whose story you've come to hear.

Productions on the drawing board for coming years include *Bridge of the Gods*, a Native American story from the Columbia Gorge; and a new Monkey King tale, to be directed by the legendary Chinese puppet master Yang Feng.

Theatre in the Grove
2028 Pacific Ave.,
Forest Grove 97116
359-5349
Season: Winter & spring
Tickets: $7-$9

An amateur community theater troupe formed in 1974 to produce musicals, Theatre in the Grove continues to thrive in a remodeled Forest Grove movie theater. Its season consists of six shows, two of which are musicals for children.

Casting for these productions is often a family affair—with parents and children on stage side by side—and you can bet the audience is,

too. *Cinderella* debuted as the most recent holiday musical. *Hansel & Gretel*, loosely based on Engelbert Humperdink's opera, was performed in the spring for local school groups.

Tygres Heart Shakespeare Company
309 SW 6th Ave., Suite 102,
Portland 97204
222-9220
Season: October-June
Tickets: $6-$30; season subscription available

Founded in 1989 by artistic director Jan Powell, Tygres Heart Shakespeare Company has developed a winning formula of innovative staging and natural, vivid delivery, which results in productions that are fresh and bold. Staged in the unique courtyard setting of the Winningstad Theatre (1111 SW Broadway), the plays are also intimate. *Othello, Richard III,* and *A Comedy of Errors* debuted in 1996-97.

Though full-length productions are probably more than most children can attend to, the company's narrated, abridged Sunday Family Matinee series makes a fine introduction to the Bard. Each play in the three-show season receives this special treatment once during its run.

Tygres Heart Shakespeare Company offers special abridged matinees, which are ideal for children.

TIPS

Three local theater companies—Tygres Heart, Northwest Childrens Theater, and Oregon Children's Theatre Company—make an effort to reach disabled persons with special sign-interpreted and audio-described performances. Call the box offices for dates and other details.

U.S. Bank Broadway Series

Dan Bean Presents
510 SW 3rd Ave., Suite 425,
Portland 97204
224-7384, 790-ARTS (Ticketmaster)
Season: September-April
Tickets: $23-$45; season subscription available

Launched in 1994, the Broadway Series has set the stage for musical-theater entertainment in Portland by consistently bringing to town blockbuster sell-outs. The promoter, Dan Bean Presents, got its start booking similar series at Seattle's Paramount Theatre before branching out to service other West Coast cities.

Make no mistake: There's nothing daring about these five-show lineups. Still, the tried-and-true crowd-pleasers (*The Sound of Music, West Side Story*) continue to fill Civic Auditorium (SW 3rd Ave. & Clay). And when the show itself isn't legendary, the star is (Carol Channing, Robert Goulet, Jerry Lewis). ∎

Before Barnes & Noble and Borders Books & Music were vying for prime real estate on every Main Street in America, our own Powell's had a national reputation as the book emporium to beat all. Some still swear by Powell's flagship store, which occupies an otherwise undistinguished block on W. Burnside. New and used books are filed side by side at Powell's, and the store has a disordered, lived-in feeling more suitable to bibliophiles than the antiseptic atmospheres of its competitors. Nonetheless, if location is half the battle, Powell's has a war on its hands. Barnes & Noble and Borders now occupy frontage in several of the metro area's most heavily trafficked shopping centers.

Fortunately for us, local booksellers are offering increasingly diverse and interesting free programs in hopes of enticing wallets inside. Most bookstores schedule weekly children's storyhours. Others—namely Powell's, Barnes & Noble (all locations), Borders (all locations), and A Children's Place— also feature monthly calendars of readings/signings, demonstrations, and activity sessions with notable children's authors and illustrators. Barnes & Noble stumbled on a bonanza with its Goosebumps Gross Out parties and American Girl Teas. These events require reservations. Call to be added to your favorite bookstores' mailing lists, and follow the monthly storytelling listings in *Portland Parent* newsmagazine.

Public Libraries

Libraries around town also offer scheduled storyhours throughout the school year. Toddlers and preschoolers are typically treated to separate sessions, and several libraries have instituted a periodic Book Babies series for parents and infants ages 6-18 months.

Multnomah County branches host an impressive array of craft sessions, pajama parties, puppet shows, and other special events year-round, but pull out the stops during summer vacation to inspire young readers to continue practicing.

Drop by your local library to pick up a program flier, or call the appropriate department below for information about branches in your neighborhood.

- **Multnomah County Library**
  Administration: 248-5402
  KidsPage:
  www.multnomah.lib.or.us/lib/kids/

- **Washington County Cooperative Library:** 642-1544

- **Library Information Network of Clackamas County:** 655-8550

- **Vancouver What's Happening Line:** 360-699-8800 ∎

T aking the kids to a movie isn't the dress-up experience many parents recall from their own youth. Kids consume movies the way their parents used to consume Pez, and much of what they're watching is no more healthful. Films are as likely to be seen in the mall multiplex as they are at home on the VCR, which takes some of the build-up out of the event.

Two movie theaters in town offer something a little different: real food. Operated by the McMenamins chain of eateries, both the Bagdad Theatre and Edgefield Power Station Theatre show second-run pictures (as distinct from first-run blockbusters) in cinemas adjacent to full-service pubs. Order from the restaurant and eat from a bench table while watching the movie.

Bagdad Theatre & Pub
3702 SE Hawthorne Blvd.,
Portland 97214
230-0895, 236-9234
Times: Sat-Sun, 2:30 pm
Tickets: $1/person
G, PG, PG-13 only

Edgefield Power Station Theatre
2126 SW Halsey,
Troutdale 97060
669-8754
Times: 6 pm nightly
Tickets: $1/person

"Crying rooms" are designed to offer a second chance to parents of children who are too young to be at the movies. The only crying rooms in town are located at KOIN Cinemas (3rd Ave. & Clay, 225-5555 ext. 4608, 243-3516), which mostly screens independent art and foreign films. Each of its two crying rooms is equipped with four seats and a monophonic sound system. Situated at the rear of the theaters, behind a glass panel, the private annexes are virtually soundproof, so Baby can carry on without disturbing anyone—except her parents. Tickets: $6; $3/senior, child; $3/before 6 pm. ∎

Chapter 3
PARKS

It doesn't take much to win the heart of a child, really: a big, shady tree, a swing, a patch of lawn, some sand. In the Portland area, there seems to be a park around almost every corner. Surely there's one your family knows best of all—where Sister mastered the rings, Brother fell from the jungle gym, and Baby ate dirt—and there's no replacing a comfortable neighborhood hangout. But some parks offer something new and unexpected: a child-designed, community-built wooden play structure; an extinct volcano; a trail under a waterfall; a bike path along a river; a koi pond; a duck pond; a water-play stream; paddle boats. Such parks are destinations, not pit stops.

RESOURCES

Call local parks and recreation offices for details about their districts. Many publish brochures with park maps and descriptions (including

continued ➡

special facilities), and accept reservations by telephone for group picnic areas.

The two larger departments—Portland Parks & Recreation and Tualatin Hills Park & Recreation District—oversee community centers, swimming pools, recreation centers, senior centers, golf courses, and tennis courts, in addition to their playgrounds and nature parks. Residents are mailed quarterly program booklets with information about their parks department's hundreds of classes, seminars, lessons, and special events. District residents have priority at registration time; out-of-district residents pay a higher fee to enroll, but are otherwise welcome to participate in most programs.

Dedicated to acquiring regional trails, open spaces, and natural areas, Metro Regional Parks & Greenspaces oversees its own assortment of more than a dozen sites throughout the region. The biannual program guide, Metro GreenScene, details Metro-sponsored hikes, tours, cleanups, bike rides, river trips, and other special outdoor events.

USEFUL PHONE NUMBERS:

- Portland Parks & Recreation: 823-2223; 823-PLAY (information hotline); 823-2525 (picnic/gym reservations; ask for brochure, How to Reserve a Portland Park for Your Picnic)
- Tualatin Hills Park & Recreation District: 645-6433
- Lake Oswego Parks & Recreation Department: 636-9673
- City of Tualatin Parks & Recreation Department: 692-2000
- Tigard Public Works Department: 639-4171
- Gresham Parks & Recreation: 669-2531; 669-2485 (reservations)
- Metro Regional Parks & Greenspaces: 797-1850
- Oregon Parks & Recreation Department State Information Line: 800-551-6949
- Reservations Northwest: 800-452-5687 (state-park campgrounds in Oregon & Washington)

B est known for their play structures, playing fields, and picnic
facilities, the following parks
are especially fun for younger kids.
At the first break in the clouds, they
will plead to be taken to a playground. Just so you don't waste a
minute of that sunbeam, be prepared with a sturdy canvas bag or
cardboard box prepacked with: pails
and shovels (one for each child),
sieve, empty yogurt containers to
use as molds and scoops, rugged toy
trucks and cars, plastic watering can,
balls (tennis, rubber, beachball, basketball, etc.), baseball bat and glove,
Frisbee, kite, sunscreen, Kleenex,
first-aid kit, picnic blanket. And
don't forget juice and a snack.
What's a park without a picnic?

Atfalati Park
6600 SW Sagert St., Tualatin

Atfalati Park encompasses an
undulating green hillside, playing
fields, basketball and tennis courts,
and an attractive fantasy playground. Little ones gravitate to the
shop, where they scoop up ice
cream delights and ply parents with
home-baked cookies. Older ones
scale the pirate ship's rope ladders
and hunt for buried treasure in the
sand. Bring tricycles and scooter
toys for an exploratory walk along
the winding, paved trails. There's little shade on the rise here, and no
picnic shelter, but Atfalati Park is
often swept by cool breezes that
miss the lowlands.

Beverly Cleary Sculpture Garden
Grant Park, NE 33rd Ave. & Brazee,
Portland

An Oregon native, award-winning children's author Beverly
Cleary mastered reading at a gram-
mar school in northeast Portland,
not far from the Klickitat Street she
made famous in *Henry Huggins* and
her many other books about child-
hood—and not far from Grant Park,
site of this monument.

TIPS

Thirty-eight of the developed
parks in the Portland Parks &
Recreation district are equipped with
wading pools. Unfortunately, in this era
of budgetary belt-tightening, not all
pools are open each summer. In 1996, 27
wading pools were in service. To inquire
about the wading pool at your favorite
Portland park, call 823-2223. (See also
Active Play: Indoor Fun, Swimming Pools.)

Dedicated in October 1996, the
Beverly Cleary Sculpture Garden for
Children features a central fountain
surrounded by bronze statues of
Ramona, Henry, and his mongrel,
Ribsy. Local sculptor Lee Hunt took
pains to make the sculptures accessible to children (even toddlers can
sit on Ribsy's back) and realistic,
though whimsical: Henry is wearing

Blue Lake Park is one of the region's largest recreational areas.

a Band-Aid and Ramona has on rainboots. Restrooms are adjacent to the nearby playground.

Blue Lake Regional Park
Off Sandy Blvd. & NE 223rd Ave., Portland
797-1850, 665-4995

$3/vehicle

Operated by Metro Regional Parks & Greenspaces, Blue Lake Park is a 185-acre recreational paradise. The big draw is the lake. Rent a paddle boat, canoe, or rowboat.

TIPS

A popular location for corporate picnics, Blue Lake Park can get crowded on summer weekends. Plan instead a Wednesday visit, to coincide with the eight-week Especially for Kids program (mid-June–mid-August, 2 pm). Each 45-minute performance spotlights premier local talent in a puppet show, play, concert, or demonstration of educational value.

Nature Crafts, another summer kids' program, is a series of four hour-long art sessions that features take-home projects using spruce cones, clay, dried nettles, and origami paper (late June–early August; Tuesdays, 1 pm; $2/child).

Music by Blue Lake is a weekly concert event in summer; families are welcome (mid-June–mid-August; Thursdays, 6:30 pm).

Let the kids wade and splash in the swim park (no lifeguards) or water-play area.

But there's more to do than get wet at Blue Lake. Bring bikes to tour the interior or to explore the scenic 40-Mile Loop Trail (see Nature Parks), which runs adjacent to the park. Fish for largemouth bass, bluegill, green sunfish, and catfish from the docks. Hang from the jungle gym, slurp on a popsicle. Then try a new sport, like horseshoes or archery, or an old favorite, like a nature hike. (Most sports gear is provided on loan; bring your own fishing and archery equipment.)

Picnic tables and shelters abound, as do restroom facilities. Bring a lunch or purchase hot dogs and other snack foods at the concession stand.

Cedaroak Park
4515 S. Cedaroak, West Linn
657-8721

A wooden fantasy castle designed, with the input of schoolchildren, by noted playground architect Robert Leathers of New York (see also Columbia Park and Hallinan Park), this play structure was built in 1988 by parents, children, and staff members on the grounds of Cedaroak Elementary School. Twice a year volunteers from the community return to refurbish and repair the structure, which is surrounded by gravel.

There are playing fields, a tennis court, and a few picnic tables here, but not much shade and no restrooms. The playground is open

to the public from dawn to dusk on weekends and holidays, during summer vacation, and on school days after 3:05 pm. Park in the school parking lot, not on the street.

Columbia Park
1600 SW Cherry Park Rd., Troutdale

Columbia Park is famous for its community-built wooden play structure, yet another Robert Leathers design (see also Cedaroak Park and Hallinan Park). Erected in 1994 behind Reynolds High School, Imagination Station is a circular, castlelike construction on a springy ground-cover cushion. The park itself, with its extensive playing fields, benefits from continued improvement. Recent upgrades: a picnic shelter, restrooms, concession stand, and forest trails.

Cook Park
South of Durham Rd. at end of 92nd Ave., Tigard

At 51 acres, Cook Park, Tigard's prized play park, has long been attracting metro-area families with its expansive playground, well-groomed fields, and clusters of shaded picnic tables. Toddlers are content on the swings and slides, while older children get involved in games of volleyball, basketball, and horseshoes. Adults tend to venture toward the Tualatin River, where there's a fishing dock, boat ramp, and paved, mile-long trail (wheelchair-accessible). Reservations for the large picnic shelter go fast in summer, so call early: 639-4171.

Hallinan Park
16800 Hawthorne Dr., Lake Oswego
635-0353

Erected by the Hallinan Elementary School community following an ambitious fundraising campaign in 1988, the extensive play structures here were designed by New York playground architect Robert Leathers (see also Cedaroak Park and Columbia Park). Tucked away in a quiet, suburban neighborhood, the park is largely unknown outside its immediate environs. Facilities include picnic tables, playing fields, a running track, and portable toilets. The playground is open dawn to dusk on weekends, holidays, during summer vacation, and on school days after 4 pm.

Ibach Park
10455 SW Ibach St., Tualatin

Ibach Park was scarcely complete before the word was out among local families and they began arriving to see for themselves what the fuss was all about. Surrounded by brand-new suburban sprawl, Ibach Park is indeed an oasis. Young children rush to explore the dinosaur bones, splash in the waterplay stream, scale the meteor, ride the trolley. Older children are no less inspired; they've never quite imagined a playground like this. Adults talk about it the way they would a work of art, and there are intriguing and varied sculptural references to many of the fixtures.

Learn of the Atfalati tribe, natives of the Tualatin River Valley, from interpretive signs posted along a paved pathway. Bring baseball equipment and tennis racquets. Spread a picnic cloth on the vast lawn, or in the picnic shelter, and stay all day. The sapling trees offer little shade, so wear sunscreen and hats in summer.

TIPS

Downtown Tualatin was underwater during the 1996 flood, and people are still paddling around. Actually, the shops and parking lots that turned into lakes are high and dry now, but a concessionaire on the banks of the 5-acre manmade Lake of the Commons rents three-person paddle boats in season (Wed–Sun, noon–8 pm; $5/half-hour). Swimming is prohibited, but children may wade.

The surrounding park is lovely, with picnic tables and a computerized, run-through fountain. Bring food for the ducks, then feed yourself at one of the nearby family restaurants. In summer the Tualatin Commons hosts a free outdoor concert series on Friday evenings. For information, call 692-2000.

Rose Garden Children's Park

SW Kingston Blvd., adjacent to International Rose Test Garden, Washington Park, Portland

As if the zoo, Japanese Garden, and Rose Test Garden weren't reason enough for families to make regular pilgrimages to Washington Park, since 1995 there has been an even better reason in the minds of young children: Rose Garden Children's Park. Originally envisioned by the Rotary Club of Portland as the nation's first park designed to fulfill the specific needs of children with disabilities, the place may be too good to be true.

So surreptitious are the special

TIPS

In 1871, when Portland's population stood at 8,000 and the city was surrounded by forest, hills, and the river, the city purchased more woods—41 acres—from a private citizen for the then-steep price of $32,624. The 1901 Park Commission's report reads: "The purchase was at first regarded by most citizens with disapprobation or contempt." Fortunately, nothing came of this general dissatisfaction, and Washington Park, now grown to 129 acres, is among Portland's best-loved and most-used parks. (See Rose Garden Children's Park, International Rose Test Garden, Japanese Garden, Metro Washington Park Zoo, and World Forestry Center.)

The park also boasts one of the metro area's few designated archery ranges. The flat green field, located downhill from the Rose Garden Children's Park, is equipped with hay bales. Archers are asked to bring their own gear and targets.

handicapped aids—handrails, arm-
rests on benches, Braille instructions—one scarcely notices them.
But then, it's hard to concentrate on
much of anything in the hustle-bustle of children here. Wildly popular
with kids, the Rose Garden
Children's Park is showing some
wear and tear. Park superintendents
acknowledge they have had trouble
keeping up with necessary repairs.
Of deeper concern is talk that disabled children appear to be staying
away, perhaps intimidated by the
rowdy crowds.

Even at its worst—on a sunny
weekend when it's a beehive of
activity and parking is scarce—this
park is best. Themed "pods" feature
a castle, spaceship, clock tower, and
tree house. In addition, there are a
sand play area and water-fight fountains, tube slides, a variety of
swings, and shaded lawns for picnicking. Nearby, the old zoo's
Elephant House, once a haven for
drug dealers, has new life as a picnic shelter with restroom facilities. ■

I n Portland you need not drive far to feel far away. Any of these metro-area parks can provide an escape from the ho-hum hum-drum. There's lots to do on a nature walk: Breathe the fresh air, slop in the mud, listen for woodpeckers, watch a twig boat navigate the eddies of a stream, turn a somersault in a sunny meadow, tickle a slug.

Let the kids whine, fuss, drag their heels, feign a limp or charley horse. Once you're in the woods, they're sure to stand taller and walk faster. With their animal instincts on red-alert, they're frisky as kittens—and you are, too.

TIPS

Just because it's sunny and hot at your house doesn't mean the weather's the same in the forest. Many of the region's wooded hillsides and deep, steep ravines are damp and shaded year-round. The state's reputation for rain translates into mud on unpaved nature trails, and those that receive the least sunshine can remain gooey for weeks after the last downpour. Dress appropriately, in layers for flexibility, and in sturdy walking boots or shoes for comfort and protection. Bring along a daypack to carry the cast-offs, along with a canteen of water, high-energy snack, first-aid kit, sunscreen, Kleenex, and a notebook and pencil for "scientific observations."

Champoeg State Heritage Area
Champoeg Rd., St. Paul
678-1251
Fee: $3/vehicle

To an outsider, 615-acre Champoeg (pronounced "Sham-poo-ee") State Park looks like any other. The Willamette is slow and wide here, the trees dangle lichens and ferns, and the frogs offer a serenade. But Champoeg wasn't always so serene.

On this site on May 2, 1843, farmers who had settled the area voted 52 to 50 to establish a provisional government, the region's first. With its strategic location on the river, Champoeg was a regular stop for stagecoaches and steamboats, and a thriving village (pop. 200), until a record flood washed out the town in 1861. Visitors today can peek in at the Manson Barn, which was salvaged from the flood. Two other structures are open to the public in season: the Pioneer Mothers Cabin Museum (503-633-2237), a massive log structure built in 1931; and the Newell House (678-5537), which was reconstructed by the Daughters of the American Revolution.

Many are content instead to enjoy the setting. Hike in the woods near the river, or bring bikes for a ride along the 3.5-mile paved trail (wheelchair-accessible). There are three picnic shelters here, and expansive meadows and lawns on which to spread out. The campground features 46 tent sites, 48 sites with electrical hookups, and 12 walk-in tent

TIPS

Champoeg State Park keeps more than its history a secret. Another surprise is to discover that it's outfitted with a nine-hole disc (Frisbee) golf course. Located near the Oak Grove Day-Use Area, the field is equipped with nine baskets into which players try to launch their flying discs. There is no fee to play, but you must bring your own equipment. Pick up a course map at the visitors' center on entering the park.

On hiatus for several years, the Historic Champoeg Pageant plans to return for a 10-day run during 1998. With a new script that traces the history of Oregon through the eyes of a Columbia Gorge petroglyph, the musical epic will play in the park's 2,000-seat amphitheater on consecutive evenings. Call for details: 678-1251.

sites. To reserve, call Reservations Northwest: 800-452-5687.

Crystal Springs Rhododendron Garden
SE 28th Ave., 1 block north of Woodstock, Portland
771-8386
Season: March-early September, 10 am-6 pm daily
Fee: $2/adult; free/Tues-Wed

Operated by the Rhododendron Society on land owned by Portland Parks & Recreation, this 6.5-acre enclave is a paradise of birds. All manner of ducks and other water-

E M METCALFE

Crystal Springs Rhododendron Garden is loveliest in spring.

fowl flock here, and local bird-watching groups regularly visit to take a new census. Bring binoculars, cracked corn, and a notebook to keep tally of the varieties you see: mallards, wood ducks, domestic ducks, widgeons, buffleheads, pie-billed grebe, and coots. The wooden boxes nailed to tree trunks are for wood ducks (with round door openings) and bats (without).

TIPS

Save your stale bread for croutons and French toast. Ducks prefer cracked corn, and so do park supervisors. As it turns out, the molds in old bread can make birds sick. Furthermore, uneaten morsels attract rats, and what rats refuse pollutes the water. A produce stand adjacent to Crystal Springs sells cracked corn, as do local bird shops. It costs about 30¢ a pound.

Surrounded by the Eastmoreland Golf Course and fed by 13 different springs, the peaceful gardens are planted with hundreds of rhododendron species and azaleas, which generally reach their peak blooming season in late April and early May. Winding, paved trails loop around lakes, over bridges, past waterfalls and fountains, along a lagoon. There are neither tables nor shelters, but picnicking is allowed on the lawn.

Forest Park

"Whose woods these are ..." In Portland, these woods—the 5,000-acre Forest Park—belong to everybody, and we couldn't be luckier. The largest natural area in any U.S. city, this expansive tangle of firs, alders, and maples is crisscrossed by some 50 miles of trails. Navigating the wilderness with children takes some forethought, though, because few of the paths make loops. Hoyt Arboretum (4000 SW Fairview; 228-8733) has free Forest Park trail maps and staff who can offer suggestions for family walks.

An obvious place to start is at the end of NW Thurman St. (continue west from NW 25th Ave., across a small bridge to the dead end). Especially popular with cyclists, Leif Erickson Dr. begins here. Once a public throughway that was closed in the 1950s, this broad trail is still paved in spots, and relatively flat. Though it continues for about 7 miles, you will likely tire before then and turn for home.

Sample another bit of Forest Park from Cumberland Rd. (ascend Westover from NW 25th Ave., then continue up Cumberland to the dead end). The dappled Cumberland Trail hugs the hillside along a ravine. Connect with Wildwood Trail, then Upper Macleay Trail, and emerge on Macleay Blvd. for a short walk back to the car. Ambitious (and strong) hikers can remain on Wildwood Trail for a steep climb to Pittock Mansion (*see Kid Culture, Exhibits & Museums*).

TIPS

Portland Parks & Recreation sponsors Forest Park hikes on Saturdays in
season (9 am–2 pm; $2/person). Seven
miles long, with elevation gains of
600–900 feet, the guided outings
may be too challenging for some children. Participants meet at Wallace
Park (NW 25th Ave. & Raleigh) and
car-pool to the trailhead. Call ahead
for details: 823–5132.

Hoyt Arboretum
4000 SW Fairview Blvd., Portland
228-8733

Established in 1928, the 175-acre
Hoyt Arboretum boasts one of the
nation's largest collections of
conifers, including Brewer's weep-
ing spruce, Himalayan spruce, dawn
redwood, Chinese lacebark pine,
and a maturing grove of coast and
giant redwoods. This city-owned
garden of wood is adjacent to
Washington Park, and many of its
10 miles of trails dip into its neigh-
bor and link with Forest Park
byways beyond.

The Vietnam Veterans Memorial
Trail and Bristlecone Pine Trail are
wheelchair-accessible; most other
trails are rugged and steep at times.
Scenic outlooks over Portland and
toward mountain peaks are worth
the climb, even when you're toting
a child. Wildflowers in spring, and
colorful foliage and wild mushrooms
in fall, are other seasonal treats.

TIPS

When you arrive in Hoyt
Arboretum for a walk, stop first at
the visitors' center to get oriented
(9 am–3 pm daily). The restrooms are
here, and a large picnic shelter is
directly across the street. Seasonal
trail maps for spring's wildflower
displays and autumn's fall foliage
fiesta cost 50¢ each. A self-guided
tour booklet is available for $1. While
you're here, pick up a free Forest Park
trail map to add to your collection.

Free, guided 90-minute tours
of Hoyt Arboretum are offered on
weekends from April–October (2 pm).
Reservations are not required, but you
might call ahead to assess suitability
for children. In addition, the arboretum hosts a series of preschool nature
classes in fall and spring ($1/child per
class, reservations required), and special
family events, also in fall and spring
($5/family, reservations required).

International Rose Test Garden

400 SW Kingston Ave., Washington
Park, Portland
823-3636

From its terraced hillside above
the city, the International Rose Test
Garden is more to Portland than a
botany laboratory. But to serious
rose hybridizers, this idyllic spot
represents a confluence of conditions too good to be true.

Since 1917 the 4.5-acre rose garden, one of only 25 such sites in the
country, has been methodically conducting research into the performance levels of new rose varieties.

PHOTO COURTESY OF THE PORTLAND OREGON VISITORS ASSOCIATION

On a clear day, the view from the International Rose Test Garden is among the city's finest.

TIPS

Tourists visit all the time; Portlanders prefer to come on lazy Sunday afternoons after church, or for wedding portraits against the scenic skyline backdrop. (Blooms are at their best from early June–early November.) Whether native or not, visitors to the International Rose Test Garden bring their cameras.

Children may quickly lose interest in row upon row of flowers (8,000 plants, 532 varieties). Encourage them to study just a few closely, and soon they'll initiate a hunt for a family favorite—be sure to factor in aroma, as well as color, shape, and texture. Enjoy a giggle at the roses' funny "celebrity" names, then ask your children to select the varieties by which they would choose to be immortalized.

The adjoining 2-acre amphitheater, which hosts summer concerts, is a great place to run and romp. Restrooms and picnic shelters are located near the tennis courts and parking lots up above on Kingston Ave., as are a seasonal concession stand and the zoo train depot. The Rose Garden Children's Park (see Playgrounds) is an easy walk farther down Kingston.

"Best Rose" winners are exhibited chronologically in the Gold Medal Garden. Roses still in the guinea-pig stage are designated by numeral only. Improvements in handicapped access are expected shortly.

TIPS

Portland isn't called the Rose City for nothing. Here are two other public rose gardens to visit:

Peninsula Park Rose Garden; 6400 N. Alberta: 823–3636

Ladd's Addition; south of Hawthorne Blvd., bounded by SE Hawthorne Blvd., Division, 12th Ave., & 20th Ave.: 823–3636

Japanese Garden
611 SW Kingston, Washington Park, Portland
223-4070
Hours: Spring/fall, 10 am-6 pm daily; summer, 9 am-8 pm daily; winter, 10 am-4 pm daily
Fees: $5/adult; $2.50/senior, student; free/child under 6 years

In 1990, at the 25th anniversary of the Japanese Garden, no less than the ambassador to the U.S. from Japan proclaimed this "the most beautiful and authentic Japanese garden in the world outside of Japan." Ambassador Matsunaga was merely confirming what loyal visitors have long suspected: The Japanese Garden is a spiritual oasis.

It's serene, quiet, and meditative on this Washington Park promontory, with views out over downtown Portland and on to Mount Hood. Among the pristinely manicured shrubs, deftly raked pebbles, and artfully designed bamboo fences, children subconsciously sense an indefinable otherness. If you're lucky, they'll act with careful, cautious reverence. If you're not, they'll act like children.

Kids just have too much fun here. And who can blame them? There are peek-a-boo pathways along a cascading stream, creaky boardwalks through a marsh, mysteriously intriguing carp, rocks to climb, and rocks to throw. Within the 5.5-acre spread are representations of five separate garden styles: Strolling Pond Garden, Tea Garden, Natural Garden, Sand and Stone Garden, and Flat Garden. Ask your kids to identify them (without reading the plaques!).

Jenkins Estate
8005 SW Grabhorn Rd., Aloha
642-3855
Grounds hours: Winter, 8 am-5 pm daily; summer, 8 am-8 pm daily

Originally owned by heiress Belle Ainsworth Jenkins, the 68-acre Jenkins Estate was purchased by the Tualatin Hills Park & Recreation District in 1975. The main house—built to resemble an English hunting lodge—and stable have been restored and are available by reservation for private receptions and business functions. The carriage house, greenhouse, pumphouse, and water tower await their turn.

With winding, hide-and-seek

TIPS

The Japanese set aside a day each year when to be a child is to be king. The Japanese Garden has merged the traditional Boys Day and Girls Day into Children's Day (early May; Sunday, 1–5 pm). Bring the kids then, when their exuberance will go unnoticed, or they'll be so focused on origami workshops, tea ceremonies, dancing, and martial arts demonstrations that they'll forget to misbehave.

TIPS

If the Jenkins Estate's lush landscaping and big, weird fish aren't reward enough for your children, entice them with images of a pot of gold at trail's end. Walk south past the teahouse to Camp Rivendale, a clearing where outdoor sessions for youths with physical and learning disabilities are held each summer. There's a fine play structure here, an ample lawn, and picnic shelter. (The camp is in use on weekdays in summer until 4 pm.) Best of all, well away from the peaceful estate, your kids are free to shake their sillies out.

gravel paths, a rockery, and koi pool, the gardens were designed in a traditional English Picturesque style. Rhododendrons and wildflowers are at their best in spring; the perennial gardens peak in summer.

. Bring a picnic to spread out on a lawn, park bench, or covered table. But be mindful that there are no public restrooms, save one portable toilet in Camp Rivendale (see Tips).

Mount Tabor Park
SE 60th Ave. & Salmon, Portland

To visit Mount Tabor Park is to experience a brush with danger ... but not really. This peak is an extinct volcano, one of only two found in cities in the continental U.S. (Bend has one also.) On a clear day, the climb provides a view of downtown Portland and Mount

Hood. Below there are basketball and tennis courts, a playground, picnic shelters, an off-leash dog area, and restrooms. Cinders discovered in the park were used to surface its roads. Send the children off to hunt for volcanic rocks.

Oxbow Regional Park
3010 SE Oxbow Parkway, Gresham
797-1850, 663-4708
Fee: $3/vehicle

Evidence indicates Native Americans inhabited the Oxbow Regional Park area 9,000 years ago, and it's easy to see what drew them here. Oxbow's 1,000 acres encompass an ancient forest and a switchback of the Sandy, one of the state's most scenic rivers. Owned and man-

TIPS

When the nationally renowned Olmsted brothers arrived from Boston in 1904 to propose a park system for Portland as part of the planning for the Lewis & Clark Exposition, they recommended a 40-mile loop trail that would encircle the city and connect the region's scenic parks like pearls on a necklace.

Since then Portland has grown. Likewise the 40-Mile Loop. Though it will stretch 140 miles when complete, and connect 30 metro-area parks along the Columbia, Sandy, and Willamette rivers, it still goes by its historic moniker. Bits and pieces are already in place, with Forest Park's Wildwood Trail (see Nature Parks) and the Springwater Corridor (see Active Play: Outdoor Fun, Biking) making the most significant contributions.

To order a colorful 40-Mile Loop trail map, send a $3 check made out to "City of Portland" and a stamped, self-addressed envelope to: Portland Parks & Recreation, Receptionist, 1120 SW 5th Ave., Room 1302, Portland, OR 97204.

aged by Metro Regional Parks & Greenspaces, Oxbow, the system's largest park, has been left relatively undeveloped.

Come to hike, bike, or ride horseback; there are 30 miles of trails throughout the park. No motorized boats are allowed, but canoes, kayaks, and rafts are welcome, as are fishermen (consult park staff regarding regulations). In season several small, rocky beaches provide access to the river for swimmers (brrr!).

Picnic tables and shelters dot the park, and there are two playgrounds. Forty-five campsites are available on a first-come, first-served basis.

Earmarked for improvements courtesy of a 1995 bond measure, Oxbow Park will look a little different in coming years. Though the natural character of the area will be maintained, trail access, signage, nature-interpretation exhibits, and restroom facilities will soon be updated. At present the park is equipped with pit toilets only.

TIPS

Oxbow Regional Park hosts regular nature programs for families throughout the year, but in summertime it's especially busy. Schoolchildren investigate park ecosystems and animal habitats in Discovery Days, a series of four hour-long sessions (July–mid-August; Tuesdays, 1 pm). Weekly Saturday campfire programs spotlight history lessons, storytellers, and birds of prey (July–late August, 8 pm). Call the park for a schedule of guided nature walks and other special events: 797-1852.

Oxbow Park is also the site of the annual Salmon Festival, which coincides with the return of spawning Chinook salmon to the Sandy River in mid-October. Tiptoe beside the river for a chance viewing. Learn about the life cycle of these anadromous fish from park guides. Stay for a salmon-bake lunch, live entertainment, and children's craft activities. Fee: $6/vehicle.

continued ➡

METRO REGIONAL PARKS AND GREENSPACES

Bring a canoe to Oxbow Park and explore the Sandy River.

TIPS

Metro Regional Parks & Greenspaces' group picnic facilities at Oxbow Park and Blue Lake Park (see Playgrounds) are hot commodities in summer. The reservation lines open October 1, and by June 1 all weekends are booked. Reserve a weekday and receive a 20 percent discount. Picnic reservations include the use of a baseball diamond for two hours, plus equipment for volleyball, horseshoes, and basketball.

Park regulars may wish to consider purchasing an annual pass for $35. Good for entry and parking at Oxbow Park, Blue Lake Park, Chinook Landing Marine Park, and the James M. Gleason Boat Ramp, the Metro Parks pass is valid October–September. Pick one up at Oxbow Park, Blue Lake Park, or at the Metro Greenspaces office (600 NE Grand Ave.).

Portland Audubon Society
5151 NW Cornell Rd., Portland
292-6855

Nestled against Forest Park's southwestern flank, the Portland Audubon Wildlife Sanctuary is deep, dark, and tranquil. Home to the Giant Pacific salamander (it barks like a dog and grows to be a foot long) and bats (look for wooden bat houses nailed high up in trees), in addition to a variety of bird species, the 150-acre park consists of dense forest and 4 miles of rugged trails. The maze of trails weaves and loops over bridges and boardwalks, past a pond, below a rough-hewn picnic hideout, alongside Balch Creek, and up and down steep hillsides. Two longer loops begin south of Cornell (be alert when crossing this busy road).

Stop by the trailhead at the Wildlife Care Center, where volunteers tend to injured birds and other forest creatures. Peek in the windows to see them gently handle baby birds and drip nutrients into their beaks using syringes.

Permanent residents, whose cages face the outdoor courtyard, include two hawks, a pygmy owl, barn owl, and Mexican free-tailed bat.

Enter the Nature Center (Mon-Sat, 10 am-6 pm; Sun, 10 am-5 pm) for an up-close look at the backyard birds and squirrels which come to feast at a large platform feeder, and at the display of birds, nests, and eggs. Walk down Cornell Road to Macleay Park, which sports green grass, picnic tables, and additional restrooms.

Kids hunt for creatures in Balch Creek.

Silver Falls State Park
20024 Silver Falls Hwy., Sublimity
503-873-8681
Fee: $3/vehicle

At 8,700 acres, Silver Falls is the largest of Oregon's state parks. From the main day-use parking lot it's a short, flat walk to a viewpoint that looks directly down on the 177-foot South Falls. But the park has nine

School groups visit the Portland Audubon Wildlife Sanctuary to learn about native flora and fauna.

TIPS

The Portland Audubon Society hosts a regular selection of nature programs for families and children. Day-camp are offered during winter, spring, and summer vacations. Field trips and workshops are scheduled throughout the year.

Free, guided nature walks (or slide shows in bad weather) are held every Saturday, 1:30–2:30 pm. Guest speakers make presentations at Nature Night, second Tuesday of each month, 7 pm. Call ahead to assess suitability for children.

TIPS

Cousins of the hummingbird, Vaux's swifts migrate up from Central and South America in spring to mate and hatch their young before returning south when the weather gets colder. Like the swallows who return each year to California's San Juan Capistrano, these tiny birds have established a traditional communal roosting place in the chimney at Chapman School (NW 25th Ave. & Pettygrove).

Sometime in late August (the timing is not predictable), as many as 25,000 swifts begin a bedtime ritual that continues, nightly, until the cold season arrives in late September. Come as dusk approaches, and sit on the hillside by the baseball diamond (bring a blanket, as the grass is prickly). Then look up.

At first they look like tiny watermelon seeds dancing against the sky, chirping a singsong melody. Then, as quickly as they came, they are off to swoop over Forest Park, collecting friends. The tiny birds return as an ever-larger group, circle the chimney, flutter away, come again. The chimney whirlpool intensifies until, one by one, the swifts drop inside, where they cling by their claws, en masse, to the brick flue. Sleep tight!

The entire performance can last about 45 minutes. If you're lucky, the Portland Audubon Society will be on hand with informational fliers, examples of swifts and their nests (they stick twigs together with saliva), binoculars, and volunteers who can answer questions.

According to PAS, swifts roost together for several reasons: to avoid predators, to keep warm, to provide role models for their young, and to locate one another before the long migration.

---

other hidden treasures, which are visible from the popular 7-mile Trail of 10 Falls. (This hike is arduous, so think twice about embarking on it with small children.)

Stop by the visitors' center for trail maps and advice. The lodge also features a snack bar, fireplace (a great place to warm up), nature displays, and a small gift shop.

Few children (or adults) can pass up an opportunity to stand behind a waterfall, so you'll likely want to descend into the canyon and slog through the mud and mist to crouch under the massive rock outcropping, sheltered from the spray and deafening rush.

Bring bikes for the paved, 4-mile loop trail, or rent horses (in season) and explore the equestrian trails (14 miles). Picnic tables and shelters are scattered throughout the park, as are restrooms.

In summer the river is dammed south of the parking lot for swimmers. The beach is rocky, not sandy, and the water is cold—but that doesn't seem to discourage children, who are also attracted to the wooden play structure.

The Silver Falls campground is outfitted with 51 tent sites and 54 sites with electrical hookups. (To reserve, call Reservations Northwest: 800-452-5687.)

Tryon Creek State Park
11321 SW Terwilliger Blvd., Portland
636-4398

Nestled in a shady canyon between Lewis & Clark College and Lake Oswego, Tryon Creek State Park is a 645-acre forest with 14 miles of trails for hikers, bikers, runners, and equestrians. Pick up a trail map at the nature center, and ask advice on activities appropriate to your family's stamina.

Shorter legs are happy enough with the 0.35-mile Trillium Trail, a paved, all-abilities loop. Older children may prefer to venture farther into the wilderness to explore the creek and its bridges. Bicyclists stay to a 3-mile paved path that runs parallel to Terwilliger Blvd. (this is not a loop trail). Horseback riders have two packed-gravel loops to

choose from, for a total of 5.2 miles.

Restrooms are found in the nature center. A large pavilion shelter is equipped with benches, but no tables.

TIPS

Sunday-afternoon programs are a Tryon Creek tradition. Though fall and spring bring nature lectures for adults, in summer the park hosts a concert series (see Kid Culture, Music), and special Sunday events for schoolchildren are scheduled four times a year, in October, December, April, and August (nominal fee). Site of a popular summer day camp, Tryon Creek also offers a twice-monthly series of nature classes for preschoolers and their caregivers ($12/class, reservations required).

Tualatin Hills Nature Park
(formerly St. Mary's Woods)
North of Tualatin Valley Hwy., adjacent to SW 170th Ave., Tualatin Hills

Scheduled to open in November 1997, this 200-acre nature park, once owned by St. Mary's Home for Boys, is being developed courtesy of a 1994 bond measure that earmarked $2 million. A smaller version of Tryon Creek State Park (see above), its wetlands, forest, and wildlife sanctuary encompass the region where Cedar Mill Creek and Beaverton Creek merge.

Designed for contemplation and walking, Tualatin Hills Nature Park features 4 miles of trails (one of them handicapped-accessible), a visitors' center, and covered shelter. No bicycles or horses are allowed, and there are no picnic facilities.

Willamette Greenway Trail
SW Macadam & Nebraska, Portland
Fees: $2/vehicle; $3/vehicle plus trailer in summer

Relatively flat and smooth, the Willamette Greenway Trail traces the west side of the river from just south of Willamette Park through Johns Landing, and is great for strollers, toddlers, and still-wobbly bicyclists. Plans are under way to extend the footpath north to the downtown waterfront and south to Sellwood Bridge. But at present, just about a mile of trail is negotiable by foot or bicycle. Park near the playground at Willamette Park and watch the activity at the boat ramp, then follow the trail north as it meanders past condominium apartments and office buildings.

Popular with runners and cyclists, the narrow, paved footpath gets crowded on sunny weekend afternoons; give your kids a wide berth if their steering and braking is uncertain. Take time to skip stones

and watch the boats at one of the rocky "beaches." Then stop for refreshments at a nearby restaurant (Who-Song & Larry's has a kids' menu), or retrace your steps to the playground for a picnic.

Follow the path south from Willamette Park, through the adjoining neighborhood, and emerge in Butterfly Park. In spring and summer the native shrubs, trees, and meadowlands here are particularly attractive to and other colorful flying insects. ■

TIPS

Both the Wild Bird Center (646-6907) and Backyard Bird Shop (635-2044) host an impressive variety of guided walks, workshops, and presentations year-round, many of which are ideal for families and youngsters. At Wild Bird Center, children learn to build birdfeeders and birdhouses. Backyard Bird Shop operates a summer day camp for schoolchildren interested in nature. Call for details.

Chapter 4

ACTIVE PLAY: OUTDOOR FUN

Psst! Can you keep a secret? It doesn't always rain in Oregon. But when there's a break in the clouds, everyone takes a break—outdoors. The Portland metro region is one of the country's most scenic. The wilderness is relatively unspoiled: Mount Hood is snow-capped year-round, the rivers run fast and clear or slow and sure, the lakes are well stocked with fish and rental boats.

Let's keep it that way. Promise you won't tell a soul, or what you like to do on a nice day won't be so nice anymore.

Enchanted Forest

Exit 248 off I-5 in Turner
503-363-3060
Hours: March 15-September 30,
9:30 am-6 pm daily
Admission: $6.50/adult;
$4.95/senior; $5.75/child 3-12
years; free/child under 3 years
Extras: $1/Haunted House;
$1.50/Ice Mountain Bobsleds;
$2/Big Timber Log Ride

Lovingly constructed on a wooded hillside near Salem, Enchanted Forest is a dream come true for little kids. A grandfather now, Roger Tofte has been crafting storybook castles, village huts, and amusement park rides for more than 30 years. And he's probably still not completely satisfied, though many of his customers are. Recent additions include English Village and Big Timber Log Ride, a tour-de-force attraction.

In summer, local college and high school students put on five fairy-tale shows a day in the outdoor Fairweather Theatre. But for preschoolers it's enough just to romp along the twisted trails, peering into the Seven Dwarves' cottage, wiggling into a bunny hole near Alice in Wonderland's toadstool, and slipping down a bumpy slide at the Old Woman's Shoe.

This is no Disneyland, so the challenge is to amuse older children. The scary haunted house, log ride, and bobsled roller coaster may be enough. But nobody should miss Fantasy Fountains, a charming water-and-light show in the English Village.

There are snack and lunch foods here, as well as picnic tables if you pack your own. The steep, winding pathways can be slippery and muddy in poor weather, and the dense trees keep the temperature cool. Come on a hot, sunny summer afternoon for a welcoming patch of shade.

The newest attraction at Enchanted Forest is the Big Timber Log Ride.

Family Fun Center
29111 SW Town Center Loop W.,
Wilsonville 97070
685-5000
Hours: Winter; Sun, 10 am-9 pm;
Mon-Thurs, 11 am-9 pm;
Fri, 11 am-11 pm; Sat, 9 am-11 pm.
Summer; Sun-Thurs, 9 am-10 pm;
Fri-Sat, 9 am-11 pm
(hours extended in fine weather).
Mini-golf: $5/adult; $3.50/senior,
child 12 years & under
Go-karts: $4/driver; $1.50/
passenger
Bumper boats: $3.50/driver;
$1.50/passenger
Batting cages: $1-$25

An exceptionally clean and welcoming facility, Family Fun Center
has it all: Kidopolis (see Active Play:
Indoor Fun, Indoor Playgrounds),
Bullwinkle's Family Restaurant,
arcade games, and outdoor miniature
golf, go-karts, and bumper boats.

Golfers choose from one of two
18-hole courses—a castle theme
with cave and waterfall, or a
Western town with totem poles and
sawmill. Putters come in three sizes.

Go-kart drivers must be at least
4 feet 9 inches tall, and passengers
must be at least 4 years old. Cars
race each other on the 1,000-foot
road course, which features dips
and hairpin turns.

With 20 boats and a cascading
waterfall at the bumper-boat pond,
everybody's bound to get soaked,
so plan accordingly. Drivers must be
at least 3 feet 8 inches tall, and passengers must be at least 4 years old.

The eight batting cages offer a
range of pitching speeds, from slow-
pitch softballs to 70-mile-an-hour fast-
balls. Bats and helmets are provided.

TIPS

The outdoor facilities at Family
Fun Center are open year-round,
regardless of weather, and are well-
lit at night. Dress appropriately for
the season, but if you're caught off-
guard in a rainstorm, the center sells
ponchos for $1.

Malibu Grand Prix
9405 SW Cascade Ave.,
Beaverton 97008
641-0772
Hours: Winter; Mon-Thurs, 11 am-
10 pm; Fri, 11 am-midnight; Sat,
10 am-midnight; Sun, 10 am-10 pm.
Summer;1 1 am-midnight daily.
Racetrack: $2.50-$19.95
Batting cage: $1/16 pitches

A popular birthday-party destination, Malibu Grand Prix showcases two racetracks and three different go-kart models. The larger, half-
mile road course accommodates the
Virage (a 3/4-scale, gas-powered
formula Indy car) and the Sprint
racer. Equipped with brake and gas
pedals (the transmissions are auto-
matic), the cars can reach speeds
of up to 30 miles an hour in races

Malibu Grand Prix features two racetracks and three different go-kart models.

against the clock.

The small, oval racetrack accommodates a simpler go-kart called the Slick. On this track, drivers race each other. All drivers wear helmets and are strapped in using a four-point harness. On-track supervisors monitor the activity at all times. The tracks are least crowded after school, on weekend mornings, and during the dinner hour.

There are eight outdoor batting cages where players can practice

---

TIPS

Not all children are tall enough to handle the steering wheels at Malibu Grand Prix. Drivers must be at least 4.5 feet tall to drive the Slick and Sprint cars, and 3.5 feet to accompany an adult driver. To drive the Virage without a driver's license, youths must complete the Car Control Clinic and be at least 14 years old.

---

using a variety of balls and speeds. Bats and helmets are provided.

Indoors, the 100 video games and mechanical kiddie rides do good business in inclement weather. Snack foods are available.

Mount Hood SkiBowl Action Park
Government Camp 97028
503-272-3206 ext. 234, 222-BOWL (information line)
Hours: Late May-mid-September; Mon-Fri, 11 am-6 pm; Sat-Sun, 10 am-7 pm
Adventure Pass: $25; $20/half-day

The question isn't what's here; the question is, what *isn't* here. In summer, Mount Hood SkiBowl hosts legions of revelers—no doubt many of them the very same daredevils who schuss down the slopes in winter. They are drawn back to the mountain by the region's only Alpine slide (a half-mile, side-by-side model) and more than a dozen other amusement-park activities, many of which defy description.

There are the obvious: a scenic chairlift ride to the summit; Indy go-karts; pitching, batting, and golfing machines; Gyroscope; Kiddie Jeeps (tots steer the miniature gas-powered vehicles themselves); 18-hole miniature golf course; children's play park with ball bin and wooden play structure; guided equestrian trail rides; pony rides; and 40 miles of rugged trails for mountain biking.

Then there are the downright outrageous: motorized skateboards (wear protective gear and closed-toe shoes); Velcro flytrap (dress in a Velcro suit, jump on an air mattress, and hurl yourself onto a Velcro wall); body-nerfing (slink into a Nerf cylinder and roll downhill); a bungee trampoline (do flips and other gymnastic moves with the aid of a belt attached by bungee cords to poles on either side of a trampoline); and a 100-foot double bungee tower (get the picture?). If the person who dreamed up these attractions hasn't already killed himself playing guinea pig, he should have his head examined.

Spread over 960 acres, the park is divided into west and east sides. The west features the chairlift, which provides access to the Alpine slide and upper bike trails. A half-mile east lies the bulk of the action, and the nature of the majority of these attractions precludes the participation of small children. Kids older than age 6 begin to have a fiendishly good time, however.

Rides with restrictions include: Alpine slide (child under 4 feet tall rides free with adult); Indy cars (must be 4 feet 4 inches tall and at least 12 years old to drive); horseback riding (must be at least 6 years old to ride solo); motorized skateboards (minimum age 10 years); body-nerfing (minimum age 10 years); bungee trampoline (minimum weight 60 pounds); bungee tower (minimum weight 80 pounds; youths under age 18 must present parent-signed release form and have parental supervision).

To avoid crowds, come on a Monday, Tuesday, or Wednesday. A cafeteria is available, but picnics are also welcome (barbecuing is prohib-

ited). Corporate picnickers swarm the grounds on weekends, so call ahead (222-BOWL) to ensure the entire park hasn't been reserved for a private party. Check also on weather conditions, which can close the Alpine slide and chairlift.

TIPS

The Adventure Pass ($25; $20/half-day) is SkiBowl Action Park's best ticket package for die-hard thrill-seekers. The pass entitles each visitor to unlimited rides on the Alpine slide and unlimited use of all east-side attractions, except the go-karts, bungee activities, and horses. Discounted tickets for these attractions are available to all Adventure Pass-holders.

If you're interested in mountain biking and little else, call the park (503-272-3206 ext. 244) to assess the trail options at your skill level and request a trail map. Many of the trails are gravel service roads; others are even more rugged. Helmets and permits ($3/day) are required of all riders, and should you decide to try the upper trails, you'll also need to purchase chairlift tickets ($5/round trip).

Oaks Amusement Park

Foot of SE Spokane St.,
Portland 97202
233-5777

Hours: Spring break & weekends until mid-June, noon-dusk. Mid-June-early September; Tues-Sun, noon-9 pm (later on weekends). September-mid-October, weekends, noon-dusk.

Admission: $8.50/4-hour limited bracelet (excludes roller coaster, bumper cars, & Sea Dragon); $10.75/4-hour deluxe bracelet; go-karts, miniature golf, and carnival games priced separately

Built in 1905, Oaks Park is the nation's oldest continuously operating amusement park, and as such it has entertained generations of Oregonians from its rambling facilities on the banks of the Willamette River. Home to Ladybug Theater *(see Kid Culture, Theater)* and the West Coast's largest roller rink *(see Active Play: Indoor Fun, Roller Skating)*, in addition to a full complement of rides, this place may lack high-tech razzmatazz, but it serves up generous portions of old-fashioned charm.

Spread over 44 acres, Oaks Park was once a hang-out for delinquent teen-agers. Now operated as a nonprofit community resource, the amusement park has overcome its bad reputation. Its managers, themselves parents, are committed to creating a safe and friendly environment for families. To that end, they

TIPS

Oaks Park means to be affordable. Special discounts ($5.75/limited bracelet; $8/deluxe bracelet) are available with coupons from local sponsors on weekdays throughout the summer. Past participants have included Burger King, Safeway, and KFC. Call Oaks Park in late spring for details about upcoming programs.

Free rides are typically offered on opening day, the first Saturday of spring break. Patrons wearing DARE and GREAT T-shirts ride free for four hours, beginning at noon. Girl Scouts and Campfire groups are treated to free-ride days later in the season. Two other free-ride events—the Rosebud Picnic for disabled children and their families, and Foster Family Day—are open to invitees only.

Annual holiday festivities are planned for Easter and July 4th, and Oaks Park usually hosts one family concert a year. Parking is the major drawback at such events; it can take two hours to get out of the lot after the fireworks bash on July 4. If you decide to attend a special event, plan to use public transportation *(see Trains & Trolleys, SamTrak).*

have tightened security, instituted rigorous employment requirements, and banned alcohol and personal fireworks from the popular annual July 4th party.

The result: Oaks Park is teeming with young children again (teens don't find much of interest here), and corporate picnics fill the amusement park on summer weekends. Bring lunch from home, or feast on snack foods from the concession stands. Dozens of picnic tables overlook the river, and shelters that are booked by groups on weekends are vacant on weekdays and in the evening.

The park is continually re-evaluating its mix of rides, but current favorites include: a miniature train, bumper cars, ferris wheel, Tilt-a-Whirl, Matterhorn, Sea Dragon, Hammer, Haunted Mine, Scrambler, and a brand-new, $1 million roller coaster from Italy. Kiddieland features a historic wooden carousel, Jump Cycles, Ladybugs, bumper boats, and an outdoor modular play structure. Height restrictions apply to the bumper cars, Sea Dragon, and roller coaster, the same rides that are excluded from the limited-bracelet package.

Thrill-Ville USA
Exit 248 off I-5 in Turner
503-363-4095
Hours: Spring break & weekends until Memorial Day, 11 am-6:30 pm; Memorial Day-Labor Day, 11 am-6:30 pm daily; Labor Day-October 1, 11 am-6:30 pm weekends (hours extended summer weekends)
Admission: $15.95 per

person/unlimited rides

If you haven't been to Thrill-Ville USA in a while, it's worth another look. Virtually every year since opening in 1990, this small amusement park adjacent to Enchanted Forest has installed a new ride or made another improvement. Recent additions have included paved pathways, shade trees, and grassy knolls.

The lineup of attractions is impressive. There is a go-kart track, ferris wheel, Tilt-a-Whirl, Sidewinder, and Octopus, plus bumper boats, side-by-side water slides, and the Ripper roller coaster, Oregon's largest. Kiddieland features Little Ripper roller coaster; an old wooden carousel; Bulgy the whale; and helicopter, car, and train rides.

Purchase snack foods, or bring a picnic to enjoy in the covered grove near Kiddieland or on the lawn by the water slides. ■

TIPS

Corporate picnics in summer are big business at Thrill-Ville USA. So it's best to visit on a Monday, Tuesday, or Wednesday in season, or to call ahead to avoid lines on weekends. Another option is to schedule an early evening excursion; in summer, an unlimited ride pass costs just $10 per person on Fridays and Saturdays after 4 pm.

Once the kids stop arguing over who gets the blue ball, who gets to keep score, and who gets to putt first, you can start having fun. After all, isn't that why you came?

OUTDOOR COURSES

■ **82nd Ave. Miniature Golf**
2806 NE 82nd Ave.,
Portland 97220
253-0902
Hours: Winter; Mon-Fri, 9 am-9 pm; Sat-Sun, 8 am-9 pm. Summer; Mon-Fri, 9 am-11 pm; Sat-Sun, 7 am-11 pm. Fall; Mon-Fri, 9 am-10 pm, Sat-Sun, 7 am-10 pm.
18 holes: $3/adult; $2/child
Driving range: $3/bucket of balls

■ **Family Fun Center**
(See Amusements.)

■ **Family Mini-Golf & Hoop**
19655 SW Tualatin Valley Hwy.,
Aloha 97006
591-8590
Hours: March-May; Fri, 4-10 pm; Sat, 10 am-10 pm; Sun, noon-8 pm. June-August; 10 am-11 pm daily. September-October; Fri, 4-10 pm; Sat, 10 am-10 pm; Sun, noon-8 pm.
Fees: $2.25/9 holes; $4.25/18 holes
Motorized Basketball Hoop Shoots: $3.50/adult; $2.50/child 11 years & under

■ **Oaks Amusement Park**
(See Amusements.)

■ **Golden Bear Golf Center at Sunset**
16251 SW Jenkins Rd.,
Beaverton 97006
626-2244
Hours: 9 am-10 pm daily
18 holes: $3.50/adult; $2.50/child 12 years & under
Driving range: $2.50/half-bucket of balls; $5/bucket

INDOOR COURSES

■ **Chocolate Chipper**
Eastport Plaza, 4000 SE 82nd Ave., Portland 97266
777-6219
Hours: Mon-Fri, 2-9 pm; Sat, 10 am-6 pm; Sun, 11 am-5 pm
Fees: $2/round; $3/2 rounds

■ **Tee-Time Mini-Golf**
9244 SW Beaverton-Hillsdale Hwy., Beaverton 97005
297-7080
Winter hours: Tues-Thurs, 3-8 pm; Fri, 3-10 pm; Sat, 11 am-10 pm; Sun, 11 am-6 pm
Summer hours: Tues-Thurs, 11 am-8 pm; Fri-Sat, 11 am-10 pm; Sun, 11 am-6 pm
Fees: $3/18 holes; $4/unlimited golf

Had enough of windmills, castles, and loop-de-loops? Perhaps you're ready for something a bit more challenging.

The Children's Course
19825 River Rd., Gladstone 97027
722-1530
Hours: Winter, 7:30 am-dusk daily; summer, 6:30 am-dusk daily
Fees: $5-$7/9 holes; $8-$13/18 holes; discounts during off-season

Opened in July 1996 to provide children—particularly under-privi-leged and at-risk youths—with the opportunity to learn golf, the layout of this nine-hole, par-3 outdoor course is ideal for youngsters. Holes range from 130-265 yards, and a third set of tees provides further advantages to kids. Junior golfers are encouraged to enroll in lessons and special clinics. Those who pass a written rules and etiquette test receive greens-fee discounts.

Tualatin Island Greens
20400 SW Cipole Rd., Tualatin 97062
691-8400
Hours: April-September, 8 am-10 pm daily; October-March, 8 am-9 pm daily
18-hole putting course: $5/adult; $3/child 15 years & under
Driving range: $4-$8/bucket of balls

The putting outdoor course here consists of 18 famous golf holes that were copied and reduced to scale (30-50 yards each), including an island green that's accessible only by bridge. Many of the 62 driving-range tees are covered and heated for year-round play on a synthetic surface. The facility features a pro shop, restaurant, and junior golf programs. ■

The butt of many jokes across the country, Portland's wet weather is legendary. There is a silver lining to all those winter clouds, however: snow. Just enough of it falls in town to remind us that Mother Nature still has the upper hand. And within a little more than an hour's drive, there's enough to ski on all year long.

Even before your kids are ready to ski (or you're brave enough to teach them), the Mount Hood area offers ample winter recreation opportunities. For toddlers it's often enough just to taste a snowflake, make snow angels, and launch a few snowballs. *(See also Excursions, Mount Hood.)*

Whatever your intentions, always check the weather conditions before heading up to the mountain. Call the Oregon Department of Transportation (541-889-3999) for an update; Slope Talk (800-593-2021), a hotline sponsored by the Oregon Ski Industry Association; or any of the resorts' dedicated snow phone lines (see below).

Be prepared with traction devices and emergency supplies. And dress the children appropriately: in multiple layers, starting with long underwear or tights and two pairs of socks, and finishing with a wool sweater and hat, gloves, and a thick winter parka. Pack a change of clothes for each family member; everyone's bound to be cold and soggy after an hour or two in the snow. Sunscreen is another necessity. In fine weather the sun reflects off the snow and burns unprotected skin.

TIPS

To park in many of the western states' winter recreation areas from November 15–April 30, drivers are required to purchase and display in their vehicles valid Sno-Park permits. Available at Department of Motor Vehicles offices, sporting goods stores, gas stations, and ski resorts (which tack on a service fee), permits come in three sizes: 12-month ($9), three-day ($2.50), and one-day ($1.50).

Alpine Skiing

Anyone who has ever learned to downhill-ski as an adult will tell you they wish they hadn't waited so long. It goes without saying that a child's body—with its supple bones and low center of gravity—is better designed for the slopes than an adult's. So if your kids show even the slightest interest in skiing (or snowboarding), let them try it out before they're old enough to creak and ache.

Mount Hood, the state's highest peak, boasts some of the nation's most extensive ski resorts, and many runs are groomed for skiing even in summer. Several local resorts make it especially affordable for parents to introduce their little kids to the sport by allowing youngsters under age 7 to ski free with a paying adult.

If alpine skiing is not your idea of a good time, wait a few years until your kids are a little more self-sufficient. Schoolchildren are eligible to participate in special weekend ski-lesson packages that include bus transportation to and from the slopes (see Tips, pages 97, 98 and 100).

Ski Rentals

Depending on your circumstances, it might make sense to lease ski equipment in Portland, not at the mountain. Of course, your vehicle must be equipped to carry a family's worth of gear, and you have to plan ahead to get outfitted. But with a little forethought you can circumvent the resort rental shops' frustrated and frantic early-morning crowds, and likely save money.

Several outdoor retail stores in the Portland area—including REI, G.I. Joe's (Delta Park store only), and Breeze Ski Rentals—and similar outlets in Sandy, Welches, and Government Camp, lease alpine and nordic ski equipment and snowboards. Expect to pay about $14 for adult alpine equipment, $10 for child alpine equipment, considerably more for snowboards, and less for cross-country skis. (For comparison, Mount Hood Meadows charges $18 for alpine rentals, $15 for nordic equipment, and $28 for snowboards.)

Call in advance to inquire about children's gear and availability. Then take your time to ensure that the ski boots really fit. REI offers

long-term leases of four, six, and eight weeks—a good option for families who expect to spend lots of time on the slopes.

TIPS

Once you and the kids get hooked on skiing, you'll want to own your own gear. Many local families are as addicted to ski swap meets as to the sport. In fall, high school ski teams often host weekend sales to raise funds for their endeavors. Sellers bring outgrown skis and related equipment (already priced), then donate a portion of their proceeds to the ski team. For news of such sales, watch your local community newspaper or call your neighborhood high school to inquire.

The grandaddy of all ski sales takes over the Expo Center (2060 N. Marine Dr.) during the first weekend of November. Sponsored annually by the Oregon Ski Industry Association, the Portland Winter Ski & Snowboard Show features representatives from local ski resorts, as well as dozens of vendors selling new equipment. For details, call 541-387-3700.

TIPS

Though your instincts might tell you to teach the kids to ski in the summer when it's warm, they'd be wrong. The only snow on Mount Hood in July covers the steepest slopes, and the only skiers are Olympic athletes and wannabes.

Resorts

Cooper Spur Ski & Recreation Resort

11000 Cloud Cap Rd.,
Mount Hood 97041
541-352-7803, 230-2084 (Portland)
Season: Winter only
Hours: Thurs, 4:30-10 pm; Fri-Sat, 9 am-10 pm; Sun, 9 am-4:30 pm (closed Mon-Wed except holidays and vacation weeks)
Lift tickets: $12/adult; $8/child 11 years & under; free/under 7 years with parent; $5/night

This smaller resort on the eastern slopes of Mount Hood reopened under new management four years ago. Popular with families in the 1940s and '50s, Cooper Spur still markets itself primarily to families and novice skiers.

What you see is what you get: A T-bar provides access to 10 runs. But the price is right; Cooper Spur is the cheapest around. Children under age 7 ski free with a paying adult. The Learn-to-Ski package costs $30 per adult, and $20 per child 11 years & under (rental equipment included). And night skiing is free when you rent ski or snowboard equipment.

Mount Hood Meadows Ski Resort

Hwy. 35, Mount Hood 97041
503-337-2222, 227-SNOW (snow phone)
Season: Mid-November-early July
Hours: Mon-Tues, 9 am-4 pm; Wed-Sun, 9 am-10 pm
Lift tickets: $35/adult; $21/child 7-12 years; $6/6 years & under; $17/night; discounts in late spring; season passes & family rates available

With 10 chairlifts, 82 runs, and 2,150 acres, Mount Hood Meadows is the largest day-ski resort in the U.S. Equipment rentals, lessons, and groomed slopes and tracks are available for alpine and nordic skiers and for snowboarders.

The Mount Hood Meadows Ski School oversees a variety of youth lesson packages:

Children ages 4-12 are grouped by age and ability in daily, supervised KidSki programs. Choose a half-day ($50, rentals included) or full-day ($70, rentals and lunch included) session.

Available daily to children from age 10, Learn to Ski features a 90-minute lesson and Buttercup lift ticket ($35; $30/nordic; $45/snowboard; rentals extra.)

TIPS

For kids who are really gung-ho about skiing (and parents who are not), Mount Hood Meadows has arranged a charter bus service that operates from many local schools on weekends in January and February. Ideally suited to those who are enrolled in multiweek ski-school programs, children in grades 1–12 are grouped with their peers on chaperoned private buses. Buses depart designated sites early on Saturday and Sunday mornings, and return from the resort late in the afternoon. Expect to pay about $64 per child for a four-week session. For details about the route in your neighborhood, call the Mount Hood sales office: 246-1810.

Bus-Lift, another charter service that transports skiers to Mount Hood Meadows on weekends in season, makes five stops in the metro area. Children 13 years and older may travel unaccompanied. Tickets are available from Ticketmaster ($20/bus ride; $49/bus, plus adult lift ticket; $38/bus, plus youth lift ticket). For details, call BUS-LIFT: 287-5438.

If you're the one driving to the mountain, remember that there is an alternate route to Mount Hood Meadows. Take I-84 east along the Columbia River to Hood River, then take Hwy. 35 south to the resort. Traveling this way may add about 15 minutes to the 90-minute trip, but you'll avoid the congestion that typically clogs Hwy. 26.

You can save money on lift tickets, lessons, and rental equipment by planning your ski trips in advance and enrolling your children in one of the following multiweek ski-school packages, offered in January and February only:

Children in grades 1-8 are eligible to participate in Sno-Blasters, a supervised, all-day ski-school program that meets for four consecutive weekend sessions ($260; $292/snowboarder; rentals included).

Children in grades 6-8 who no longer require supervision can enroll in the Middle School Program, which includes four half-day lessons in alpine skiing or snowboarding ($152; $192/snowboarder; rentals included).

Mount Hood SkiBowl
Government Camp
503-272-3206, 222-BOWL (snow phone), 254-0847 (ski school)
Season: Winter only
Hours: Mon-Tues, 1-10 pm; Wed-Thurs, 9 am-10 pm; Fri, 9 am-11 pm; Sat, 8:30 am-11 pm; Sun, 8:30 am-10 pm

Lift tickets: $14-$30/adult; $18/child 7-12 years; free/child under 7 years

Mount Hood SkiBowl, the resort nearest Portland, is also one of the last to get snow. But when it does, SkiBowl offers the nation's largest night-ski area, with night skiing on 34 lit runs beginning daily at 3:30 pm. Sixty-five day runs are served by four chairlifts and five surface tows, including 600 acres of expert slopes. *(See Amusements for details regarding the summer season's Mount Hood SkiBowl Action Park.)*

A variety of ski and snowboarding packages are available to kids. Mogul Busters is an intensive, four-session program for children ages 4-13. Two instructors share responsibility for leading groups of six to eight children in two 2-hour lessons each day ($210; $60/one-day session; rentals extra).

Ski and snowboard lessons for beginners are offered daily. Students are grouped by ability, not age, in these 90-minute sessions. ($25; $34/snowboard; rentals and surface-tow pass included).

TIPS

While your kids are in ski school, you can be, too. Parents whose children are enrolled in a four-session Mogul Busters program are treated to a special, concurrent lesson package at Mount Hood SkiBowl: four 90-minute lessons and all-day lift passes ($95, regularly $160).

The Mogul Busters program features optional weekend charter bus service from depots on Portland's west and east sides. The cost for transportation over the four-week session is $65/child. Call for details: 254-0847.

TIPS

In continuous operation since 1927, Summit may not be the glitziest mountain resort, but for families trying to satisfy skiers of varying abilities, it's often the best choice. Enroll the older kids in snowboarding classes and the younger ones in ski school, then take the pouting nonskier tubing on the nearby slope (see also Sliding Areas below), or on a trek in snowshoes (they're available for rent for $10). Nordic skiers—and their babies—may prefer a cross-country sled ($12) to an infant backpack.

TOM IRACI

Dress appropriately for a day on the slopes, where all that's predictable about the weather is its unpredictablility.

Summit Ski Area

Government Camp
503-272-0256
Season: November-April
Hours: 9 am-4 pm weekends
& holidays
Lift tickets: $12; $10/half-day;

$7/rope tow only

The second oldest developed ski area in the nation, Summit is another good option for beginners. Its single chairlift provides access to six runs. In addition, there is one rope tow and a small lodge with cafe and rental shop.

Summit's ski-lesson packages include a class, all-day lift ticket, and rental equipment ($35/alpine; $45/snowboard).

Timberline

Hwy. 26, Timberline 97028
231-7979 (ski area), 222-2211 (snow phone), 231-5402 (ski school)
Season: Year-round (upper lifts closed September-October)
Hours: Sun-Tues, 9 am-4 pm; Wed-Thurs, 9 am-9 pm; Fri-Sat, 9 am-10 pm
Lift tickets: $26-$32/adult; $19/child 7-12 years; free/child under 7 years; $11/night

The grand, historic Timberline Lodge, built in the 1930s as a WPA project, sits near the summit of Mount Hood and oversees the activity on six chairlifts and 32 trails. Timberline hosts the nation's most extensive spring/summer skiing season.

Lesson packages are available for alpine and nordic skiers as well as

TIPS

Timberline sells adult lift tickets through Ticketmaster at a discount. Good for any day of the week in season, 9 am-closing, each ticket costs $25 (that's a savings of $7 off weekend rates).

Ticketmaster outlets also offer the Bus & Ski Package. This round-trip, chartered bus service to Timberline makes stops daily in season at G.I. Joe's stores in Beaverton, Gresham, Vancouver, and Portland. Passengers pay $30 per weekday, $35 per weekend or holiday, lift ticket included. (The trip is not chaperoned, and there is no discount for children.) For information, call 231-9979.

snowboarders. Bruno's Children's Learning Center, a full-day program offered daily to children ages 4-12, includes rental equipment and lunch ($60). Snowboarding instruction is available to youths from age 8.

As the name implies, Mom and Me is designed to involve parents in their children's ski lessons. Offered on three or five consecutive Wednesdays, these popular, 90-minute, midweek classes provide helpful tips to parents intent on nurturing their kids' interest in skiing ($144/3 sessions; $220/5 sessions).

Nordic Skiing

Whereas many Mount Hood resorts feature groomed trails for cross-country skiing, as well as nordic rental equipment and ski lessons, their emphasis is on the alpine and snowboarding customer, who will purchase a lift ticket. At Mount Hood Meadows, where nordic skiers are treated to 15 kilometers of tracks, the trail fee is $9 per person.

If you'd prefer a more "backwoods" experience, the Mount Hood region is a maze of trails for all abilities. To receive a comprehensive list of nordic ski trails near Government Camp, call the Mount Hood Information Center: 622-4822 or 622-7674.

The trails below are short, sweet, and relatively flat and easy—good for youngsters just learning.

- **Summit Trail:** flat, 2-mile marked road begins at east end of SkiBowl parking lot.
- **Snow Bunny Trail:** more difficult, marked 2-mile road begins at Snow Bunny Sno-Park.

- **Pocket Creek Trail:** first mile of this 4.5-mile trail is relatively flat. Begins on east side of Hwy. 35, 3 miles north of Mount Hood Meadows.
- **Meadows Creek Tie Trail:** easy, 1.2-mile trail off Pocket Creek Trail (see above).
- **Clark Creek Trail:** easy, 2-mile marked trail begins at Clark Creek Sno-Park on Hwy. 35.

Sliding Areas

Sliding using saucers, inner tubes, sleds, and toboggans may look like child's play, but on a crowded, unsupervised hill, it can be more dangerous than skiing. Teach your children the basic rules: 1. Know your abilities and stay on appropriate slopes. 2. Only one slider on the hill at a time. 3. Ascend along the sides of the slope, not up the middle. 4. Don't build jumps. 5. Clear out from the bottom as soon as you stop. (Most accidents occur there.)

These designated areas are the only spots in the Mount Hood region where sliding is allowed:

Little John Snow Play Hill

31 miles south of Hood River on Hwy. 35
541-352-6002

Built by the U.S. Forest Service, Little John Snow Play Hill has two open slopes—one easy, the other more difficult. Bring your own discs, saucers, or inner tubes; sleds, toboggans, and snowboards are prohibited. Outhouses and a wooden shelter outfitted with a stove are open

TIPS

Little John Snow Play Hill is located on the edge of the snow zone, so it's wise to call ahead for snow conditions before planning an outing.

to the public. Haul some firewood from home so you can prepare a warm snack.

Snow Bunny Snow Play Area

Government Camp
503-272-0256
Season: November-April
Hours: Sat-Sun & school holidays, 10 am-4 pm
Fee: $7/tube rental

Monitored by the ski patrol, Snow Bunny Snow Play Area, just 2 miles from Summit Ski Area, features two hills with five lanes each, a small snack bar, and an outhouse. No personal sliding devices are allowed; all patrons must use (and pay for) Snow Bunny inner tubes. Kids are also allowed to tube on a designated slope at Summit Ski Area (9 am-5 pm daily, $7/tube). ■

There will be skinned knees and elbows, and close calls Mom needn't know about. Learning to ride a two-wheeler is a child's first true accomplishment—and first true taste of freedom. Because kids often have more stamina biking than hiking (they're just so excited to be going fast!), bike rides are sometimes a better option for families. And in Portland there's no dearth of nature trails for cyclists.

The following is a sampling of parks that feature paved bike trails *(see Parks for details)*:

- **Blue Lake Park**
- **Champoeg State Park**
- **Forest Park**
- **Oxbow Park**
- **Silver Falls State Park**
- **Tryon Creek State Park**
- **Willamette Greenway Trail**

(See also Amusements, Mount Hood SkiBowl Action Park; and Fishing, Henry Hagg Lake and Sauvie Island.)

Springwater Corridor

The major southeast segment of the 40-Mile Loop *(see Parks, Nature Parks)*, Springwater Corridor was originally an interurban electric railway corridor that carried passengers between Portland and Estacada from 1903 to 1953. Today its smooth, 16.5-mile paved path makes it ideal for bikers and equestrians. Acquired by the City of Portland in 1990, the trail parallels Johnson Creek and travels from just east of SE McLoughlin Blvd. to Boring, past wetlands, farmlands,

nature parks, and residential and industrial neighborhoods.

Trailheads with parking, restrooms, and picnic tables are found near SE Johnson Creek Blvd. at 45th Ave., and in Gresham at SE Hogan Rd. Eventually this trail is set to connect to the Pacific Crest Trail through Mount Hood National Forest. To obtain a trail map, call Portland Parks & Recreation: 823-2223.

TIPS

All Tri-Met buses and MAX trains are equipped with bicycle racks. To use one, a cyclist must attend a short training session and purchase a special permit that costs $5. Regular permits are issued to anyone 16 years or older. Youth permits are issued to children ages 8-15, and these young riders must be accompanied on buses and trains by adults with permits.

Permits are available at Tri-Met offices in Pioneer Courthouse Square and at 4012 SE 17th Ave. Several area bike shops also carry them. For more information about the Bikes on Tri-Met program, including MAX restrictions, call 239-3044.

Bike Rentals

These shops rent bicycles and trailers by the hour or day. Tot-size bikes are harder to come by. One option is a tandem bicycle; another is a trail-a-bike. This training attachment designed for kids features a seat, handlebars, and back-wheel unit that hooks to a rack at the rear of an adult bicycle. Call ahead for availability. Helmets are usually included, but if you have ones that you know fit, use them.

Bike Central Co-op

835 SW 2nd Ave., Portland 97204
227-4439
Hours: Mon-Fri, 7 am-7 pm;
Sat-Sun, 9 am-6 pm (10 am-4 pm in winter)
Bicycle: $12/day (child); $20 & up/day (adult)
Trail-a-bike: $12/day
Trailer: $20/day
Tandem: $75/day
Helmet: $1-$2/day

Small, one-speed kids' bikes and training wheels available. Reservations advised, especially on weekends in summer.

Bike Gallery

821 SW 11th Ave., Portland 97205
222-3821
Hours: Mon-Sat, 9:30 am-6 pm;
Sun, noon-5 pm
Mountain bike: $5/hour; $40/day
Trailer or trail-a-bike: $5/hour;
$30/day

Four other area locations.

Fat Tire Farm

2714 NW Thurman, Portland 97214
222-3276
Hours: Mon-Fri, 10 am-8 pm; Sat, 8 am-6 pm; Sun, 10 am-6 pm
Bicycle or trailer: $5/hour; $30/day
Tandem: $10/hour; $60/day

Ideal location a few blocks from Forest Park's Leif Erickson Dr. *(see Parks, Nature Parks)*, Portland's cycling heaven. ∎

P oised at the confluence of two rivers, Portland made its mark early as a significant seaport. Though the River City now relies less on the shipping industry for economic vitality than it once did, the rivers continue to be a focal point of tourism and recreation, which suits kids just fine.

Take a sightseeing cruise on a sunny afternoon and marvel at a new perspective. Children may have little patience for scenery, but they'll enjoy tossing crumbs to the seagulls, counting bridges, waving to passing watercraft, and watching the captain navigate.

Choose a smaller vessel for a more intimate and vivid boating experience, and test the waters first with a shorter excursion. The atmosphere aboard larger yachts leans toward "floating restaurant," and their exotic, gourmet dinner cruises are not particularly suitable for children. How would you like to share your romantic anniversary date with a stranger's bored (and hungry) brood?

Call ahead to check on availability and to make reservations.

Cascade Sternwheelers
1200 NW Front, #110,
Portland 97209
223-3928
Season: Year-round (in winter, Cascade Queen available only to groups)

  (Columbia Gorge only)

Authentic replicas of sternwheelers from a previous century, the *Columbia Gorge* and *Cascade*

Queen are Portland's most distinguished vessels. The latter, the smaller of the two, is patterned after paddle boats of the Mississippi, with two decks and double smokestacks. The former resembles local sternwheelers of the 1890s—specifically, the *Bailey Gatzert*—and can accommodate 600 passengers.

With two docks downtown and one in Cascade Locks, these boats maintain an active schedule of narrated cruises on the Willamette year-round and on the Columbia in summer. The two-hour Portland harbor tour is ideal for families. Choose to include a brunch buffet ($23.95/adult; $18.95/child 4-12 years; free/child under 4 years) and feast on eggs and crepes, or opt to go without and save $11 per person. Children have access to the pilot house and can stand aft to watch the paddlewheel up close.

Great Rivers Cruises and Tours
1308 SW 2nd Ave., Portland 97201
228-6228, 800-720-0012
Season: May-late November

Great Rivers II, a 132-passenger, trilevel catamaran, departs three days a week at 9 am in season, bound for Bonneville Dam on a 7 1/2-hour, round-trip adventure. Schoolchildren are entertained by the lively narration and open pilot house. Younger children are rocked to sleep by the undulating currents. There are two outside decks and an enclosed, heated one. Lunch is served, though the ship also has a

snack bar ($35/adult; $14/child;
free/infant).

Another option is the three-hour
lunch cruise, which departs at 11 am
every Saturday in season. The narrated excursion to Willamette Falls and
back features a substantial gourmet
meal ($24/adult; $17/child 11 years &
under). Operators indicate they may
soon institute a children's menu.

TIPS

There's no food on board
(except for whatever stale snacks
you may have stashed in the glove
compartment), and it's not particularly romantic, but the Canby
Ferry (655-8521), in operation
almost continuously since 1914, has
a loyal following all its own.

A small, simple platform that
holds nine vehicles and stays on
course by means of an underwater
cable, the ferry receives power
via an overhead line. It shuttles
cars across the Willamette from
Mountain Rd. in Stafford to Locust
St. in Canby, and in nice weather
families out for a drive in the country often complement a train ride
at Flower Farmer (see Farms, Special
Farms) with a trip on the Canby
Ferry. There may be a wait on such
afternoons. Bring a few toys, books,
and travel games just in case.

Hours: 6:45 am-9:15 pm daily
Fee: $1.25/car

Portland Spirit
842 SW 1st Ave., Portland 97204
224-3900, 800-224-3901
Season: Year-round

Scenery takes a back seat to food
aboard the three-story, 350-passen-
ger yacht *Portland Spirit.* Operating
from a dock at Front Ave. and SW
Salmon, the vessel focuses on dinner
cruises, with live entertainment and
an attractive menu of excursion
options and special events.

Best for families is the two-hour
champagne brunch cruise
($34/adult; $18/child 4-12 years;
free/child under 4 years) to Lake
Oswego, which features an impressive spread and an array of finger-
foods favored by kids. Passengers
may forgo the meal to concentrate
on the sights ($14/adult; $9/child 4-
12 years; free/child under 4 years).

Sternwheeler Rose
6211 N. Ensign St., Portland 97217
286-7673
Season: Year-round

Built in 1987 from the wood of
an old barn, this jaunty little red-
and-white paddlewheeler accommodates up to 130 passengers on two
levels. Available for charter, the *Rose*
also offers a regular schedule of
public cruises south to Lake
Oswego from its dock at OMSI.
Families might prefer the hour-long
harbor tours ($10/adult; $6/child 3-8
years; free/child 3 years & under) to
the more formal, two-hour dinner

($35/adult; $17.50/child; free/child under 4 years) and brunch cruises ($25/adult; $13.50/child; free/child under 4 years). Better still are Santa cruises (weekday mornings in early December, $6/person).

Yachts-o-Fun
Foot of SE Marion St.,
Portland 97202
234-6665
Season: May-October; select weekends in winter

Yachts-o-Fun is the smallest of Portland's commercial boats. A 49-passenger catamaran with an enclosed lower deck, open upper deck, and snack bar, the yacht makes daily harbor cruises from its pier at OMSI. The 90-minute narrated excursions journey just far enough downriver to include a handful of bridges ($10.50/adult; $6/child 3-12 years; free/child under 3 years). Dinner and brunch cruises are also available.

Boat Rentals

You can sail the Columbia, canoe the Tualatin, raft the Sandy. The metro area offers any number of recreational boating opportunities on rivers that crisscross the region. But before you rent a vessel with your children, be sure you feel comfortable in the skipper's seat.

Ask for pointers from the rental agents; most offer instructional programs for all ages and abilities. Discuss your planned route as well, especially if you're going rafting,

and pick up a map of the river or harbor to help you navigate. Check the craft for appropriate safety equipment before setting out. Life jackets are required for all passengers and should be provided, but not all outfitters offer a wide selection of sizes. If your children are small, it's wise to bring life jackets you know fit them. One old-time sailor recalls tying his toddlers by a length of lead to the boat to ensure that, were they to fall overboard, they wouldn't be gone long.

Pack a picnic, and tie up at an island or beach, or pull up and dock at a waterfront restaurant. After a few hours in a cramped boat, everyone will welcome the opportunity to stretch their legs.

The following outfits rent vessels and provide tips to beginners. Call well ahead for reservations on summer weekends. (See also Parks, Playgrounds, Blue Lake; and Fishing, Hagg Lake.)

Alder Creek Kayak & Canoe
250 NE Tomahawk Island Dr.,
Portland 97217
285-0464
Hours: Winter; Mon-Fri, 10 am-6 pm; Sat-Sun, 8 am-7 pm. Summer; Mon-Fri, 10 am-7 pm; Sat-Sun, 8 am-7 pm.
Canoe: $27/half-day; $40/day
Double kayak: $40/half-day; $50/day

Put in at harbor on Columbia. Paddlers must have prior experience. Shop must approve itinerary.

TIPS

Alder Creek does more than rent boats. Its ambitious lineup of classes and tours features many offerings for families.

The last Sunday of each month is set aside for parents and youths who are interested in learning the basics of sea kayaking. At the 11 am class, kids ages 6–10 are free with paying adults ($45/person). The 2 pm class is for youths ages 11–17 ($25/person).

Beginning in March and continuing into October, Alder Creek leads all-day family canoe outings in the Ridgefield National Wildlife Refuge. Equipment, instruction, and lunch are included.

Fees: $60/adult; $40/youth 11–17 years; $20/child 6–10 years

Kids Kayak Week, a summer day camp for youths ages 11–17 years ($195/person), convenes at Lake Oswego Water Sports Center, then moves to the lower Clackamas River to practice in rapids.

Ebb and Flow Paddlesports
0604 SW Nebraska, Portland 97201
245-1756
Hours: Tues-Fri, 11:30 am-6 pm;
Sat, 9:30 am-5 pm; Sun, noon-5 pm
Canoe: $15/half-day; $19/full day
Double kayak: $26/half-day;
$39/full day

Cross the street and put in on the Willamette near Ross Island.

Island Sailing Club
515 NE Tomahawk Island Dr.,
Portland 97217
285-7765
Hours: 9 am-6 pm daily
Sailboat: $140-$250/full day; $100-
$200/half-day; $25-$50/reservation
deposit

Fleet of 28 sailboats, 20-27 feet long. Knowledge of sailing required; sailing certificate required to rent 27-foot boat.

REI
1798 Jantzen Beach Center,
Portland 97217
283-1300
7410 SW Bridgeport, Tigard 97224
624-8600
Canoe: $35/day; $70/weekend
No roof racks, but REI supplies foam pads and straps for mounting on car.

River Trails
336 Columbia River Hwy.,
Troutdale 97060
667-1964
Hours: May-September, 9 am-6 pm
daily
Raft: $50-$65/day
Canoe: $25/day
Sixty to 70 rafts in inventory, plus canoes. Shuttles transport craft and passengers to and from Sandy River at 9:30 am and 11:30 am daily

TIPS

Oxbow Park leads guided raft-ing trips along the Sandy River on weekends in June and July. Ideally suited to beginners and families, the eight-hour outings feature an 11-mile, Class I (no white-water) stretch of the river, from Oxbow Park to Lewis & Clark State Park.

Meet at River Trails (see above) to pick up rafts and gear, then ferry to the park for a brief orientation session. Adults and interested youths gain experience maneuvering rafts while a trained guide follows in a kayak. Everybody learns something about the region's natural history.

These excursions are very popu-lar, so reserve early by calling 797-1834. Fees were not available at press time, but expect to pay about $35 per person. To see the greatest selection of wildlife, pick a date early in the season and depart early in the day (9:30 am). Think twice about bringing along toddlers, who tend to feel confined in rafts, or older kids who may find the scenery and slow pace tiresome.

in season. Rafts outfitted with oars or paddles, ice chests, and river bags at no extra cost. No guides provided. Two designated excur-sions: Dodge Park to Lewis & Clark State Park (Class III white-water, no children under 5 years permitted),

and Oxbow Park to Lewis & Clark State Park (see Tips). Reserve well in advance for summer weekend.

Sportcraft Marina
1701 Clackamette Dr.,
Oregon City 97045
656-6484
Hours: Winter; Tues-Sat,
9 am-5 pm. Summer; Tues-Sun,
9 am-6 pm.
Canoe & kayak: $30/day
Skiff: $60/day

Thirty canoes in fleet. Put in at floating shop, 1 mile below Willamette Falls. No reservations; boats provided on first-come, first-served basis. ∎

TIPS

Tualatin Riverkeepers, a citizen-based, nonprofit waterway-preserva-tion organization, leads half-day guided canoe trips on the Tualatin River from March-October, in cooper-ation with other local nature groups. Limited space is available for partici-pants without boats, so people are strongly encouraged to bring their own canoe and equipment. The fees were not available at press time, but organizers say they are nominal.

Discovery Day, begun in 1990, generally attracts as many as 300 boaters to a scenic stretch of the Tualatin River on the last Saturday in June. Reservations are required for all events. Call for a calendar: 624-0855.

B ait a hook with a wiggly worm, drop it in the water, and you'll have a child's attention, if not a bite. Grown men and women have been known to spend countless hours trying to outsmart fish in lakes, rivers, and oceans—only to come up empty-handed and, in the process, lose the interest (and respect) of their kids. Go fishing, not to catch a record-breaker, but to have fun outdoors.

If you're a novice angler, do a little research first, and you and your kids will get more out of the experience (and probably more fish, too). Where do fish bide their time? When, what, and how do they eat? Fishing is a living, breathing science lesson that goes way beyond guts and gore.

In Oregon, children under age 14 can fish for warm-water pan fish, such as trout and bass, without a license. Youths ages 14-17 are required to purchase an annual Juvenile Angling License ($6.25). An adult license costs $17.50 per year. Special annual tags are issued to all anglers who fish for salmon, steelhead, halibut, and sturgeon ($6-$10.50). Licenses and tags are sold at local sporting goods stores, including G.I. Joe's and Fred Meyer, and at Department of Fish and Wildlife offices. When purchasing licenses, ask for a copy of *Oregon Sport Fishing*, a booklet of information and regulations that's updated each December.

The best fishing for kids is in lakes. Rivers with fast-moving currents are much more dangerous. Choose lakes that are flushed and cleaned naturally, either by tidal action or inflowing rivers. Fish from a raft or canoe only if your child knows how to swim. Otherwise, find a spot on the bank where your child can nab frogs, skip rocks, and hunt for snakes, should your patience and persistence outlast hers (and it likely will).

Several hundred copies of *Guide to Warm Water Fishing, Portland Metropolitan Area*, a 47-page leaflet published in 1985, are still available from the Oregon Department of Fish and Wildlife. To order one, call 872-5264, ext. 5365 or 5367.

The following lakes and ponds are among the region's finest for families:

Henry Hagg Lake

Off Hwy. 47 near Gaston, south of Forest Grove
359-5732, 681-3692 (information line)
Hours: Late April-late October, sunrise-sunset daily
Fees: $3/vehicle; $3.50/with boat
Seasonal pass: $25/vehicle; $30/with boat
Electric motorboat: $10/hour
Other watercraft: $7/hour

Owned by the U.S. Bureau of Reclamation, and maintained and operated by Washington County, Hagg (pronounced "Haig") Lake (a reservoir) is stocked with about 100,000 rainbow trout—including 60,000 fingerlings—each spring. But smallmouth-bass anglers are lured by the prospects of nailing a record-breaker. The current state record-holder was caught here in September 1994.

The best thing about Hagg Lake may not be the fishing, however. This park is a recreational paradise. Divided by a buoy line that designates allowed boat speeds, the lake is popular with water-skiers and other boaters in summer. Rent a canoe, kayak, paddle boat, or small fiberglass boat with electric motor, and cruise the slow zone. Especially hospitable to young anglers, the grassy banks sport picnic areas, drinking water, restrooms—and lots of other little fishermen.

Swimming is allowed, though there are no lifeguards on duty. A 15-mile hiking/biking trail follows the forested shoreline, and adjoining Scoggins Valley Park boasts a 10.5-mile bicycle lane. Disabled visitors are catered to as well, with a short, accessible trail, and special picnic sites and boat ramps.

Roslyn Lake is annually stocked with rainbow trout.

Portland General Electric Recreational Areas

PGE has made available to the public nine recreational areas that are in the vicinity of some of the utility's hydroelectric facilities. The following two parks feature fine fishing for local families:

■ **Promontory Park**
Hwy. 224, 7 miles east of Estacada
630-5152
Season: June-October
Skiff: $50/day
Pontoon: $125/day

Located on the 350-acre North Fork Reservoir, behind North Fork Dam, Promontory Park features campsites, picnic facilities, boat rentals and docks, and restrooms. Like Hagg Lake (see above), the reservoir is divided into two speed zones, with the upper portion more conducive to angling. However, kids have an even better reason to come to Promontory Park to fish: Small Fry Lake, a shallow, 1-acre pond developed and stocked for the exclusive use of young anglers. The daily catch limit per child is three fish.

> ## TIPS
>
> In spring, when the water temperature is warmer on the lake bottom, that's where you'll find the trout. Use a slip-sinker, BB weight, marshmallow (to float the hook), and worm. In summer, trout move closer to the surface. Fish with a bobber and worm in warmer weather.

■ **Roslyn Lake Park**
From Sandy, north off
Ten Eyck Rd.
668-5690
Season: Late April-early
September
Fee: $2/vehicle, weekends only
Kayak: $5/hour
Paddle boat: $7/hour

The forebay of PGE's Bull Run
Hydroelectric Project, Roslyn Lake is
stocked annually with rainbow trout.
Fishing is best from the east side of
the lake, near the incoming stream.
A day-use area with five picnic areas
(two with shelters), in addition to
playing fields, horseshoe pits, a concession store, and boat rentals, the
park is particularly suited to families.
No motorboats or alcoholic beverages are permitted on the premises.
Wheelchair-accessible features
include a fishing dock, picnic area,
sunbathing area, and restrooms.

TIPS

Be among the throngs of
beginning anglers to hook a trout
at the statewide Free Fishing
Weekend. Held annually in early
June, the metro-area event takes
place at Bonneville Hatchery.
Children work their way through
activity stations, learning about
fish identification, water safety,
and knot-tying, before "graduating" to Mitchell Creek—which is
dammed and stocked for the occa-
sion. Equipment and instruction are
provided. For more information, call
657-2000. (See also Excursions,
Columbia Gorge.)

Promontory Park's wooded picnic facilities provide shelter from the warm summer sun.

Sauvie Island
Off Hwy. 30 north of Portland

A popular destination for fruit-pickers in summer and fall *(see Farms, Special Farms)*, Sauvie Island boasts nice beaches along the Columbia River, hiking and biking trails, and lakes, rivers, and sloughs for anglers. For a map, stop at the Wildlife Area Office (18330 NW Sauvie Island Rd., 621-3488; Mon-Fri, 8 am-noon & 1-5 pm). The kiosk outside is well stocked for weekends.

Visitors to the wildlife area are required to purchase parking permits ($3/day; $10.50/year), which are available from island merchants and at G.I. Joe's and Fred Meyer stores. Bring a picnic blanket if you plan to lunch outside; there are no picnic facilities in the wilderness, though many farmstands have tables.

Sauvie Island offers several good fishing options for families. Gilbert River is accessible via two fishing piers: one on the west side at Big Eddy, off Sauvie Island Rd.; the other on the east side on Gilbert River Boat Ramp Rd., off Reeder Rd. Expect to catch bullhead and channel catfish, walleye, crappie, and perch. The following two ponds are also recommended for kids:

■ **Haldeman Pond**
Take Reeder Rd. to
Oak Island Rd.
Season: February 1-
September 30

This 2-acre pond on Oak Island is stocked with rainbow trout several times in late spring and early summer. Come in early April and return home with a bucketful for supper. Stay on the south side of the pond, where the bank is less steep, and for insurance have the kids wear life jackets. Restrooms are found at the parking lot.

■ **Webster Pond**
Take Reeder Rd. to
Oak Island Rd.
Season: February 1-
September 30

The Oregon Bass & Panfish Club has adopted this 5-acre pond, and is developing and improving its population of warm-water fish species.

Rainbow Trout Farm
52560 E. Sylvan Dr., Sandy 97255
622-5223, 774-0088
Hours: February-October,
8 am-dusk daily
Fish priced by size

Nobody leaves the Rainbow Trout Farm without catching a fish. With 10 ponds full of ravenous trout and years of experience helping school groups land the big ones, the owners virtually guarantee you'll get lucky, and supply lessons in fish physiology at cleaning time. Bring your own equipment and bait, or borrow from the farm at no charge. Bring a picnic, too, to enjoy in the parklike setting. ■

Horseback riding isn't for everyone. Some people exude the scent of anxiety that tips horses off to their vulnerability. The very riders who are praying not to trot are the first to veer off the trail in a cloud of dust. But for true horse-lovers—the kids who collect plastic horses, wear cowboy hats, and walk bow-legged—there's no rest until they've had a chance to handle the reins of a real beast.

The following ranches rent horses and ponies for use on their property. When you call to arrange a ride, provide information regarding your group's equestrian experience. Children must be about 6 years old to ride solo; doubling up with an adult is not allowed.

Dress appropriately in long pants (blue jeans are best) and lace-up shoes or boots. Leave pocketbooks and purses in the car, and stow valuables in a backpack or fanny-pack. *(See also Amusements, Mount Hood SkiBowl Action Park.)*

Beaverton Hill Top Kennels & Stables

20490 SW Farmington Rd.,
Beaverton 97007
649-5497
Season: Year-round
Fee: $20/hour per horse

Choose from a guided trail ride through Hill Top's 50 scenic, wooded acres (trotting and cantering allowed), or exercise instead in the indoor corral. Pony rides are available for children under age 5 if par-

ents are willing to lead the animals ($20/hour; $12.50/half-hour). Hill Top accepts same-day reservations for individuals and families only. Larger groups are asked to provide advance notice.

Lakeside Horse Rentals

22551 S. Eaden Rd.,
Oregon City 97045
631-4502
Season: February-November
Fee: $13/hour

With 108 acres of flat, fenced-in farmland and more than 80 horses accustomed to kids, Lakeside is an especially safe place for beginners. Guides are not provided, but supervisors circulate throughout the property to check on visitors. Horses bearing child riders can be tied to adults by leads so they don't stray.

Promised Me Farm

1850 SW Ek Rd., West Linn 97068
638-0921
Season: Year-round
Fees: $20/hour; $10/half-hour

Even the youngest has a chance to saddle up at Promised Me Farm. Small ponies offer rides to toddlers, and older kids can try full-size horses, but everyone remains in the 7,000-square-foot, covered arena. Bring a picnic lunch to enjoy at the shaded tables.

Rocking Horse Ranch

Fall Creek & Hwy. 224, 3 miles east of Estacada
637-3031, 630-5180
Season: May-October
(weather permitting)
Fee: $12/hour

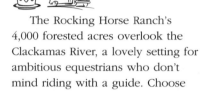

The Rocking Horse Ranch's 4,000 forested acres overlook the Clackamas River, a lovely setting for ambitious equestrians who don't mind riding with a guide. Choose from 75 horses. Carriage, hay-wagon, and covered-wagon rides are an added specialty.

Equestrian Trails

There are many options locally for horse-owners looking for new trails to blaze. Each of the parks listed below allows horseback riding on some of its trails (see Parks, Nature Parks for details).

- **Forest Park**
- **Oxbow Park**
- **Silver Falls State Park**
- **Tryon Creek State Park**

(See also Biking, Springwater Corridor.) ■

Like a high-pitched whistle that only dogs can hear, the clickety-clack of trains and ding-dong of trolleys elicit visceral reactions in children. Take them on a ride. It needn't be a big-deal, all-day affair. Sometimes the spontaneous afternoon treats are the most fun.

Amtrak

Union Station, 800 NW 6th Ave., Portland 97209
800-USA-RAIL

The destination is beside the point when a "grown-up" train is going to get you there. Amtrak offers daily service to Vancouver, Wash., and back on two distinctly different trains ($5-$8/adult; $2.50-$4/child 2-15 years; free/child under 2 years). Take the *Cascadia*, a double-decker with an upper lounge car, north from Union Station at 8:50 am. Wait two hours at the Vancouver Amtrak station, then return aboard the *Talgo*, a sleek, first-class Spanish train, and arrive at Union Station in time for lunch.

The trip may be quick (about 20 minutes each way), but there's a lot to see: Cross three bridges, walk between coaches, gaze at the Portland skyline. Snacks are allowed on both trains, but it's surely more fun to splurge on a treat from the onboard snack bar.

Built in 1910, Mount Hood Scenic Railroad has been designated a National Historic Site.

Reserve ahead, especially for weekend travel, and arrive about 30 minutes before departure. All-day parking at Union Station costs $3.75.

Molalla Train Park
31803 S. Shady Dell Dr., Molalla 97038
503-829-6866
Hours: May-October; Sun & holidays, noon-5 pm
Fare: $1/ride

This 4-acre park is equipped with eight operating 1/8th-scale model trains (engines are gas, steam, and electric) and just under a mile of rails. Climb aboard and make tracks through woods, over bridges, across a pond, and along a canal.

Mount Hood Scenic Railroad
110 Railroad Ave., Hood River 97301
800-872-4661
Season: April & September, Wed-Sun; July, Tues-Sun; November-December, Sat-Sun
Departures: 10 am & 3 pm daily (mornings only in winter)
Fares: $21.95/adult; $13.95/child 2-12 years; free/child under 2 years

You don't need to love trains to love this ride. A four-hour, 44-mile round-trip excursion from Hood River to Parkdale, the route snakes through orchards and along country back roads. With its restored rail cars from the 1910s and '20s, locomotives from the 1950s, a refurbished depot from 1911, and original tracks laid in 1906, the entire railroad is designated a National Historic Site. Events, including train robbery re-enactments, seasonal specials, and holiday festivities, are scheduled monthly. Call for details.

TIPS

Ride the Mount Hood Scenic Railroad in spring and autumn to see the orchard landscape at its peak. Reservations are strongly advised, and you are encouraged to arrive at least a half-hour before departure to pick up tickets.

The trip to Parkdale takes about 90 minutes, and time passes quickly, especially if younger children have brought along a few favorite travel games and lap activities. Ask to sit in the Timberline car, where banquettes face tables. Let the kids walk the aisles to get a feel for the dimensions of the train, and they'll likely make friends among the other young passengers. There's an open-air car at the rear, and a snack bar.

If you take the morning train, plan to eat lunch during the hour-long layover in Parkdale, where there are a few cozy cafes, a general store, and picnic tables.

Phoenix & Holly Railroad

(See Farms, Special Farms, Flower Farmer.)

SamTrak

653-2380

Stops: Sellwood Bridge at Spokane St. on the hour; OMSI on the half-hour

Hours: May-early June & September-October, 11 am-4 pm weekends. Mid-June-early September; Tues-Sun, 11 am-5 pm.

Fares: $4/adult; $1.50/child 1-4 years; $1 extra/caboose cupola

It's our own version of the Little Engine that Could. SamTrak's 150-horsepower diesel engine pulls two open-air cars on a route that links Oaks Park and OMSI. The 6-mile round trip through the Oaks Bottom Wildlife Sanctuary lasts an hour. Choose to stop off at either attraction, then pick up the train later for the return.

Willamette Shore Trolley

222-2226

Stops: Downtown Lake Oswego & RiverPlace

Season: January-February, weekends only; March-May & October-December, Fri-Sun; June-September daily

Departures: 10 am-4:30 pm

Fares: $5/adult; $3/child 3-12 years; free/child under 3 years

A sightseer's delight, two cars (one double-decker from England that was "modernized" in 1928; the other, a Portland Broadway trolley from 1932) trace the river between Lake Oswego and RiverPlace four times daily in summer. The round trip lasts 1 3/4 hours. Stop off at Willamette Park or at either terminal for window-shopping, and return on a later trolley.

TIPS

The same folks who operate the Willamette Shore Trolley also maintain a trolley collection that was once housed at the Trolley Park in Banks and recently moved to Western Antique Powerland (3995 Brooklake Rd. NE, Brooks, 97303, 503-393-2424). Here you can see trolley cars from around

continued ➡

Willamette Shore Trolley operates between Lake Oswego and RiverPlace.

the world: an Australian open car circa 1912, a Canadian Urban Car circa 1910, a Council Crest car circa 1904, and San Francisco trolleys from the 1950s. The Oregon Electric Railway Museum (222–2226) is mostly outdoors.

A cooperative venture of a dozen clubs dedicated to the preservation of antique farm machinery, Western Antique Powerland has been in operation on its farmland acreage for about 26 years. Various groups display representative equipment. The Willow Creek Railroad offers rides aboard its miniature train. The Pacific Northwest Truck Museum features antique trucks, parts, and memorabilia, including a 1917 Maxwell 1–T Peddler—a farmstand on wheels—and a Portland–built 1949 Freightliner cab. The Powerland Museum houses a collection of tractors.

Days and hours vary, and much of the equipment is kept outdoors, so call ahead before scheduling a visit, or plan to attend the Great Oregon Steamup. Held on two consecutive weekends in late July and early August, the annual event showcases antique farm equipment at work. See threshing, log–sawing, flour–milling, tractor pulls, and a farmyard parade. Then hop aboard a historic trolley for a short ride. Fees: $5/adult; $2/child 6–12 years; free/child under 6 years.

Zoo Train

(See Kid Culture, Exhibits & Museums, Metro Washington Park Zoo.) ■

Hillsboro Aviation

3565 NE Cornell Rd.,
Hillsboro 97124
648-2831
Hours: Sat, 10 am-noon (weather
permitting)
Fees: $19.50-$48

Home to Metro Traffic and news-station helicopters, Hillsboro Aviation offers a wide array of local scenic tours by air, most of which are designed for adults. Saturdays' quick-ie tours of Washington County are better for kids, who get to strap on a headset and sit right up front with the pilot in a two-seat helicopter. Passengers choose from five-, 10-, and 15-minute circuits, and are ad-vised to arrive early; rides are allocat-ed on a first-come, first-served basis.

Pearson Air Museum

*(See Kid Culture, Exhibits &
Museums.)*

Vista Balloon Adventures Inc.

701 SE Sherk Pl., Sherwood 97140
625-7385
Season: April-late October, daily
(weather permitting)
Fees: $175/person; $150/person in
groups of 4 or more

Arrive before dawn, when the air is cool and still, to help set up and inflate the hot-air balloon. Climb into the basket and find a comfortable spot in which to stand. Glide for an hour, wherever the wind takes you—over the rolling vineyards, orchards, and farmlands of the Willamette Valley. Then touch down in an open field and await the ground crew. Return to the

TIPS

It's not worth a special trip, given the airport's limited parking situation, but Kids' Flight Deck, a 1,200-square-foot, interactive play area at PDX, is a welcome diversion for traveling families in limbo. Similar in concept to a popular structure at the San Jose airport, Portland's features a mock airplane, air-traffic control tower, and weather cen-ter—all connected by intercom.

In the cockpit, "pilots" steer; in the cabin, "passengers" watch in-flight movies. The jet engine is a slide. The control

tower has a radar map of air traffic and computer monitors that supervise incoming planes and control runway lights. The weather center is equipped with a com-puterized barometer that measures cur-rent conditions in Portland.

In designing its miniature airport, Portland-based Sienna Architecture Company gathered ideas from the Children's Museum, OMSI, and airport employees. Kids' Flight Deck is located near the Delta and United terminals. For more information, call 460-4234.

launch field for a picnic of tasty gourmet hors d'oeuvres, desserts, and sparkling cider. It's a special-occasion outing, to be sure, but one you won't soon forget.

With a fleet of five state-of-the-art hot-air balloons, Vista Balloon Adventures has been in business nine years without mishap. It recommends this trip for children 8 years and older only. (For one thing, the basket is 4 feet high.) Reservations are required. ■

TIPS

Commonly referred to as the Spruce Goose, the Hughes Flying Boat (or H−4 Hercules) currently resides in a temporary, weatherproof facility on the grounds of Evergreen International Aviation Inc. in

The historic Hughes Flying Boat is housed in a weatherproof facility in McMinnville, awaiting the construction of an aviation museum.

McMinnville (3850 Three Mile Lane, 503−472−9361). Constructed in the early 1940s of laminated wood (birch, not spruce), a "nonessential" material in wartime, the single−hull, eight−engine aircraft weighs approximately 400,000 pounds. Surmounting increasing skepticism about the viability of the project, Hughes and his team of engineers labored on, and in late 1947 Hughes himself piloted the Flying Boat in a successful trial flight. The plane lifted 70 feet off the water, flew one mile in less than a minute at a top speed of 80 miles an hour, then made a perfect landing.

The Spruce Goose is the cornerstone of Evergreen Aviation's vintage aircraft collection, and the focus of its efforts to raise the funds necessary to build the Captain Michael King Smith−Evergreen Aviation Educational Center. For now, visitors are welcome to tour the company's restoration hangar and view the other historic aircraft on display (two ME 109G−10's, a 1938 CW−A22 Falcon, and a 1942 Piper J−3 Cub), and to drive by the office buildings and get a peek at the Flying Boat through the protective fencing. Hours: Mon−Fri, 9:30 am−4 pm.

Chapter 5

ACTIVE PLAY: INDOOR FUN

Cabin fever. It's a dreaded, chronic malady known to cause irreparable damage to the nervous systems of otherwise healthy mothers and fathers. How can you avoid falling victim to this perplexing and potentially disabling condition? Get out of the house!

You don't have to be a skier to enjoy winter weather. You just have to be a little creative. Bundle the kids up against the rain and cold, and go looking for fun. There's plenty of action indoors at these local establishments.

Q: How did our parents manage before the invention of the indoor playground?

A: They didn't; look at us.

Seriously, these kid-size gerbil mazes have their detractors, but who hasn't witnessed first-hand the gleam in a child's eyes when offered the chance to burrow in ball pits, tumble down tube slides, get sweaty, disheveled, and bounced silly? Adults have even been known to think it looks like fun, only to pulverize a kneecap, throw out a back, or get wedged in a tunnel. Indoor playgrounds take the groans and grunts out of the weather. Much more good fortune and we'll lose our rights to complain.

Whether it's SuperPlay, Kidopolis (at Family Fun Center), or Discovery Zone, the setup is basically the same: a colorful, modular multilevel plastic obstacle course, complete with ball pits, tube slides, bouncing mats, and climbing ropes; arcade-style redemption games; and a snack bar.

On busy days (rainy weekends, usually), kids swarm the play structures in great numbers, and the facilities' humidity readings top out at locker-room levels. Bring a hand towel to mop your child's brow, and a water bottle to slake his thirst. Remember, too, that socks are required (for sanitary purposes), and that most play facilities lend out kneepads to save patrons' joints (and jeans).

Discovery Zone

7809-B Vancouver Plaza, #180, Vancouver, WA 98662
360-254-2900

Hours (subject to change):
Mon-Thurs, 10 am-8 pm; Fri, 10 am-10 pm; Sat, 9 am-9 pm; Sun, 11 am-8 pm

Fees: $5.99/child 36 months-12 years; $3.99/child 12-36 months; free/adult

The indoor playground pioneer in this market, Discovery Zone grew too fast, and was forced to close its Portland-area facilities several years ago. Vancouver still boasts a Zone, as does Salem.

Kidopolis

Family Fun Center, 29111 SW Town Center Loop W, Wilsonville 97070
685-5000

Hours: Winter; Mon-Thurs, 11 am-9 pm; Fri-Sat, 9 am-11 pm; Sun, 10 am-9 pm. Summer; Sun-Thurs, 9 am-10 pm; Fri-Sat, 9 am-11 pm (hours extended in good weather).

Fees: $4.75/child from 2 years-5 feet tall; free/child to 2 years, 2 adults per child

Open since 1994, the Family Fun Center likes to remind you that "Fun" is its middle name. They're on to something here. The indoor playground differs hardly at all from the other options around town, but when you factor in the redemption games and video arcade; full-service restaurant with animated, computer-

TIPS

Generally, the main play structures at these facilities are best for kids from about age 4. Younger children are variously entertained by pint-size versions and freestanding, preschool-style equipment, but will invariably yearn for something better. Don't invest in a visit for a toddler only unless you plan to take him through the larger unit—again and again. And don't bank on being able to supervise at both structures simultaneously; that's not always possible. Though some places hire monitors to oversee the play, adults are required to remain on the premises to watch their kids.

To get your money's worth, you really ought to stay for about two hours. Fuel up the kids beforehand, then treat them to a snack at halftime (no outside food or drinks allowed).

You probably won't be able to get out the door before dropping a few quarters in the arcade, and after you do, the schlocky prizes are likely to break on the way home. So set a limit on how much you'll spend, and be firm. If your kids are inveterate gamblers (or whiners), suggest they bring spare change from their piggy banks.

ized entertainment and fountain water show; and the outdoor facilities—miniature golf, bumper boats, go-karts, and batting cages—you've got a winning formula, especially when it's sunny.

Take the whole family and the oldest will disappear (do you really want to know where?), leaving you to focus on the youngest. Set a time to rendezvous at Bullwinkle's Restaurant. The kids can have pizza; there are better options for you, including barbecued ribs and a salad bar. *(See also Active Play: Outdoor Fun, Amusements.)*

TIPS

Their faces told the story: For many local parents, life would never be the same. The aged carousel in the Burlingame Burger King (7601 SW Barbur Blvd.; 10 am–9 pm daily; 245–1238) had broken down and couldn't (or was it wouldn't?) be repaired. When they weren't worried about how they would survive the rainy winter months without it, these parents fretted over the fate of its operator, a young

continued ➡

woman who smiled a lot (and had lots of time to read).

The indoor play structure that came to replace the vintage, wooden merry-go-round represents progress, right? Then how come only the kids are smiling?

Still, nobody can beat the price ($1/child per hour)—or, as far as the kids are concerned, the food. Rules: Parents must remain on the premises to supervise, and children under 3 years must be accompanied on the play structure by an adult.

SuperPlay

270 NW Burnside, Gresham 97030
661-7529
10894 SE Oak St., Milwaukie 97222
652-7949
17455 SW Farmington Rd., Aloha 97007
848-7529
Hours: Mon-Thurs, 10 am-9 pm; Fri-Sat, 10 am-10 pm; Sun, 11 am-8 pm
Fees: $5.95/child 25 months-12 years; free/adult, child to 24 months

Locally owned and operated, SuperPlay beat the local Discovery Zone franchise at its own game and is now King of the Padded Mountain. Itchy to keep innovating, the owners have spent the last year experimenting with pizza recipes.

Plans are to begin marketing the facilities as pizza restaurants with great on-site playgrounds and arcade games: Purchase a large pizza, and everyone plays for free.

In another departure from its tried-and-true formula, SuperPlay recently opened SuperPlay Kids Club at Spirit Mountain Casino. This drop-in childcare center for kids 6 months-12 years features a movie room, computers, Barbie Land, Construction Land, and separate infant and toddler facilities. Security is extra tight. For prices and other details, call 800-760-7977. ∎

TIPS

SuperPlay does not hire playground monitors, so parents are responsible for watching their own children. At Milwaukie and Aloha facilities, where toddler-size ball pits and mats are located in a separate room, a single parent supervisor will get as good a work-out as his kids. Avoid the confusion by visiting as a two-parent family or with a friend and her children.

Come on a weekday to take advantage of special admission discounts: Monday, pay your age; Tuesday, two-for-one; Wednesday, five free game tokens with admission; Thursday, $2 off with a can of food; Friday, super dinner deal.

Almost every community in the metro area boasts at least one indoor park. A gathering place for caregivers and a freeform free-for-all for their young children, indoor parks meet in church social halls, community centers, and gymnasiums.

Most commonly operated as nonprofit cooperatives, these groups gather at minimum once a week for two hours throughout the school year. Members are responsible for running the club: collecting dues, maintaining a collection of toys, paying rent on the facility, etc. Caregivers are usually required to remain on the premises to supervise the play, and invariably they meet others like themselves—as do their kids.

Any listing of local indoor parks

TIPS

Of the nine community centers under the Portland Parks & Recreation umbrella, all but one operate indoor parks. Their schedules and rules vary, but the majority allow drop-in visitors and charge just $1. Call the community center nearest you for details.

is outdated before it's complete, because club contacts and locations change with regularity. To learn about indoor parks in your neighborhood, start by calling your local parks department, city hall, library, or elementary school. ■

Y ou can divide children into two basic groups based on their reactions to water: those who are fearful and those who aren't fearful enough. It's a challenge in either case to instill water-safety rules, yet helping your kids learn to swim may be the single greatest gift you can give them. The statistics are sobering: In Oregon, drowning is among the top four causes of death in children, and it's the leading cause of death in kids ages 1-4 years.

The state may not be blessed with months of swimming-pool weather, but as the list below indicates, there are many indoor swim centers that offer instruction and open-swim hours throughout the year.

North Clackamas Aquatic Park
7300 SE Harmony Rd.,
Milwaukie 97222
557-7873
Season: Year-round
Residents: $3-$6; free/child 2 years & under; $1/spectator; $10/family (designated times)
Nonresidents: $4-$9; free/child 2 years & under; $1/spectator; $20/family (designated times)

A Disneyland of the deep, this place has it all: a wave pool, lap pool, shallow wading pool, diving pool, whirlpool, and three water slides. The noise level and commotion on weekends turn some away,

North Clackamas Aquatic Center is a state-of-the-art swim playpark.

TIPS

The North Clackamas Aquatic Park makes a point of accommodating families and children of all ages by maintaining a varied schedule of open-swim times and other special events.

Teen Night, the first Friday of each month, 9:15–11:15 pm, features a live deejay and free inner tubes. Fee: $5.

Parents Night Out is a fully supervised program for children ages 6–12. Offered twice a month on Saturdays, 5–10 pm, the evening includes swimming (of course), dinner, games, popcorn, and a movie. Fee: $15/child, plus $15 deposit.

To beat sticker shock at the admission desk, plan your visits carefully. Arrive during the last two hours of open swim and receive $2 off each admission. Or come on a Sunday, Monday, or Wednesday during open swim, when special family rates are available ($10/resident family; $20/nonresident family).

No diapers are allowed in the pools, so children who are not yet toilet-trained should wear plastic pants.

but for many the chaos is all part of the fun. Mark Spitz never had it so good.

Children under 8 years old must be supervised at all times by a parent or guardian. Snack foods are available from the on-site cafe; food and beverages from home are not allowed. Call for a complete schedule of lesson and open-swim times.

Portland Parks & Recreation (823-5130, 823-SWIM) manages five indoor and eight outdoor swimming pools in its district, each of which offers a variety of programs, including swim lessons, water-exercise classes, and special open-swim hours. Suited to waders and beginning swimmers, most Portland pools have shallow ends that begin at 1.5 feet. (The shallow end at Sellwood Pool begins at just 8 inches!) Indoor pools are open year-round; outdoor pools are open from mid-June–Labor Day. Call your neighborhood pool for a schedule or to reserve the facility for a party. Fees: $2/adult; $1/child under 17 years.

INDOOR POOLS

- **Buckman Swim Pool**
  320 SE 16th Ave., Portland
  823-3668

- **Columbia Swim Pool**
  7701 N. Chautauqua, Portland
  823-3669

■ **Dishman Community Center & Indoor Pool**
77 NE Knott, Portland
823-3673

■ **Metropolitan Learning Center Swim Pool**
2033 NW Glisan, Portland
823-3671

■ **Portland Community College/Sylvania Swim Pool**
(lessons only)
12000 SW 49th Ave., Portland
823-5130

OUTDOOR POOLS

■ **Creston Park Swim Pool**
SE 44th Ave. & Powell, Portland
823-3672

■ **Grant Swim Pool**
2300 NE 33rd Ave., Portland
823-3674

■ **Montavilla Community Center & Swim Pool**
8219 NE Glisan, Portland
823-3675

■ **Mount Scott Community Center & Swim Pool**
5530 SE 72nd Ave., Portland
823-3676

TIPS

The Portland Parks aquatics team deserves credit for dreaming up some of the region's most creative summer-time activities. No doubt many parents find themselves fighting the urge to dive in, too.

To kick off each summer session, Portland pools offer one week of free swim lessons. Be sure to reserve in advance. Scholarships are available to those who wish to continue but find the costs prohibitive.

A free, open-swim time is scheduled at each pool weekly. Call your local pool for a schedule. The turnout is consider-able; best to come only if your kids thrive on noise and splashing.

Dive-in Movies feature second-run flicks shown on a big screen poolside. The audience, equipped with inflatable rafts and inner tubes, watches from the super-heated water. Hosted at local pools on weekend evenings in late July and August, the films are rated G or PG, and the lifeguards carry flashlights. Fees: $2.50/adult; $1/child 17 years & under.

At Fun Days, staff members lead splash fests, water games, and penny dives. Itty Bitty Beach Parties are held at Grant, Montavilla, Sellwood, and Creston pools for kids ages 6 months–6 years and their parents. Call for dates and details. Fees: $2/adult; $1/child.

- **Peninsula Park Community Center & Swim Pool**
  6400 N. Albina, Portland
  823-3677

- **Pier Swim Pool**
  N. Seneca & St. Johns, Portland
  823-3678

- **Sellwood Park Swim Pool**
  SE 7th Ave. & Miller, Portland
  823-3679

- **Wilson Swim Pool**
  1151 SW Vermont, Portland
  823-3680

Tualatin Hills Park & Recreation District (645-7454) manages five indoor pools and two outdoor pools, where swimming and diving lessons and family open-swim times are offered throughout the season. Indoor pools are open year-round; outdoor pools are open from mid-June-early September. Call your neighborhood pool for a schedule. Fees: $1.75/adult; $1.25/child 3-17 years.

Special programs for individuals with handicaps include: disabled and physically limited swimming at Beaverton and Harman swim centers; hearing-impaired and deaf instruction at the Aloha Swim Center; and drop-in swims at Harman and Sunset pools.

INDOOR POOLS

- **Aloha Swim Center**
  18650 SW Kinnaman Rd., Aloha
  642-1586

- **Beaverton Swim Center**
  12850 SW 3rd Ave., Beaverton
  644-1111

- **Harman Swim Center**
  7300 Scholls Ferry Rd., Portland
  643-6681

- **Recreation Swim Center**
  15707 SW Walker Rd., Beaverton
  645-7454

- **Sunset Swim Center**
  13707 NW Science Park Dr., Portland
  644-9770

OUTDOOR POOLS

- **Raleigh Outdoor Pool**
  3500 SW 78th Ave., Portland
  297-6888

- **Somerset West Outdoor Pool**
  NW 185th & Parkview Blvd., Beaverton
  645-1413

T hree suburbs also maintain indoor, public swim centers that host swim lessons and open-swim hours year-round:

Lake Oswego High School Pool
2400 Country Club Rd.,
Lake Oswego
635-0330
Resident: $3/adult; $2/child
Nonresident: $3.75/adult; $3/child

Mount Hood Aquatic Center
26000 SE Stark St., Gresham
667-7243
Fee: $1.50

Located on the campus of Mount Hood Community College, this swim center may be the metro area's best-kept secret. Its two indoor pools are open year-round; the Olympic-size outdoor pool is open in summer only. Family swim hours: Fridays, 6:30-8:30 pm; Saturdays, 1-4 pm.

Tigard Swim Center
8680 SW Durham Rd., Tigard
684-2100
Fee: $2/adult; $1.50/child ∎

Kids scale the wall at Portland Rock Gym.

Constructed from concrete, wood, and a variety of other materials, and punctuated by bolted-on handholds, carabiners, and dangling ropes, climbing walls are a big hit with fitness fanatics who are forced indoors during inclement weather. And it's no surprise that many kids are intrigued as well, especially those who were climbing (living room bookcases, neighbors' fences, brick chimneys ...) before they could walk.

Rock climbing is a highly technical sport, and experienced climbers take their hobby seriously, so newcomers are advised to visit first when the gym isn't busy (i.e., right after school and in summer), and to come with an adult.

Safety is of primary importance when your life is dangling at the end of a rope. Children under age 18 must produce a waiver form signed by a parent or guardian to use the equipment. Both the Portland Rock Gym and Stoneworks recommend that children enroll in an introductory class, and parents are strongly encouraged to learn to

TIPS

Don't throw away old tennis shoes. An uncomfortably tight pair of sneakers worn without socks makes a decent substitute for rock-climbing shoes, and saves a few dollars in rental fees. For bouldering (technical climbing without ropes), however, it's worth springing for the real thing. Appropriate clothing for rock climbing is anything that's comfortable and roomy.

belay so they can supervise.

Another option for beginners is to reserve a group session with several friends. Typically scheduled during off-hours, group parties include a brief instruction period and lots of practice time with a staff belayer. Call for details.

Portland Rock Gym
2034 SE 6th Ave., Portland 97214
232-8310
Hours: Mon-Fri, 11 am-11 pm; Sat, 9 am-7 pm; Sun, 11 am-6 pm
Fees: $12/adult; $6/child 10 years & under; $5/shoe rental; $3/harness rental
Annual family membership: $715/3 people

Portland Rock Gym, open since 1989, recently spawned a sister operation: The Powerplant, in northwest

Portland (see below). The former club features 8,000 square feet of climbing walls, and prides itself on its variety. Equipped with a 40-foot lead wall, 35- and 20-foot top ropes, and bouldering areas, including a "cave," the gym does its best to simulate real-life outdoor experiences.

The Powerplant
617 NW 13th Ave., Portland 97209
796-9335
Hours: Mon-Fri, 11 am-11 pm; Sat, 11 am-7 pm; Sun, noon-5 pm
Fees: $8; $4/child 10 years & under; $5/shoe rental

The Powerplant, a smaller facility with 3,000 square feet of undulating "terrain," is poised to take advantage of the surge in the popularity of bouldering. In bouldering, climbers do not use ropes. Hence, the sport requires a higher level of technical expertise and physical strength and stamina than rope climbing. The Powerplant does have one 20-foot top-rope wall, and offers an introductory belaying class.

Stoneworks Inc. Climbing Gym
6775 SW 111th Ave., #205, Beaverton 97008
644-3517
Hours: Mon-Thurs, noon-10 pm; Fri, noon-9 pm; Sat-Sun, noon-8 pm
Fees: $9; $4/shoe rental; $2/harness rental
Annual membership: $525/couple, $80/extra person

TIPS

At Portland Rock Gym, introductory classes are offered on Saturday mornings and Wednesday evenings. Each three-hour session costs $45, rental equipment included. Groups of up to six people can receive private instruction and practice with a staff belayer for $30 an hour; rental equipment is extra. Once a parent or other adult has received instruction, he is permitted to visit the gym to belay his youngster for free.

TIPS

Introductory classes are scheduled on Friday evenings and Saturday afternoons at Stoneworks. The 2 1/2-hour sessions feature instruction in equipment use, knot-tying, belaying, communication, and body position. A return visit is included in the $40 fee. Stoneworks also hosts 2-hour introductory sessions for groups of five or more for $17 per person, rental equipment included.

Kids are invited to join the Junior Program, which meets Thursdays, 4–6 pm. Participants, who compete up and down the West Coast, range in age from 8–20. Fee: $9/visit, nonmember.

The only Oregon rock-climbing club to be accredited by the Climbing Gym Association, Stoneworks caters to children. The handholds here have been purposely placed close together so kids don't have to stretch. Devoted mostly to bouldering, the facility has 3,000 square feet of climbing surface, including one 20-foot wall with a dozen top ropes. Novice climbers must enroll in a rope-climbing class before being allowed to attempt this wall.

REI
1798 Jantzen Beach Center,
Portland 97217
283-1300

*Climbing wall public hours
(subject to change):*
Thurs, 6:15-9 pm; Sat, 10 am-2 pm
7410 SW Bridgeport, Tigard 97224
624-8600
*Climbing wall public hours
(subject to change):*
Sat, 10 am-noon

Each of the metro area's two REI outdoor equipment stores features a modest-size climbing wall designed for novice rope-climbers. The walls are open to the public during select hours; the rest of the time they are used by AdventureSmith Guides for private lessons (293-6727).

An REI supervisor helps rope in and belay the climbers. Children are welcome to try scaling the wall, provided they fit into a harness (minimum weight: approximately 40 pounds). Arrive early, especially on Saturdays, and expect to wait. ■

TIPS

To be filed under: Who Woulda Thought? The Mount Hood Aquatic Center, located on the Mount Hood Community College campus (26000 SE Stark St., Gresham, 667-7243), boasts a 1,440-square-foot rock wall. To use the structure, young climbers must be at least 12 years old and accompanied by an adult.

Hours: Mon–Fri, noon–8:30 pm; Sat, noon–4:30 pm.

Fee: $4, plus $3.50/equipment rental

Bumper bowling has given new life to a sport that used to mean a night out for Mom and Dad. Bumpers are pads, or in some cases rails, that deflect the ball away from the gutters, and turn what was once a physically technical pastime into a forgiving one. In bumper bowling, even the weakest, meekest novice throws strikes. (Warning to adults: Use bumpers at your own risk; they have been known to be addictive.)

There's still reason to exercise caution around kids and bowling balls, however. Watch for delicate fingers and toes, and mounting frustration (bowling balls can be lethal weapons).

The following alleys schedule bumper bowling on select days during daytime hours. They also offer birthday-party packages for kids, and several sponsor bumper-bowling leagues on Saturday mornings for children from age 3. Other bowling alleys can accommodate bumper bowlers by reservation. It's always wise to call ahead to ensure availability.

Rental-shoe sizes vary, but if your child's feet are too small, he's welcome to bowl in sneakers or socks. Expect to pay up to $1.75 per pair for rental shoes.

Brunswick Sunset Lanes
12770 SW Walker Rd., Beaverton 97005
646-1116
Fees: $2-$3/game

Cascade Lanes
2700 NE 82nd Ave.,
Portland 97220
255-2635
Fees: $2-$3/adult; $1.95/child
17 years & under

Grand Central Bowl
808 SE Morrison St.,
Portland 97214
232-5166
Fees: $2-$3/adult; 95¢/child
12 years & under

Hollywood Bowl
4030 NE Halsey St., Portland 97230
288-9237
Fees: $1.75/game

Kellogg Bowl
10306 SE Main St.,
Milwaukie 97222
659-1757
Fees: $2/game

Pro-300 Lanes
3031 SE Powell Blvd.,
Portland 97206
234-0237
Fees: $2-$3/adult; $1.85/child

Rockwood Lanes
18500 SE Stark St., Portland 97233
665-2123
Fees: $2-$3/adult; $1.85/child

Tigard Bowl
11660 SW Pacific Hwy.,
Tigard 97223
639-2001
Fees: $15/hour for up to 6 people, shoes included

TIPS

Two local bowling alleys offer something a little different: glow-in-the-dark bowling. The lanes and pins look fluorescent under black lights (glow-in-the-dark balls are on order), and music, laser lights, and a fog machine add a disco twist to the experience.

At Tigard Bowl, families arrive in throngs on Saturdays at 6 pm; reservations are suggested. Five players are assigned to each lane, so be prepared to team up with strangers.

Hours & fees: Sun–Wed, 9 pm–midnight; $3.50/game plus shoe rental. Fri, 9:30–11:30 pm & midnight–2 am; Sat, 6–8 pm & midnight–2 am; $10/person, shoes included.

Brunswick Sunset Lanes has dubbed its version Cosmic Bowling, and offers families a chance to raise funds for a favorite local organization. On Tuesdays from 4–5:30 pm, each player is invited to fill out a special coupon that directs $2 of the $7 bowling fee to the church or school of his choice.

Twentieth-Century Lanes
3550 SE 92nd Ave., Portland 97266
774-8805
$2-$3/adult; $2/child 18 years &
under

Valley Lanes
9300 SW Beaverton-Hillsdale Hwy.,
Beaverton 97005
292-3523
$1-$2.25/game ■

Who would have predicted a sissy activity like roller skating would one day be hip? The advent of in-line skates has forever revolutionized skating—and roller rinks 'round the country couldn't be happier. Easier than ice skating, and a lot warmer, roller skating is fun for the whole family, especially now that it's no longer "just for girls."

Skaters may bring their own (in-line skates are allowed as long as they don't have black brakes), or rent them. Call for information about family skate sessions, rates (they vary according to day and time), and birthday-party packages.

Oaks Park Skating Rink
Foot of SE Spokane,
Portland 97202
236-5722
Fees: $3.75, skates included
Largest roller rink on West Coast. Special wooden rotunda floor. Equipped with genuine Wurlitzer theater organ.

Mount Scott Community Center
5530 SE 72nd Ave., Portland 97206
823-3183
Fees: $1, skates included

Skate Church
Central Bible Church
(See Best for Teens.)

TIPS

Once a week in winter, SportWorks (421 SW 2nd Ave., 227-5323), a local skate and snowboard retailer, rents Memorial Coliseum (1401 N. Wheeler Ave.) for the evening, turns up the music, and opens the polished quarter-mile concrete concourse to in-line skaters of all ages and abilities. Typically, 200 show up. Skate Night at the Coliseum is a party.

Aggressive skaters congregate with a local skate team in one corner to get tips on negotiating rails and curbs. Six certified skating instructors patrol the course and offer mini-lessons to novices. Rental skates, including safety equipment, are available on-site. Helmets—as well as knee, elbow, and wrist pads—are strongly recommended, though not required. Designated weeknights vary according to the availability of the Coliseum. Call for a schedule.

Season: October–May, 7–10 pm weekly
Fees: $7; $5/advance purchase; $7/rental equipment (parking is free)

Convenient to Waterfront Park's promenade, a popular skating route, SportWorks also rents in-line skates and equipment for outdoor use in season. Fees: $10/half-day; $20/full day; $100/credit card deposit.

TIPS

Both Skate World locations go out of their way to appeal to families, with regularly scheduled family skate hours and special sessions for home-schoolers. In Hillsboro the rink is reserved for home-schoolers the first and third Friday of the month, September–June, 11 am– 12:30 pm. In Gresham the home-schooling session takes place every Thursday, September–June, 11 am–1 pm. Fee: $2.50/person, skate rental included.

Gresham Skate World also offers Tiny Tots, a biweekly program for preschoolers and caregivers. Children receive 30 minutes of instruction, followed by games and playtime, every Wednesday and Thursday, September–June, 9:30–11 am. Adults are welcome on the rink in street shoes during these sessions, as are strollers. Fee: $2.50/child, skate rental included; free/adult.

See some of the country's best in-line skaters compete each summer at Pioneer Courthouse Square (SW Broadway, between Yamhill & Morrison). The National In-Line Skating Contest comes to town in late July, and locals who are not content to watch from the sidelines may register to participate. For details, call the event hotline: 295-8084.

Skate World
1220 NE Kelly, Gresham 97030
667-6543
Fees: $3-$5.50, skates included;
$3 extra/in-line skate rental

Skate World
4395 SE Witch Hazel Rd.,
Hillsboro 97123
640-1333
Fees: $3-$5.50, skates included;
$10/family of 4 (parent must skate, too); $3 extra/in-line skate rental ∎

Olympic skaters make it look easy, but anyone who has tried knows ice skating is a slippery proposition. You can expect your beginners to wibble-wobble on rubbery ankles and to cling to you for balance. Come prepared—both of you—with gloves and padding. You'll likely spend some time prone on the ice.

The rinks below offer lessons and birthday-party packages for children. Call for public skating schedules and other details.

Ice Chalet at Clackamas Town Center

1200 SE 82nd St., Clackamas 97266
786-6000
$6/adult; $5/child 17 years & under; $2.50/skate rental; $5/hockey-skate rental

Ice Chalet at Lloyd Center

2201 Lloyd Center, Portland 97232
288-4599
$6/adult; $5/child 17 years & under; $2/skate rental

Valley Ice

9250 Beaverton-Hillsdale Hwy., Beaverton 97005
297-2521
$6, skates included; free/child 4 years & under ∎

"Capture the Flag" meets *Star Wars*. This, in essence, is the concept behind the high-tech laser games that are so popular with kids—and many adults. Equipped with laser "guns" and computerized vest packs, groups of as many as 30 players are divided into opposing teams whose mission is to disable the enemy and claim his home base.

Disappearing into dark, mysterious, cavernlike mazes obscured by fog machines and illuminated by black lights and lighting special effects, players are immersed in a three-dimensional video game in which stealth, cunning, and quickness reap the biggest rewards.

Games last about 25 minutes, and monitors on duty throughout the arena ensure there is no running or physical contact among players. Still, arena owners do not recommend laser tag for children younger than 6 or 7 years old.

Hard-core patrons, who tend to be young adult males, come dressed in black and depart drenched in sweat. Weekdays, when the arenas are less crowded, are best for families. If you want to play on a weekend, call ahead to reserve.

Laser tag, a high-tech version of "Capture the Flag," is played in maze-like arenas equipped with computers and special effects.

Laserport

10975 SW Canyon Rd.,
Beaverton 97005
526-9501
Hours (subject to change):
Mon-Thurs, noon-10 pm; Fri,
noon-midnight; Sat, 10 am-mid-
night; Sun, 10 am-9 pm
Fees: $6/game Mon-Thurs,
$3/additional game; $7/game Fri-
Sun & holidays, $4/additional game

Laserport computers keep a running tally of game scores and relay
that information to voice chips in
players' equipment vests. Especially
popular with corporate groups and
families, the arena features a full-
service pizza kitchen, coin-operated
video and simulation games, and a
party room. Reservations are recommended for groups of six or more.

Ultrazone

Holly Farm Center, 16074 SE
McLoughlin Blvd., Milwaukie 97267
652-1122
Hours (subject to change):
Tues-Thurs, 3-10:30 pm; Fri,
3 pm-1 am; Sat, 11-1 am; Sun,
11 am-10 pm
Summer: Mon-Thurs, 1-11 pm; Fri,
1 pm-1 am; Sat, 11-1 am; Sun, 11
am-11 pm
Fees: $6.50; $5.50/member
Annual membership: $12-$37

Beyond its super sound system
and three-team format, Ultrazone
has an added wild card: An enemy
robot sentinel, programmed to fire

randomly, roves the upper level.

Teens congregate here after
school and on weekends to play
laser tag, as well as video and simulation games, and Ultrazone makes
a point of maintaining a wholesome
atmosphere. On report-card day,
students line up down the block to
cash in on discounts for A's and B's.
Sunday is Family Day, and parents
play free with paying children until
closing. Reservations are required
for large groups and birthday parties
only. ■

Her questions begin almost as soon as she can talk: "Why?" "How come?" At first you dutifully try to answer, but before long these queries don't even register. And that's okay. Like the involuntary jerk of the lower leg after the doctor taps that tender spot just below the kneecap, your toddler can't help herself; her questioning is reflexive.

Not for long. Within a year or two, you notice a change. Your ears prick up; this could get interesting. "Where does the mail come from?" "Why is cheese different colors when milk's white?" "Where do the police officers' horses go when they're tired?" "Who decides what's news?"

Maybe you get out the encyclopedia you haven't opened since college. Maybe you search the Internet or ask a librarian's advice. Maybe you go to the source, and take your child behind the scenes at the post office, dairy farm, police horse stables, or newsroom. However you choose to hem and haw your way to an answer that's both accurate and comprehensible to a young child is really inconsequential, because there's a much greater lesson involved: You're teaching your child how to learn.

School teachers have long known that one of the best ways to motivate children is not to explain, but to show. But why wait for a good teacher to work a field trip or group tour into the curriculum? The locations below open their back doors to the general public for a peek at what really goes on.

Alpenrose Dairy

6149 SW Shattuck Rd.,
Portland 97221
244-1133, reservations required well in advance
Season: Fall & spring
Hours: Mon-Tues & Thurs-Fri, 9:30 am & noon
Duration: 1 1/2 hours
Recommended ages: Grades 1-3
Group size: Minimum 10, maximum 60

Help milk Rosie the cow, then watch the pasteurization process. On the assembly line, a small plastic pellet grows into a one-gallon milk jug. Visit the on-site museum—with its assortment of historic memorabilia, including the first Portland police car and the original dairy owners' extensive doll collection—and stay for an ice cream treat. *(See also Farms, Special Farms; and Spectator Sports, Nonprofessional Leagues.)*

The Candy Basket

1924 NE 181st Ave.,
Portland 97230
666-2000, reservations required
Hours: Tues-Thurs, 9:30 am
Duration: 1 hour
Recommended ages: 6 years & older
Group size: Maximum 35

Right out of *Charlie & the Chocolate Factory*, the tour of this 60-year-old, family-run operation begins beside a 20-foot chocolate cascade. Watch the candy-making process up close, then taste the results.

TIPS

Ideal destinations for school field trips and scouts outings, the following establishments offer tours to large groups only:

- Bonneville Dam
- Fox 49 TV station
- OPB TV station
- Port of Portland, Portland International Airport
- Union Station

Chevys Mexican Restaurant

Various metro-area locations
Hours: Mon-Thurs, 9 am & 2 pm (times may vary)
Recommended ages: 3 years & older
Group size: Minimum 10 (at least one adult for every 5 children)

You have to feel good about a restaurant that's willing to let you in the kitchen. Follow a patron's order from computer to chef to table. The famous El Machino tortilla press turns out 900 tortillas an hour—that's one every 53 seconds! Finish with a free kids' meal and complimentary sombrero. *(See also Basics, Restaurants.)*

Franz Bakery

340 NE 11th Ave., Portland 97232
232-2191 ext. 365, reservations required
Season: October-June
Hours: Wed & Fri, 9:30 am-noon; Tues & Thurs, 9:30 am-4:30 pm
Duration: 1 hour
Recommended ages: 7 years & up
Group size: Minimum 10, maximum 40

From sifting flour, to packaging loaves of bread, to loading them on delivery trucks—visitors see it all. Try samples as you go, but be sure to wear closed-toe shoes; no sandals allowed.

TIPS

Production schedules vary from year to year at Franz Bakery, and so do tour schedules.

TIPS

Even if you don't come to Chevys with a group, you can peek in the kitchen when it isn't too busy. The hostess will gladly arrange a short, five-minute tour for your family. Just ask.

KGW Channel 8 News

1501 SW Jefferson, Portland 97201
226-5000, reservations required
Hours: 9-11:30 am & 1-3:30 pm weekdays
Duration: 1 hour
Recommended ages: 7 years & older

Begin the tour with a brief video,

which explains what goes on in a newsroom, then see the real thing. Watch reporters and anchors gather facts and draft scripts. Visit the master control room, where the taping takes place; the director's control booth; and the weather center.

Mounted Police Horse Stables

1036 NW 9th Ave., Portland 97209
823-2100, reservations required
Hours: Tues-Sat, 1 pm
Duration: 30 minutes
Group size: Maximum 20

Follow an officer through the stables and learn about the care and training of the Portland Police force's nine horses.

TIPS

Most local fire stations are willing to provide tours of their facilities on a drop-in basis. See fire engines up close, visit the firefighters' private quarters, and examine their tools and attire. Call your neighborhood station for details.

Oregon Candy Farm

Hwy. 26, Sandy 97055
668-5066
Hours: Mon-Fri, 9 am-5 pm;
Sat-Sun, noon-5 pm

Watch the candy-making process from large viewing windows, and receive a free sample.

The Oregonian

1320 SW Broadway, Portland 97201
221-8336, reservations required
Hours: Tues & Thurs, 10 am-noon
Duration: 2 hours
Minimum age: 12 years
Group size: Maximum 12

Begin at the Broadway building, where you'll watch a brief instructional video, visit the newsroom, and see how the paper is laid out. Then move on to the plant, at 16th Ave. & Taylor, to watch the plate-making, printing, and mail-room processes.

TIPS

The two *Oregonian* facilities are about 15 blocks apart, and tour groups are asked to provide their own transportation.

A Phoenix, the Manikin Shop

16950 NW St. Helens Rd.,
Portland 97231
289-9202, reservations required
Hours: 9 am-4 pm weekdays
Duration: 20-30 minutes

Meet store owner Russ Varner and his mascot, Joe Manicat. Then peruse hundreds of mannequins that date back several decades. See how mannequins are restored and prepared for store display, and examine character heads like Santa Claus' and Ben Franklin's, which are often leased for parties. If time allows, watch a casting demonstration.

A tour of the Portland Center for the Performing Arts is as good as a backstage pass.

Portland Center for the Performing Arts

1111 SW Broadway, Portland 97205
248-4335
Hours: Wed, 11 am; Sat,
11 am-1 pm (every half hour);
1st Thurs of month, 6 pm
Duration: 1 hour

Visit the regal Arlene Schnitzer Concert Hall, built in the 1920s, and the Intermediate and Dolores Winningstad theaters in the contemporary New Theatre Building next door. Together with the Civic Auditorium, these buildings make up the Portland Center for the Performing Arts, one of the largest in the nation. Learn about the theaters' histories, art, and architecture, and—if you're lucky—get a peek at a dress rehearsal.

Portland Main Post Office

715 NW Hoyt St., Portland 97208
294-2306, reserve at least 2 weeks ahead
Hours: January-mid-November,
9:30 am-noon weekdays
Duration: 1 1/4 hours
Group size: Minimum 4,
maximum 35

See how mail is processed and sorted. View the post-office-box section. Visit the philatelic counter to learn about stamp collecting, then explore the truck docks, where mail is loaded and unloaded.

Steinfeld's Products

10001 N Rivergate Blvd.,
Portland 97203
286-8241, reservations required
Hours: 7 am-3:30 pm weekdays
Duration: 45 minutes
Recommended ages: 6th grade
& up

See the assembly line in motion at Steinfeld's.

TIPS

The best time to tour the Steinfeld's plant is during harvest season (late July–late September), when cucumbers are delivered fresh from the fields.

Watch as cucumbers are received, sorted, pasteurized, pickled, made into relish and other condiments, and packaged into 6-ounce jars, 55-gallon drums, and everything in between.

Tillamook Cheese Factory
Hwy. 101, Tillamook 97141
503-815-1300 ext. 1149
Hours: Fall, winter, & spring, 8 am-6 pm daily; summer, 8 am-8 pm daily

Begin the self-guided tour in the exhibit hall. Here a mechanical cow demonstrates the milking process, and a short video provides a history

TIPS

In summer you can also visit the Tillamook Dairy Farm and help milk the cows. Offered daily at 3 pm, the tour takes approximately 1 1/2 hours. Round–trip transportation from the Tillamook Cheese Factory is provided. Call ahead for reservations: 503–815–1300.
Fees: $8/adult; $6/child 5–16 years; free/child under 5 years; $15/family of 4, $5/additional

of the Tillamook factory. Then move upstairs, where three videos help explain the cheese-making process on view on the factory floor below. End the tour with complimentary samples of cheese. (Many can't resist buying an ice cream cone, though it's hard to choose from among the 40 flavors.) ■

I t's an awkward stage. Teen-agers think they're all grown up, and you wish they were. They demand to be treated like adults, but they vow never to act like them (or, more pointedly, like you).

The following represent entertainment alternatives suitable, but not exclusively, for young adults. You may want to go, too, but are probably not invited. *(See also Climbing Walls and Laser Tag Arenas.)*

City Paintball

631 NE Grand Ave., Portland 97232
233-1105
Hours: Tues-Sat, 3-10 pm
Fees: $15/2 hours, air gun, safety equipment, & carbon dioxide included ($18 in summer); $7/bag of 100 paintballs

The state's first indoor paintball arena, City Paintball opened in 1992 in a 12,000-square-foot space designed, like a stage set, to resemble a city street scene. Kids ages 10 years and up come to play structured strategy and elimination games using paintballs as markers.

Fired from air guns at 200 miles an hour, paintballs break open and sting on impact, so players are required to cover their arms and legs (City Paintball rents coveralls). Most regulars wear dark, loose, sloppy clothing.

Especially popular with teens (youths under 18 years must turn in a waiver form signed by a parent or guardian), City Paintball caters to beginners. New games begin every 10 minutes, and referees monitor all

contests. Novices are encouraged to attend an early session, midweek, when the place isn't so crowded.

Hit & Run Paintball

8900 SW Commercial St., Tigard 97223
968-9579
Hours: Mon-Fri, 3-9 pm; Sat-Sun, noon-9 pm
Fees: $5-$20/2 hours, pump gun, goggles, & carbon dioxide included (upgrades available at additional charge); $7/bag of 100 paintballs

The 12,000-square-foot indoor facility at Hit & Run Paintball features three different rooms with three different scenarios: Western pioneer town, cityscape, and desert. Players in groups of two to 40 try Capture the Flag, Center Flag, and Basic Elimination, among dozens of game options under the watchful eyes of several referees.

Children must be at least 10 years old to participate. Youths under age 18 are required to submit a waiver form signed by a parent or guardian. Because the paintballs burst open and sting on impact, players are advised to wear long-sleeved shirts, long pants, and gloves.

Malibu Grand Prix

(See Active Play: Outdoor Fun, Amusements.)

OMSI's Laser Light Shows

Murdock Sky Theatre, 1945 SE
Water Ave., Portland 97214
797-4646
Hours: Wed, Thurs, & Sun, 8:15 pm
& 9:30 pm; Fri-Sat, 8:15 pm,
9:30 pm, 10:45 pm, & midnight
Fee: $6.50

Produced by Laser Fantasy
International, OMSI's Laser Light
Shows are intricate, hour-long multi-
media presentations that mix lasers
and planetarium choreography with
popular music or classic rock and
roll. Each show spotlights the repertoire of a particular band, such as
Pink Floyd, Led Zeppelin, Metallica,
Smashing Pumpkins, and Nirvana.
Be forewarned: The music is played
rock-concert loud. Free earplugs are
available on request.

Ever-popular with a core audience of teens, these shows often sell
out. The weekend midnight showing
of "Laser Floyd's Wall" always plays
to capacity crowds in the 200-seat
theater. Arrive at least 15 minutes
before showtime (earlier on weekends) to purchase tickets. Music
Millennium and Washington Square
OMSI stores carry two-for-one discount coupons for Wednesday and
Thursday shows. For a schedule of
upcoming events, call the laser hotline: 797-4646.

Quest

126 SW 2nd Ave., Portland 97204
497-9113
Hours & fees: Thurs, 9:30 pm-
2 am; $3/until 11 pm, $5/after

11 pm. Fri, 9:30 pm-4 am; $7.
Sat, 9:30 pm-3 am; $7

In business since 1986, Quest is an
all-ages nightclub that's strict about
enforcing its policy (no-alcohol/no-
drug). While the teen crowd is dancing, mingling, playing pool and video
games inside, the four bouncers, two
metal detectors, and three video cameras outside are ensuring they continue to have a good time (and "good"
means safe and sober). A deejay picks
the tunes—dance music from the '80s
and '90s, mostly—and the "bar" sells
soft drinks and candy.

Quest is popular. Long lines
snake around the block on weekends, when average attendance
reaches 800. Teens are advised to
come early. No one under 16 is
admitted; after midnight, patrons
must be at least 18 years old to enter.

SKATEBOARD PARKS

■ **Burnside Park**
East end of Burnside Bridge
Built, managed, and operated by
local skaters for skaters, this challenging concrete course, sheltered under
the Burnside Bridge, has quite a following, but few hard-and-fast rules.

■ **Davis Park**
NE 194th Ave. & Glisan, Gresham
618-2531
Developed and managed by
the Gresham Parks Department,
which recommends that all users
wear safety equipment, this small,
concrete skate park is ideal for
beginners. Situated in a quiet neighborhood and bordering an elemen-

tary school, Davis Park features two benches and a low mountain.

■ Skate Church

Central Bible Church, 8815 NE Glisan St., Portland 97220
252-1424
Hours: Grades 6-8; Mon, 6:30-9 pm. Grades 9-12; Tues, 6:30-9 pm. In-line skating, grades 6-12; Tues, 3:45-6 pm.
Fees: $5/year; $2/visit

Opened in September 1996, the warehouse building at Central Bible Church is equipped with a skate park made of wood and masonite. It features a mini-halfpipe, vertical halfpipe, and bowl. As many as 100 teens show up at designated weekly skate sessions to use the warehouse and basement street course, and to participate in half-hour Bible classes (attendance is mandatory). Other church rules: To register, skaters must present a current school ID card and waiver form signed by a parent; and all participants are required to wear safety gear when skating in the warehouse.

Teen Night, North Clackamas Aquatic Park

(See Swimming Pools.) ■

Archers Afield

Tigard Plaza, 11945 SW Pacific Hwy., Tigard 97223
639-3553
Hours: Mon-Fri, 9 am-9 pm; Sat, 9 am-6 pm; Sun, 10 am-6 pm
Fees: $3/day; $10/recurve bow rental; $15/compound bow rental

Archers Afield, a carpeted indoor archery range and store, features 30 shooting lanes and 60 targets. Serious archers come here for lessons and practice. Curious beginners are welcome, but are encouraged to enroll in the 90-minute group lessons ($9/ person) that are offered on Saturdays.

No uncommon physical strength is required by the sport, so children as young as 5 years old are capable of mastering it. Archers Afield stocks rental equipment for kids this little, and rental fees may be applied toward equipment purchases at the store.

Patrons are allowed to bring snacks from home to enjoy at the booths.

Family Country Dance

Location not available at press time
245-2185
Season: September-May; 2nd Sat of odd months, 5-8 pm
Fees: $5/adult; $3/child under 16 years; free/infant; $15/family maximum

The motto of the Portland Country Dance Community, which organizes bimonthly Family Country Dance potluck gatherings, is: "If your kids can walk, they can dance. (So can you.)" Now in its third year, this family dance series is designed for beginners—both adults and children.

A caller offers instruction in a variety of American folk dances, and the steps are purposely kept rudimentary. Kids like best the live folk bands, with their fiddles, guitars, mandolins, and pianos.

Wear comfortable clothes and shoes, bring a dish for the potluck that follows, and expect to meet new people; about 100 typically attend. Contra-dancing for adults and older children begins after supper.

The Ramblin' Rod Show
KPTV-12, 211 SE Caruthers, Portland 97214
230-1200
Reservation line: 736-0456

He's a grandfather now, to 12 grandchildren and much of Portland's youth as well. Ramblin' Rod, a.k.a. Rod Anders, has taped some 8,500 of his popular children's cartoon shows in a television career that has spanned 34 years, and he's now greeting audience members whose parents—even grandparents—sat in the same studio seats and produced the same smiles on cue. Wearing a trademark sweater festooned with hundreds of pin-on buttons (his collection numbers 20,000), Ramblin' Rod has a gentle, friendly manner that goes a long way toward explaining his longevity as a television host.

The show formula is simple, and is based on the premise that everyone should have an opportunity to see themselves on TV. The 20 to 30 3- to 12-year-old children in the studio audience introduce themselves, birthday children receive special recognition, and then everyone vies for prizes in the Smile Contest. To be honored as a birthday child, one's birthday must fall within a week of the taping date.

Getting on the show can be a challenge. Reservations are taken the first three working days of each month for the following month's taping sessions. The tapings are scheduled every Wednesday at 4:45 pm, and run approximately 45 minutes.

It's a common misconception that the studio audience watches cartoons. The cartoon segments are added just prior to broadcast (Saturdays, 9-10 am, KPTV-12). ∎

Chapter 6
FARMS

To many city kids, chicken nuggets might as well grow on trees. And potatoes— don't they spring from the ground precut and fried? When your kids begin to grow suspicious of their food—to dissect their peas, spit out tomato seeds, and refuse hamburger ("This is COW?!")—it's time to visit a farm.

Plan to get dirty and to return home with something fresh and exotic for supper. Let the children help prepare the new food (farmstands can often supply recipes), and make a pact over the meal to return at each new season for another day in the country and another dietary experiment.

Portland's mild, damp weather grows more than moss, mold, and mildew. The metro area is blessed with an abundance of fresh-grown produce (chiefly apples, pears, peaches, cherries, berries, hazelnuts, and walnuts), and dozens of farmers are glad for help at harvest time. Reservations are not necessary, but call ahead to determine the course of the season. Ideally you want to plan your picking early in the harvest and early in the day for the best selection. U-pick establishments often supply containers, but take some along just in case.

(The long, flat boxes available at nurseries work best.) When you're finished, your haul is weighed and you pay by the pound.

The *Tri-County Farm Fresh Produce Guide*, published annually in the spring by an association of member farms, is a comprehensive guide to local orchards, nurseries, and farms. Copies are available at libraries, chambers of commerce, and local county extension offices. For additional information about regional harvests, call the Ripe & Ready Hotline: 226-4112 (updated weekly, mid-April-November). ∎

TIPS

When harvesting fruit, wear hats and sunscreen. Show children how to avoid thorns on berry bushes, how to maneuver among the bushes, and how to determine which fruits are ripe (perhaps the farmer will share his secrets). Some farms prohibit children from climbing ladders and trees; you may want to adopt strict rules yourself.

Pick only what you can reasonably use. Many fruits don't freeze well, but most berry varieties can be frozen if you follow this method: Remove stems, wash and drain berries on a towel. (Wash delicate raspberries by placing them in a colander first, then submerging the colander in a sink full of water. Raise the colander to drain.) Spread fruit in a single layer on a cookie sheet covered in wax paper. Place the pan in the freezer for two hours. Scoop frozen berries into plastic bags, and return to freezer.

Wear rubber boots and a smile when you go pumpkin picking.

Squirrels collect nuts. Birds fly south. People go to the pumpkin patch, another rite of autumn.

At last count, more than a dozen metro-area farms were featuring these colorful squashes in time for Halloween. Some make a month-long party of it, with hay rides, hay mazes, spooky trails, funny dioramas, and festive goodies. Call ahead to confirm dates and hours, then pray for a break in the clouds.

Fir Point Farms
14601 Arndt Rd., Aurora 97002
678-2455
Season: April-December;
9 am-6 pm daily

The annual Halloween Pumpkin Fest packs this 75-acre spread every weekend in October, when special activities include a deep, dark hay maze (carry a flashlight just in case), corn maze, pony and hay rides, half-mile haunted trail, and refreshments.

Return off-season with a picnic, and stay all afternoon. Pick your own flowers and vegetables. Examine the apiary and greenhouse. Gape at the goats who romp on ramps set amid in the treetops. Visit with chickens, turkeys, and rabbits.

Flower Farmer
(See Special Farms.)

Lakeview Farms
31345 NW North Ave.,
Cornelius 97113
647-2336
Season: October; Mon-Sat,
9 am-5 pm; Sun, 10 am-5 pm

Open to the public in October only, Lakeview Farms' 6-acre spread has lovely views out over rolling agricultural land, but most visitors are too intent on finding the perfect pumpkin to notice. This is the place to come if you prefer literally "picking" pumpkins (bring a pocket knife or garden shears). The vines are tall and prickly, so you may opt instead to peruse the supply of prepicked pumpkins in the mown meadow.

The Lakeview theme is transportation. Take the four-car miniature train to the patch through a haunted tunnel. Return across the lake by barge, but beware of a pair of vengeful pirates and a hungry shark.

The grounds—green grass punctuated by a grove of tall evergreens—also feature farm animals, a gift shop, snack shack (weekends only), hay maze, and educational displays about farming. There are no restrooms, just portable toilets.

Rasmussen Farms

3020 Thomsen Rd., Hood River 97031
541-386-4622
Season: April 1-November 15,
9 am-6 pm daily

This 20-acre farm with U-pick sunflowers and pumpkins hosts three distinct harvest festivals. The second weekend in September is reserved for the Pear Party, with free samples, pear cider, pear pie, and live music. The Apple Express follows, with free samples, apple cider, apple pie, and "aebelskivers"—tiny, Danish apple pancakes.

The Pumpkin Funland, which begins the last weekend in September and continues through Veteran's Day, is a 10-year holiday tradition. The greenhouse is decorated for fall with as many as 50 scenes and characters created from vegetables, squashes, and gourds. Other activities include a mildly scary Halloween Hut, a corn maze, and make-it-yourself scarecrows ($15 for materials).

Sauvie Island
(See Special Farms.)

TIPS

Even if the sun's shining on pumpkin-picking day, take boots along in the car for insurance. Though you'll likely have many shapes and hues to choose from, chances are the pumpkins will already have been cut from the vine, so you needn't bother with a pocket knife. If wheelbarrows and wagons are scarce, be prepared to carry what you select to a scale for weigh-in (bring sturdy shopping bags, and insist that the kids tote their own); most places charge by the pound.

Wenzel Farm

19754 S. Ridge Rd.,
Oregon City 97045
631-2047
Season: October; Mon-Sat,
7-10 pm
Fees: $2/adult; $1.50/child 12 years & under

The lighted, wooded Fantasy Trail at Wenzel Farm may be decked out for Halloween, but it's not too scary. Young children are particularly entranced by the 40-foot castle. Return December 4-23, 5-9 pm, to experience the Christmas version. ∎

F ar from the best time of year for an arduous outdoor expedition, mid-December still finds legions of hardy, determined families braving the elements in search of the perfect Christmas tree. They would never admit disappointment. Whatever fir they can agree on, then wrestle into the car, into the living room, and into a stand is the prettiest ever.

More than two dozen tree farms offer U-cut Christmas evergreens in the tri-county region alone. And you can probably find fine specimens at every one. (Remember, Oregon often supplies the White House with its holiday tree.) Many go all out for the holidays, offering hot chocolate, holiday crafts, hay mazes, hay rides, and petting zoos. For a list of some of the region's U-cut Christmas tree farms, get a copy of *Choose & Cut Guide: Christmas Tree Guide to Oregon & Washington.* Published annually by the Pacific Northwest Christmas Tree Association, it can be found at G.I. Joe's stores, chambers of commerce, and county extension offices, beginning in early November; or by calling 503-364-2942.

Backwoods U-cut trees are also available in designated areas of the Mount Hood National Forest—usually under power lines and along road right-of-ways, or in young timber stands that require thinning. Such "uncultured" trees feature sparse, open branching. Purchase a map and up to five Christmas tree tags for $5 apiece (trees must be no taller than 8 feet) at one of the ranger stations listed below after Thanksgiving, or send in a check and self-addressed envelope with 55¢ postage to receive them by mail.

TIPS

Once you've brought your holiday trophy home, put it in water right away (a gallon is not too much), and replenish the water supply daily. An average tree consumes between a quart and a gallon of water a day. Be certain to keep the tree well away from any heat sources, such as heating vents, wood stoves, radiators—even television sets and sunny windows. After the holidays, carefully move the tree outdoors for recycling. Call your local disposal service or recycling center for specific instructions. Never burn any part of a Christmas tree in a wood stove or fireplace.

Clackamas River Ranger Districts
595 NW Industrial Way,
Estacada 97023
630-6861
Hours: Mon-Fri, 7:45 am-4:30 pm

Mount Hood Information Center
65000 E. Hwy. 26, Welches 97067
622-7674
Hours: 8 am-6 pm daily

Scouting for a tree in this manner is a no-frills excursion, so be prepared for the weather. Arrive at the cutting area by 3 pm. That way you can select your tree before dark. Take along appropriate tools and equipment (e.g., saw, axe, shovel, and rope), warm clothes and beverages, and traction devices for driving in snow and ice (use gravel roadways only). ■

In spring these three Willamette Valley bulb farms put on quite a show. Arrayed in neat rows, acres of flowers—a symphony of nature's purest colors—take their bows in unison. Children are welcome to explore the display fields, which are planted with hundreds of varieties so customers can select favorites to order, but farmers ask that they take care to stay in between rows to avoid damaging the flowers.

Cooley's Gardens Inc.
11553 Silverton Rd. NE,
Silverton 97381
503-873-5463
Season: Late May, 8 am-7 pm daily
    Ten acres of iris display gardens and seedlings, weekend food booth, indoor cut-flower show.

Schreiner's Iris Gardens
3625 Quinaby Rd., Salem 97303
503-393-3232
Season: Late May-early June, daylight hours
    One-acre iris display garden, picnic tables.

Wooden Shoe Bulb Co.
33814 S. Meridian Rd.,
Woodburn 97071
800-711-2006, 503-634-2243
Season: March 20-April 20,
9 am-dusk daily
    Fifty-acre daffodil display garden, 30-acre tulip display garden, entertainment, demonstrations, picnic tables, weekend food booth. ■

Visiting a farmers' market is the next best thing to getting muddy in your own garden. Besides, a parsnip gains personality when you've met its farmer. In summer and fall, produce growers congregate in local squares and parking lots to display fresh-picked fruits, vegetables, and homemade treats and crafts. Colorful and personal, these scenes resemble the street markets that are still plentiful abroad.

- **Beaverton:** 5th Ave. & Hall Blvd.; Sat, 8 am-1:30 pm; Wed, 3:30-7 pm
- **Portland:** 1200 NW Front Ave.; Sat, 8 am-1 pm
- **Hillsboro:** 2nd Ave. & E. Main; Sat, 7:30 am-1 pm
- **Tigard:** Hall Blvd. & Burnham; Sat, 8 am-1:30 pm
- **Tualatin:** Tualatin Commons; Sat, 8 am-12:30 pm

- **Vancouver:** E. 5th St., between Main & Broadway; Sat, 9 am-3 pm; Sun, 11 am-3pm

Weekend Garden Market
158th Ave. & Cornell at Hwy. 26
359-1705
Season: May-October; Sat, 9 am-3 pm

Asphalt takes the place of manure at the Weekend Garden Market, which is located in a Tri-Met Park & Ride lot, but that doesn't seem to detract from the countryside atmosphere here. Once a month in season, the market sponsors a special children's event—from MacGregor's Garden Patch (free vegetable starts and ladybugs) to the Great Pumpkin Fest (free pumpkins, candy, and flower bulbs). As many as 60 vendors are on hand each week to peddle produce, crafts, and baked goods. Call for a schedule. ■

The Weekend Garden Market hosts special kids' events each month in season.

Alpenrose Dairy

6149 SW Shattuck Rd.,
Portland 97221
244-1133

Special events: Easter, summer,
& Christmas

In the 19th century, the rolling
hillsides of southwest Portland were
dotted with dairy farms, which were
largely operated by Swiss immigrants. One pioneering dairyman,
Florian Cadonau, owned a small
farm at SW 35th Ave. and Vermont,
and began delivering milk in 3-gal-
lon cans by horse-drawn wagon in
1891. More than a century later,
Cadonau's ancestors are still in the
dairy business. Though no longer
milking cows, the Alpenrose operation purchases milk from local
Tillamook and Willamette Valley
farms for its lines of milk, ice
cream, cottage cheese, and sour
cream. *(See also Active Play: Indoor
Fun, Behind the Scenes.)*

Local families may not associate
Alpenrose with milk, however,
because the farm has evolved to
include a unique array of entertainment facilities and an annual series
of family holiday events.

Built by Florian's son and grand-
son, Dairyville is a replica of a
Western frontier town. Its dozen
false-front shops—among them a
doll museum, old-fashioned ice
cream parlor, harness shop, and
music store—are filled with period
antiques. The grand old opera
house, with seats for 600, harbors
the majestic pipe organ that once
played in the old Portland Civic
Auditorium. Elsewhere, an impressive collection of antique music
boxes, nickelodeons, and victrolas is
on public display.

No less impressive are the
Alpenrose sports facilities: a baseball
stadium, velodrome, and miniature
racetrack. Initially built to provide
athletic diversions for Cadonau children and cousins, it wasn't long
before they were made available to
the larger community. *(See Sports,
Nonprofessional Leagues.)*

TIPS

Alpenrose deserves a blue ribbon for community service. At
Easter it sponsors the city's
largest egg hunt. At Christmas its
flocked Storybook Lane is a
sparkling winter wonderland for
small children. (Bundle up, though;
the buildings aren't heated.) In
summer the weekly Dairyville open
houses are a free-for-all. Many
families' annual traditions encompass three visits a year, and
they're not sorry.

Flower Farmer's Phoenix & Holly Railroad attracts children eager to ride the rails.

Flower Farmer

2512 N. Holly, Canby 97013
266-3581
Season: May-September &
Thanksgiving-Christmas; weekends
& holidays only, 11 am-6 pm.
October; Mon-Sat, 11 am-9 pm;
Sun, 11 am-6 pm.

Flower Farmer's main attraction
isn't its 20 acres of colorful U-cut
flowers, nor its summertime petting
zoo (weekends only). Kids come in
droves to ride the Phoenix & Holly
Railroad, a half-size, narrow-gauge
train with a 30-horsepower diesel
locomotive named Sparky and a
bright red caboose named Fred. All
aboard for a half-mile loop through
the fields, with a pit stop to feed
horses and mules ($2/adult;
$1.50/child).

For Halloween, the owners
import pumpkins from their neighboring farm; construct a spooky railroad tunnel, hay maze, and hay
mountain; and serve up cider and
doughnuts. Christmas features a special lighting display.

TIPS

The drive to Flower Farmer is
a lovely country outing no matter
how you choose to come, but the
favored route among children
hooked on transportation includes
a ride on the Canby Ferry (*see
Active Play: Outdoor Fun, Boating*).

Magness Memorial Tree Farm

31195 SW Ladd Hill Rd.,
Sherwood 97140
228-1367

Donated to the World Forestry Center in 1977, this 70-acre forest on Parrett Mountain has been developed and maintained to demonstrate different methods of woodland management—from selective harvesting to clear-cutting. View examples of the various techniques from one of the farm's two hiking trails (the third, a paved trail, is wheelchair-accessible), then scale the 60-foot fire tower for a panoramic view of the Cascades. Facilities include a picnic shelter; rustic log cabins for outdoor schools, overnight camping, and retreats; and a visitors' center with restrooms.

Northwest Alpacas Ranch & Country Store

11785 SW River Rd.,
Hillsboro 97123
257-2227
Season: January-November; Fri-Sun, 10 am-5 pm. Thanksgiving-Christmas; 10 am-5 pm daily.

Visit this 80-acre spread to get acquainted with alpacas, moody cousins of the llama. Follow a field guide to a paddock to feed some of the farm's 200 animals. (They eat special alpaca pellets.) Then relax on the front porch with juice or cider and an alpaca-shaped cookie made by Beaverton Bakery. The store carries sweaters, scarves, mit-

tens, and hats made from cashmere-soft alpaca fleece.

Philip Foster Farm

29912 SE Hwy. 221,
Eagle Creek 97022
637-6324
Season: June-September; Fri-Sun, 11 am-4 pm
Special seasonal events: May, August, & September

This historic Eagle Creek farm—home to Philip Foster, one of Oregon's early entrepreneurs—was the first settlement some 10,000 emigrant pioneers and their wagon trains encountered after embarking on the Oregon Trail. Today a farmhouse, barn, pioneer store, and blacksmith shop highlight pertinent demonstrations. Children are invited to pump water, scrub clothes, cut wood with a bucksaw, and experiment with levers and pulleys. Tour the pioneer gardens and join in a treasure hunt.

Pomeroy Living History Farm

20902 NE Lucia Falls Rd.,
Yacolt, WA 98675
360-686-3537
Season: 1st full weekend of month, June-October. Sat, 11 am-4 pm; Sun, 1-4 pm.
Fees: $3.50/adult; $2/child 3-11 years
Special events: May & October

With an operating blacksmith shop, six-bedroom log house, and extensive herb and vegetable gardens, this historic farm in the Lucia Valley of northern Clark County, Wash., depicts life as it was in the 1920s. Guests are encouraged to participate in many of the daily chores: churning butter, scrubbing clothes, grinding coffee and grain, pumping water, and feeding chickens. Special events during the season feature theatrical entertainment, live folk music, and hay rides.

Portland Nursery
5050 SE Stark St., Portland 97215
231-5050
Hours: Summer, 9 am-7 pm daily; winter, 9 am-6 pm daily

Portland Nursery, one of the state's largest retail garden centers, may not qualify as a farm, but it comes close—especially in fall, when it hosts its annual weekend Gourmet Apple Tasting event (mid-October, 9 am-5 pm). More than 50 uncommon apple varieties are sliced and arrayed on a "U"-shaped table for sampling, and many can be purchased by the pound.

Explore greenhouse No. 2, too. Transformed for one weekend into the Growing with Kids Fair, it's a hotbed of learning, with stations sponsored by the Washington County Master Gardeners, Metro Washington Park Zoo, and Backyard Bird Shop, among others. Introduce your kids to horticulture: Plant a mini-greenhouse; smell fragrant oils; discover how to

TIPS

Portland Parks & Recreation maintains 23 community gardens throughout its district. Individuals and families lease 400-square-foot garden plots on an annual basis ($25, plus $10 deposit), then plant, tend, and harvest the produce for their own use. Participation in garden cleanups and other group events is required, and use of organic gardening methods is strongly encouraged. Community gardens average about half an acre in size, and still there are waiting lists for plots. Call 823-1612 for details.

Children have a garden all to themselves at Fulton Park Community Center (68 SW Miles, 823-3180). Every summer since 1994, the Friends of Portland Community Gardens has operated a drop-in gardening day camp for kids ages 4-9. Designed to teach children about the growing cycle, safe tool-handling, and plant identification, the morning classes revolve around Fulton Park's 200-square-foot display garden. The fruits (and vegetables) of the kids' labor are used in special craft projects.

Participants are informally divided into two groups by age. Planting Pals (ages 4-6) meets from 10-10:30 am daily, followed by Urban Farmers (ages 6-9), which meets from 10:45 am-12:15 pm. Fee: $5/child (district resident).

create a beehive; meet rabbits, chickens, and ducks. Balloon artists, face-painters, and musical performers are other featured guests.

Sauvie Island
Off Hwy. 30, north of Portland

This island in the Columbia River, just north of the city, is an agricultural oasis. A haven for bicyclists, bird-watchers, and sunbathers (there are four beaches along the northeastern shoreline), Sauvie Island also boasts some of the metro area's finest produce. Come in spring for fresh berries and peaches; in fall for pears, apples, and pumpkins; or just about anytime to pick and choose from the bountiful farmstand displays of fruits, vegetables, and homemade specialty goods. *(See also Active Play: Outdoor Fun, Fishing.)*

Modern-day farms give way to a historic Sauvie Island orchard at the Bybee House.

■ Bybee House
Howell Park Rd., Sauvie Island
222-1741
Season: June-August, noon-5 pm weekends
Suggested donation: $3/adult; $2/child

Built in 1858 by pioneers who arrived via the Oregon Trail, this nine-room Classic Revival dwelling was restored in 1966 by the Oregon Historical Society. Staffed only in summer on weekends, the site hosts guided tours, a series of special living-history events called A Day in the Country, and September's Wintering-In harvest festival.

Behind the house and adjacent to the Pioneer Orchard is the Agricultural Museum, where children are welcome to explore horse-drawn farming equipment as well as harness and woodworking shops. ■

Q: What sounds like a farm and smells like a farm, but isn't a farm?

A: The Oregon State Fair.

Held each summer, this is the best place to get your fill of farm animals. You'll see barns full of cows, horses, goats, sheep, pigs, rabbit, and fowl, and exhibit halls full of farming displays. As the kids mature, they may grow less interested in livestock and more interested in carnival rides, but all generations agree that the Oregon Dairy Women's ice cream earns a blue ribbon.

The State Fair is the grandaddy, but local county fairs are fun, too, and can be more intimate. When arranging your visit, call ahead to ask about special admission and carnival-ride discounts.

Multnomah County Fair
Expo Center, Portland
248-5144, 285-7756
Late July
Admission: $5/adult; $3/senior, child 6-16 years

Washington County Fair & Rodeo
Washington County Fair Complex, Hillsboro
648-1416
Early August
Admission: $6/adult; $3/child 6-15 years

Clark County Fair
Clark County Fairgrounds, Ridgefield, WA
360-573-1921
Early August
Admission: $6/adult; $2/child 7-12 years

Clackamas County Fair
Clackamas County Fairgrounds, Canby
503-266-1136
Mid-August
Admission: $7/adult; $4/senior; $3/child 8-15 years

Oregon State Fair
Oregon State Fairgrounds, Salem
503-378-3247
Late August-early September
Admission: $6/adult; $3/child 6-12 years ■

Rufus, the mascot of the Oregon State Fair, gets a warm greeting from a young fan.

Chapter 7

SPECTATOR SPORTS

Many die-hard sports fans might argue that Portland, more sprawling town than city, is not ready for the big leagues. This is no bush-league community, however. It's home to one major player—the National Basketball Association's Portland Trail Blazers—and rumors are continually circulating about multibillionaire investor Paul Allen's future sports-team acquisitions. Still, there are thousands of folks (no doubt many of them children) who can find plenty to cheer about among the region's sports offerings.

Often it's the overlooked high school and college teams (male and female) that put on the best show. From a seat in a bare-bones gym, 10 feet from the action, the lessons in fair play, cooperation, and persistence are a visceral undercurrent. These aren't superstars, they're superkids— athletes who play, not for millions, but for glory; role models you can feel good about. And what's more, the price is right.

Portland Forest Dragons

Rose Garden, 1 Center Ct., Portland
297-BALL
Season: Mid-April-July
Tickets: $7.50-$100

Though many critics early on pooh-poohed the Arena Football League—likening the sport to such hybrids as indoor soccer and roller hockey—it might just be catching on. Portland landed a team from Memphis just this season, and three other cities, including the Big Apple, added arenaball clubs of their own for 1997.

With eight men to a side (most play both offense and defense, and routinely bounce off padded walls), and average combined scores in the 100s, this rough-and-tumble indoor sport has been described as "the game of football at the pace of basketball in the environment of a hockey game." The Forest Dragons' inaugural season in the Rose Garden features eight home games, the majority of which are played on Friday and Saturday evenings.

Portland Power

Memorial Coliseum, 1401 N. Wheeler Ave., Portland
236-HOOP, 233-9559
Season: Mid-October-February
Tickets: $11-$15/reserved

The Portland Power is a brand-new adventure in professional basketball. One of eight teams in the fledgling American Basketball League, the all-female squad played its first season in 1996-97.

Featuring local favorite Katy Steding, a native of Lake Oswego and a former Olympian, the organization has high hopes of cashing in on the region's "hoop"la.

Before the season opener in October 1996, several hundred children had already contacted the Power office to ask about a fan club. Management obliged. The Power Kids Club is open to children of all ages ($9/year). Members receive a membership card, T-shirt, team photo, and newsletter. For information, call 233-9559.

With each team playing 20 home games a season, and as many on the road, coast to coast, the ABL may struggle to fill stadiums. But its battle for market share has only just begun. In summer 1997 the National Basketball Association plans to roll out its own all-female division for a short, 10-week season.

Portland Pride

Rose Garden, 1 Center Ct., Portland
684-KICK
Season: June-September
Tickets: $4-$14

Playing a quick, hockey-style game of soccer on astroturf, the Portland Pride is a member of the Continental Indoor Soccer League, whose teams span the U.S. and Mexico. Some 6,500 fans attend each game (there are 14 home games in a season), and sit right down front where the action is.

A popular team with children, many of whom play in youth soccer leagues, the Portland Pride sponsors the Cub Club Kids Fan Club and hosts four giveaway games a year, when spectators receive balls, pennants, keychains, and T-shirts.

Portland Rockies

Civic Stadium, 1844 SW Morrison, Portland
223-2837
Season: Mid-June-early September
Tickets: $6.50/reserved; $4.50-$5.50/general admission; $1-$2.50/bleachers (day of game only)

While much of the country has grown dispirited about the fate of its national pastime, baseball in Portland is enjoying a renaissance. Portland Rockies owners Jack and Mary Cain deserve all the credit for resurrecting the game as we want to remember it. The Cains moved their team, a member of the Northwest Single-A League, from Bend in 1995, and fans here hope they never look back.

On sultry evenings, families gather in the bleachers of downtown's public diamond to crack open peanut shells, scarf hot dogs, and shag fly balls that rocket into the stands. For players it's a challenging season: 38 home games and dozens of trips up and down the West Coast. For fans it's over too quickly, just like summer. Punctuated by giveaways, contests, and down-home entertainment (the mascot is Rocky Raccoon), the games rarely drag, either.

The Portland Rockies are a welcome addition to the local sporting scene.

TIPS

The Portland Rockies are the best thing to happen to local sports since Tonya Harding quit skating. Not that the team's all that good. That's beside the point. Far more important is the experience, and this is where the Cains have scored big.

One of the city's best bargains, seats in the Rockpile bleacher section are a steal. Arrive minutes before the National Anthem and settle in near the left-field line, just above the opposing team's bullpen. The vantage point is skewed, but kids are free to mill around up here, and the restrooms and snack bar are easily accessible. Bring your own picnic supper or buy popcorn, pretzels, and Kids Meals ($3.50 for hot dog, chips, red licorice whip, and drink).

Serious fans will spend a little more for real seats and a better view. Eat at the Bullpen Barbecue, a cafe set up along the first-base line ($4 cover charge applied toward food purchases), for an up-close look at the players.

Children never seem to tire of the side-show antics: costumed characters, trivia contests, prizes delivered by sling-shot, "dog" races. Fireworks follow designated games, and giveaway games are scattered throughout the season. Plan your attendance carefully and you can outfit your rookie with bat, glove, helmet, and T-shirt.

Portland Trail Blazers
Rose Garden, 1 Center Ct., Portland
231-8000, 234-9291
Season: October-May
Tickets: $15-$80

Recently ensconced in the Paul Allen Palace, a.k.a. the Rose Garden, the Portland Trail Blazers, a National Basketball Association franchise, are the town's big ticket. An NBA powerhouse in the early 1990s, the Blazers have fallen on hard times, and are in the process of rebuilding what had become an aged squad.

Critics will argue with the tactics of the management, which has systematically let go or traded many fan favorites (Clyde Drexler, Terry Porter, Jerome Kersey, and Buck Williams). And it remains to be seen whether or not the replacements can fill their shoes, either on the court or off.

One of the league's glitziest arenas, the Rose Garden is comfortable, roomy—and expensive. Most parents would agree that a ticket to a Blazers game is a treat for a child, one that is best bestowed only when she is capable of appreciating the game— and sitting through it. Think twice about purchasing cheaper ($15) tickets, which may seat you in the rafters. Consult with a ticket agent and ask about special discounts and ticket packages. You get a price break if you purchase tickets to multiple games, then divvy them up among friends. No longer a sell-out success story, the Blazers have difficulty filling the 21,500-seat Rose Garden, and at least 500 tickets are held for day-of-game sale.

TIPS

The Blazers and Emporium have developed KidsWatch identification wristbands to alleviate the anxieties of parents who worry about losing their children in the crush of a rowdy Rose Garden crowd. Available at arena information booths and concession stands, the free bracelets have space to write in a child's name, parents' names, and seat locations. Should you become separated during an event, the information on your child's bracelet can help ensure her safe return.

Portland Winter Hawks
Rose Garden, 1 Center Ct., Portland Memorial Coliseum, 1401 N. Wheeler Ave., Portland
236-HAWK, 238-6366
Season: Late September-March
Tickets: $9-$14

A fast-paced, rough game (yes, there are brawls), hockey draws capacity crowds in the Northeast and Canada. On the West Coast, where kids are less apt to grow up on ice skates, it's an acquired taste. But there are persistent rumors regarding Trail Blazers owner Paul Allen's interest in purchasing a World Hockey League franchise for the Rose City.

The Winter Hawks, a Portland fixture for 21 years, have developed a loyal following. In 1996 this major junior-league team, member of the Western Hockey League, reached the first round of post-season playoffs.

Saturday Morning Workout Show
Portland Meadows, 1001 N. Schmeer Rd., Portland
285-9144
Season: October, November, March, & April

A trip to Portland Meadows doesn't have to be a gamble. Visit the track with the kids well before the starting gun for a behind-the-scenes look at the sport of horse racing. The annual series of four free Saturday Morning Workout Shows features pony rides, face-painting, and clowns. But the real action takes place in the Winner's Circle, where children meet jockeys and trainers; watch horses in training; learn about the bandages, blinkers, starting gates, and other equipment—even see a training race. Leave by 10 am to avoid the crush of bettors, or stay on until 12:30 pm to watch the races at no charge. ■

Civic Stadium, in downtown Portland, plays host to PSU's home football games.

Portland State University
506 SW Mill St., Portland 97207
725-5677, 725-5635
Football season: September-
November
Civic Stadium, 1844 SW Morrison,
Portland
Tickets: $7-$19; $2 off/child under
12 years
Men's basketball season:
November-February
Rose Garden, 1 Center Ct., Portland
Tickets: $4-$20; $2 off/child under
12 years

Portland State University,
assigned to Division I-AA for the
1996-97 season, has high hopes for
its athletics department. And all eyes
are on the big revenue producers:
football and men's basketball.

Your best bet for watching football locally, PSU's team plays six
home games at Civic Stadium. Men's

basketball has returned after a 15-
year hiatus, and it holds court at the
Rose Garden for 10 home games.
Ticket packages include Fun for
Five ($20-$40), your pick of any five
home games, and a season pass
($40-$80).

Sports addicts—or fans who
can't make up their minds—have
another discount option. The All
Sports Pack ($50 a year) is good for
admittance to one football game,
one men's basketball game, and
unlimited soccer, women's basketball, tennis, volleyball, baseball, softball, wrestling, and track events.

University of Portland
5000 N. Willamette Blvd.,
Portland 97203
283-7117, 283-7525 (box office,
Wed-Fri, 1-5 pm)
Soccer season: September-early
November
Merlo Field, University of Portland

Tickets: $4-$9/reserved & general
admission

Soccer is the big fall sport at
University of Portland, which does
not compete in football. The east-side
school consistently fields nationally
ranked soccer teams, thanks in large
part to coach Clive Charles. His
women's team, especially, has
amassed a sterling record the last several seasons. Players of the caliber of
graduates Shannon MacMillan and
Tiffeny Milbrett, who were instrumen-
tal in the Olympic women's team's
gold-medal performance in 1996,
continue to enroll at the university.

Also in fall, women's volleyball
(there is no men's team) competes
for attention in the 5,000-seat Chiles
Center gymnasium. Seating is by
general admission, and the concession stands are open. Purchase a
booklet of 10 tickets for $20, or buy
single tickets for $2-$3.

Basketball is another popular
sport at a school whose women's
team regularly competes in the
National Collegiate Athletics Association post-season tournaments, and
whose men's team flirts with qualify-
ing. For a full night of basketball,
attend one of the season's three
double-headers. Some reserved seats
are available at Chiles Center for
men's games. Seating at women's
games is by general admission only.
Expect to pay $4-$10 per ticket; a
booklet of 10 tickets to women's
games costs $40.

The baseball team (men only)

TIPS

If your child really likes soccer,
chances are she plays in a weekend youth
league in autumn, which means you'll have
to rely on good karma to get you to a
weekend University of Portland soccer
game. Make it happen. Sportswriters
across the country are talking about
these teams, so it's almost a matter of
civic duty to support them. Besides, the
best fans are players, and the best players often began as avid fans. (Organize
an excursion for your child's team and
receive a group discount.)

These events are popular, and campus
parking, which is free, can get scarce
close to game time. Arrive extra early
for the big season-ending games and
double-headers, when men's and women's
teams play back-to-back. Reserved seats
aren't usually necessary, unless you just
have to sit right down front. Often you
can get almost as close without spending
the extra money (buy popsicles instead).
If the weather cooperates, you may prefer to sit in the bleachers behind the
near goal post, where it's shady. Coolers
and food from home are allowed at
Merlo Field, but no glass bottles, please.

has struggled of late. Recently promoted to the West Coast Conference, it now meets with stiffer competition from California schools. If the weather holds, Pilot Stadium, which seats 2,400, is a good stepping stone to Civic Stadium and the Rockies (see Professional Sports). Concession stands are available, but food from home is also allowed. Single tickets cost $2-$3 each.

Alpenrose Dairy
6149 SW Shattuck Rd.,
Portland 97221
244-1133

No longer a working dairy farm, Alpenrose remains a local fixture, known just as well for its sprawling sports complexes and special holiday events as for its milk and ice cream. *(See Farms, Special Farms for details.)* Developed to accommodate the hobbies of the children and grandchildren of the founding Cadonau family, the athletic facilities include a 3,000-seat baseball stadium plus two smaller diamonds, an oval racetrack for quarter-midget cars, and a velodrome for racing bicycles. In season the place is crawling with families who've come to compete, watch, or both.

■ Little League Softball World Series
736-9128
Season: Mid-August (13 games)

Each August since 1994, more than 100 of the world's pre-eminent female youth softball players gather on the three grass Alpenrose diamonds to crown their league's champions. Selected as all-stars from their respective regions, these 11- and 12-year-olds represent Europe, the Far East, Latin America, Canada, and the eastern, western, southern, and central U.S. The players have already endured a grueling double-elimination tournament to get here, and in six short days it's all over.

Spectators are admitted free, but are encouraged to purchase food and souvenirs from the concession stands to support the tournament (food from home is allowed).

■ Alpenrose Velodrome
244-1133
Season: May-September;
Thurs, 6:30 pm

A banked, 268-meter concrete track that resembles a giant cereal bowl, this 200-seat velodrome is specifically designed for technical, Olympic-style events that feature fixed-gear bikes without brakes. One of only 19 in the U.S., it is the scheduled venue for cycling competitions during the Nike World Masters Games in 1998.

Spectators are admitted free to the weekly races, where they picnic in the bleachers (there are no concession stands). Children are encouraged to bring their own bicycles (trikes, training wheels, two-wheelers) for pre-event, noncompetitive, 1-kilometer races on the infield track. All participants receive ribbons.

■ Quarter-Midget Racing

Season: March-October;
weekends
649-3442

Sponsored by the Portland Quarter-Midget Racing Association, these afternoon events feature competitive races among child drivers, ages 5-16. Seated at the wheel of a gas- or alcohol-powered miniature race car equipped with a one-cylinder engine, the driver can reach about 30 miles an hour on the banked, oval racetrack. To race, you must be a member of the PQMRA and bring your own vehicle and safety equipment.

Spectators are admitted free to the bleachers. A snack bar is available; food from home is also allowed.

High School Sports

Deafening bands and milling crowds of teens compete with center court for an audience at high school games, but it can be fun to follow the early career of a baby sitter or other teen friend, or to play talent scout and try to spot incipient star-power.

Call your local high school in the fall for a schedule of home games in your sport of choice. If you'd prefer to be more selective, plan to attend one of the state's all-star games. Held in June and July at venues throughout Oregon, these contests provide an opportunity to see the year's best crop of athletes. Each year Portland hosts the Oregon

vs. Washington girls' and boys' all-star basketball games, and the all-star girls' volleyball game. Contact the Oregon Coaches Association in May for the upcoming schedule: 503-399-9132.

Introduced in 1997, the Great Northwest Shootout capitalizes on the regional rivalry between Oregon and Washington high schools with two seniors-only basketball games: one for men, one for women. Selected by the coaches' associations, most of the team's 12 graduating seniors have, until this night, been rivals. Here they must forget the feuds and work together as a team. Held in mid-June at the Chiles Center (University of Portland) and televised locally, the double-header is sponsored by the Multnomah Athletic Foundation (223-6251). Tickets cost $4-$8. ■

Chapter 8
EXCURSIONS

Y ou can fill an entire book with suggestions of things to do as a family in the Portland area. Then you can fill an entire year doing them. But even if you never tire of the tried-and-true local parks, museums, and activities, the time will come when a couple of hours in the car with the kids won't sound so bad.

Perhaps it's the visiting in-laws who want to glimpse Mount St. Helens, or the kids who want to see Keiko. Whatever the impetus, don't hesitate. Pack up the car and go.

There are numerous destinations within a few hours' drive of downtown that will provide your family with a deeper understanding of the region's culture and history. You'll know your neighborhood better for having gone away.

T hough Portland straddles the Willamette River, it's the Columbia that gets more attention. And well it should. Just 40 miles east of the city is some of the state's finest scenery—fir-speckled basalt cliffs and granite outcroppings, bubbling brooks, cascading waterfalls, and peaceful pastureland. Crown Point Vista House and Multnomah Falls attract crowds of tourists in season, but there are dozens of lesser-known natural spectacles just off the beaten path.

From Portland, take I-84 east—then, if time allows, follow signs for the **Historic Columbia River Hwy.** (exit 17 at Troutdale). A masterpiece of engineering know-how when it opened in 1915, the 22-mile roadway winds along a high bluff past nine waterfalls and six state parks. Look for original Italian stonework walls that still line sections of the route, and stop for a panoramic view at the **Portland Women's Forum Overlook** or at **Crown Point.**

Plan to get out of the car to explore at least one waterfall up close. The gently sloping lower trail at Latourell Falls is ideal for little kids. Wear hiking boots or other sturdy shoes, and tote rain gear. The trails are often muddy and damp from rain and mist, and the dense forest keeps the sun at bay. For trail maps and other information, contact the Columbia Gorge National Scenic Area Forest Service: 541-386-2333.

You really must stop at **Multnomah Falls**—if you can find a parking space. At 620 feet, it's the nation's second highest waterfall, and it's spectacular. Little kids can paddle in the stream. Older children will want to hike to the top. Take the steep, 1.25-mile paved trail at your own risk; there are no railings, and several perilous drop-offs. Built in 1925, the historic lodge (695-2376) features a cozy restaurant, restrooms, and snack bar.

TIPS

Pam Vestal of Drive-It-Yourself Tours created *The Columbia Gorge* with families in mind. Both educational and entertaining, the 77-minute audiocassette begins in downtown Portland, then follows the Columbia River Hwy., with eight stops at waterfalls, scenic overlooks, and landmarks. Even if you've been before, a trip with built-in soundtrack has lots to recommend it. Learn of volcanic explosions, political wrangling, a quest for gold, and cataclysmic flooding.

Available for $14.95 at Powell's Books, Borders, other area bookstores, and the Portland Oregon Visitors Association office, the self-guided driving tour can also be ordered by calling 699-8398.

Rejoin I-84 at exit 35 and continue east to Cascade Locks (exit 44). This is the best place to break for a meal or snack. The **Charburger** (714 Wanapa St., 541-374-8477) grills made-to-order hamburgers to go with its spectacular view of the river and Bridge of the Gods, and the gift shop sells delicious home-baked cookies. Just down the street at the **East Wind Drive-In** (541-374-8380), a skyscraper of soft-serve ice cream costs just $2.

Cross the Bridge of the Gods into Washington, then head east on Hwy. 14 to Stevenson, home to **Skamania Lodge** (800-221-7117). Open since 1993, the lodge sits regally on a rolling meadow facing the Columbia River. Constructed of heavy timbers, with a massive stone fireplace in the lobby and Mission-style furnishings throughout, this place is reminiscent of Timberline Lodge *(see Mount Hood)*.

Come on a Sunday to indulge in

TIPS

While geologists believe a natural bridge spanned the Columbia at the present-day site of Bridge of the Gods some 1,000 years ago, Native Americans use an enchanting legend to explain the topography of this region.

Caught in a battle for the affections of Squaw Mountain, two brothers, Klickitat (Mount Adams) and Wy'east (Mount Hood), grew violent; they stomped their feet, spat ashes, fire, and clouds of smoke, and hurled hot rocks at each other. When their stone-throwing destroyed the bridge, their father, the Great Spirit, intervened. Wy'east, the smaller of the brothers, graciously relented.

Squaw Mountain dutifully took her place beside Klickitat, but her heart was broken, for she had loved Wy'east best. Presently she sank into a deep slumber at

Klickitat's feet. She is now known as the Sleeping Beauty, which lies just west of Mount Adams. On observing his squaw's countenance, Klickitat dropped his head in shame.

Meanwhile, Loo-Wit, an old woman who had been assigned by the Great Spirit to guard and protect the bridge, had been clobbered and badly burned during the brothers' fight. When the Great Spirit learned of her injuries and her faithfulness, he offered to grant her a wish.

Loo-Wit asked to be made young and beautiful again. And so she took her place among the other great mountain peaks—but at a polite remove, befitting her aged spirit. Today she is called Mount St. Helens, the youngest of the Cascade Mountains.

the sumptuous brunch buffet ($18.50/ adult; $9.95/child 8-12 years; $5.95/ child 3-7 years; free/child under 3 years; reservations encouraged). Then stay to work off the meal.

Three mile-long nature trails meander past golf courses and ponds. The fitness center and pool area are open daily ($6/adult; $3/child under 12 years). The rock-pool hot tub outside is fun for kids in nice weather. On a rainy day they can splash instead in the indoor whirlpool and lap pool. Locker rooms are equipped with saunas, hot tubs, showers, and towels.

Don't return home before visiting the **Columbia Gorge Interpretive Center** (990 SW Rock Creek Dr., 509-427-8211). Designed to resemble the sawmills that sat here earlier in the century, this gem of a museum is located just below Skamania Lodge. Its manageable size and engaging exhibits, which trace the history of the gorge by underscoring its resources and inhabitants, make it particularly suitable for families.

Children are intrigued by the basalt cliff adornments, indoor waterfall, replica fishwheel, Corliss steam engine, and logging truck. A short slide presentation examines the geologic formation of the gorge. **Hours:** 10 am-5 pm daily **Fees:** $6/adult; $5/senior, student; $4/child 6-12 years; free/child under 5 years

On the drive back to Portland on I-84 west, turn in at the **Bonneville Lock & Dam** (541-374-8820) on Bradford Island. The glass-walled visitors' center features an observation deck, historical displays, and underwater windows that look out on fish ladders. Chinook, coho, sockeye, and steelhead salmon migrate upriver to spawn in spring, summer, and fall. Come in summer (June-September) for the best viewing. Take a guided tour of the dam powerhouse (call ahead for reservations); then, on your way out to the highway, stop to examine the Navigation Lock.

Adjacent to the dam is the **Bonneville Fish Hatchery** (541-374-8393), where approximately 20 million salmon fingerlings are raised for release into neighboring Tanner Creek each spring. The parklike setting features sculpture ponds, picnic tables, and a gift shop (closed in winter). But the real draw is the fish.

Three natural-style rock ponds teem with rainbow trout and 6-foot sturgeon year-round. Purchase a handful of pellets (25¢) to feed the trout. Adult salmon are housed in five outdoor holding ponds from September-December. Monitored indoors, fry and fingerlings are not on display. *(See also Active Play: Outdoor Fun, Fishing.)* ■

Hood River (just off I-84, 60 miles east of Portland) is a sailboarder's mecca. A walk down Oak St. reveals shops that hawk every device necessary to equip a board and sailor—as well as the requisite souvenirs. The town is quaint nonetheless, with pretty bungalows, rolling lawns, and views of the river.

If the wind is up, you can get a front-row seat at sporting entertainment down by the water. The grassy beaches at the **Hood River Event Site** (I-84 exit 63) and the sandy beaches near the **Port Marina Park** (I-84 exit 64) afford accessible views of sailboarding. The Expo Center nearby houses the offices of the Hood River Visitor Center and local Chamber of Commerce.

The Hood River region is also famous for its orchards. A large percentage of the nation's pears (Anjou, Bosc, Comice, and Bartlett) are grown here, as is the world's preeminent Newtown Pippen apple. Pick up a copy of the **Fruit Loop Map**, an annual guide to local farmstands (available at shops and restaurants in town, or by calling Hood River County Visitor Center, 800-366-3530), and take a drive in the country. Or board the historic **Mount Hood Railroad** for a four-hour, round-trip excursion along peaceful backroads *(see Active Play: Outdoor Fun, Trains & Trolleys)*.

Plan your visit around a seasonal festival to see the valley at its best: Blossom Festival (third weekend in April); Gravenstein Apple Fair (late August); Pumpkin Funland at Rasmussen Farms (late September-late October; *see Farms, Pumpkin Harvests*); or Harvest Fest (early October). ∎

TIPS

A wonderful way to approach Mount Hood is from the east. If time and stamina allow, take Hwy. 35 south from Hood River. The 44-mile route begins in flat fruit orchards, then climbs steadily and winds past mountainous, glacial terrain. From this vantage point, Mount Hood looms gracefully to fill the windshield.

Continue to the summit at Timberline Lodge *(see Mount Hood)*, then descend via Hwy. 26 and return to Portland. The Mount Hood Information Center in Welches (622-4822, 622-7674) carries free copies of *The Mount Hood Columbia Gorge Loop*, a brochure that details this scenic drive, plus trail maps, lodging guides, and other tips for visitors.

N ative Americans called it Wy'east, and at 11,235 feet, it's the state's tallest peak. Ski lifts run year-round *(see Active Play: Outdoor Fun, Snow Play)*, but even if you don't ski, the 60-mile trip to the summit at 6,000 feet is rewarding.

At the end of the road sits **Timberline Lodge** (231-7979). Built during the Depression as a showcase for the talents of local craftsmen and artisans, it is a masterpiece of hewed logs and great stone fire-places—the quintessential Northwest mountain lodge.

Take I-84 east from Portland to Hwy. 26. At Government Camp, watch for signs.

Timberline Lodge, a majestic log structure built in the 1930s, is a Mount Hood landmark.

In ski season, special Sno-Park Permits are required of lodge guests and visitors, and parking spaces may be limited *(see Active Play: Outdoor Fun, Snow Play).*

The **Magic Mile Sky Super Express Chairlift** to the base of the Palmer Snowfield is open to non-skiers in spring (10 am-1:30 pm daily) and summer (10 am-5 pm daily), weather permitting. Purchase a Sky Ride Sightseer Pass ($6/adult; $3/child 7-12 years; free/child under 7 years) for a view of the Oregon Trail's Barlow Road, and on toward Mount Jefferson and the Cascades (bring quarters for the telescope).

Lunch outdoors at Palmer Junction Barbecue or at Silcox Hut, a rustic stone-and-timber structure built in 1939 and recently reopened to the public. Then, if you're game, return to the lodge on foot. A free trail map at the front desk highlights points of interest along the 1-mile trail down.

The lodge interior manages to feel at once massive and cozy. Don't miss the slide show, which highlights the handiwork and graphic themes that are echoed through-out. Children with energy to burn after the drive have three lobby areas to explore. There's also a tabletop shuffleboard game (ask at the front desk for board games), a pub, and formal dining room. No doubt hungry kids will prefer the fast-food offerings at the adjacent Wy'east Day Lodge, which feeds crowds of skiers at lunch time.

A better dining option for families is located in Government Camp. Owned and operated by Timberline Lodge, the **Mount Hood Brew Pub** (503-272-3724) serves wholesome pizza, hamburgers, salads, sand-wiches, and chili in an informal chalet setting. ■

On May 18, 1980, Mount St. Helens erupted with the force of several atomic bombs, dramatically changing the landscape for miles in all directions. The event itself is the stuff of history books. No less intriguing is the story of the environment's natural recovery process.

Visitors to the five interpretive centers that line State Rte. 504 east of I-5 near Castle Rock are treated to panoramic views of the mountain, video and slide presentations, and educational, interactive displays and exhibits that document the eruption and its aftermath.

Pick and choose among the options; to visit each one would be to experience sensory overload. Avoid crowds of tourists by avoiding summer weekends, but pray for a clear day for the best view.

Fuel up the car in Castle Rock (I-5 exit 49). Also known as Spirit Lake Memorial Hwy., State Rte. 504 makes a sinuous 60-mile climb to within 5 miles of the volcano, and there are no gas stations en route. Carry lightweight jackets and rain gear as well as sunscreen and water. The temperature fluctuations are unpredictable near the peak, and with few trees, there's little protection from the elements. Pack a picnic to spread out on a table at one of the visitors' centers or at Seaquest State Park near Silver Lake, or lunch in the Hoffstadt Bluffs restaurant (see below) or Coldwater Ridge cafeteria.

The U.S. Forest Service recently introduced a fee structure within the Mount St. Helens National Volcanic Monument to help defray operating costs. To use visitors' centers and other developed sites in the vicinity, adults are now required to purchase three-day passes for $8 apiece ($4/senior; free/child 15 years & under). These monument passes are available at Forest Service facilities and at local businesses in Cougar, Randle, Castle Rock, and Toutle.

Mount St. Helens Cinedome Theater
Castle Rock
360-274-8000
Hours: May-October, 9 am-6 pm daily
Admission: $5/adult; $4/senior, child 6-12 years; free/child 5 years & under

Mount St. Helens erupts every 45 minutes in season on the giant 70mm screen at the 174-seat Mount St. Helens Cinedome. An Academy Award-nominated, 25-minute documentary, *The Eruption of Mount St. Helens* is more experience than movie. The screen is three stories high and three rows of special seats at the rear vibrate with the roar of the volcano. Children under 5 years may be overwhelmed by the sound system; older kids will likely be enthralled.

Mount St. Helens Visitors Center
360-274-2100
Hours: 9 am-5 pm daily

The exhibits at this U.S. Forest Service facility on the shores of Silver Lake provide an introduction to the eruption, with a walk-through volcano mock-up, 20-minute film, and 10-minute, multiprojector slide show of the event, plus views of the mountain (on a clear day) through telescopes.

Hoffstadt Bluffs Visitor Center
360-274-7750
Shop hours: Mon-Thurs, 10 am-4 pm; Sat-Sun, 10 am-8 pm
Restaurant hours: Wed-Thurs, 10 am-4 pm; Fri-Sat, 10 am-8 pm

Built by Cowlitz County, this post-and-beam, Alpine-style building houses a gift shop and full-service family restaurant with a view of the Toutle River valley. In summer, helicopter tours ($69/person) and covered-wagon rides ($20/adult; $10/child 11 years & under) depart regularly from the parking lot.

Forest Learning Center
360-414-3439
Hours: May-October, 10 am-6 pm daily

The "volcano" playground at the entrance to the Forest Learning Center is visible from Hwy. 504, so you'll probably have to stop to

appease the kids in the back seat. Stretch your legs on the half-mile trail, then try to spot elk through the telescopes.

Inside there's a replica helicopter, three different video presentations, and a model forest. Exhibits stress the eruption's effects on private timberland, and the timber industry's efforts to salvage, replant, and recover lost acreage. Weyerhaeuser, the Rocky Mountain Elk Foundation, and the state Department of Transportation collaborated on this facility.

Coldwater Ridge Visitor Center
360-274-2131
Hours: Winter, 9 am-5 pm daily; summer, 10 am-6 pm daily

From its bluff directly opposite the mountain's lopsided crater, the U.S. Forest Service's Coldwater Ridge center underscores the region's recovery process, with interactive exhibits that detail native lifeforms before, during, and after the eruption. Take a walk along the paved trails beside Coldwater Lake (once a river), and scout for hummocks—the rocky mounds that were blasted from the volcano.

Johnston Ridge Observatory
360-274-2140
Hours: 9-6 pm daily; closed in winter

This is the end of the road, and probably as close as you'll want to get to the still-steaming crater.

Opened in May 1997, Johnston Ridge Observatory represents Mount St. Helens National Monument's crowning glory. The brand-new, $8.3 million U.S. Forest Service facility features a large, formal theater; a 15-minute, wide-screen, computer-animated video program; and a jaw-dropping view right down the throat of the mountain. The engaging exhibits examine the geologic events surrounding the eruption and subsequent eruptions, and the techniques used by scientists to monitor active volcanoes. ■

F rom Portland, Newport (about 2 1/2 hours away by car) may not be the nearest coastal beach, but in fair weather and especially in foul, it's surely among a child's top picks. And that's largely because of its first-rate aquarium.

When the **Oregon Coast Aquarium** (2820 SE Ferry Slip Rd., 541-867-3474) opened to enthusiastic crowds in 1992, visitors raved about the innovative exhibits. Designed to trace the pathway of a raindrop as it journeys from the forests of the Coast Range to the Pacific Ocean, the aquarium uses its theme, plus colorful, naturalistic indoor and outdoor display areas, to emphasize the diversity of flora and fauna native to the Oregon coast.

Kids waved at the mischievous otters frolicking underwater in their outdoor pool, then ran inside to tickle an anemone and experiment with the video microscope. Adults giggled at the puffin parade in the walk-through seabird aviary, the largest of its kind in North America, then watched the tide recede from a peaceful platform overlooking Yaquina Bay. Toddlers slid down the back of the playground's great stone seal and leaped from the shell of the turtle, then slurped on ice cream cones from the nearby cafe. The entire family stood silently before the jellyfish tank, transfixed by the graceful undulations of the ethereal moon jellies.

And this would have been enough, for the aquarium felt intimate (never too crowded), yet comprehensive. Then came Keiko.

Known to legions of children around the world as the film star from *Free Willy*, this enfeebled orca

Playful otters entertain legions of eager children at the Oregon Coast Aquarium.

TIPS

The Oregon Coast Aquarium is at its most peaceful in the off-season, from October–March (with the exception of holiday weeks), as well as first thing in the morning and just before closing. Come early or late to avoid the crowds, which tend to congregate at Keiko's tank.

About 10 volunteers dressed in royal-blue jackets, sweatshirts, or T-shirts are present on any given day, circulating among the galleries and outdoor exhibits. Trained to greet visitors and answer their questions, they are friendly and knowledgeable. Some offer ad-hoc tours of the aviary. For an in-depth tour of the entire aquarium, consider renting an audio headset ($3); there's even a special children's version.

Short lecture presentations, called Keeper Encounters, are offered daily in summer and on weekends in winter in the Whale Theatre. Look for a schedule in the lobby. Feeding times are purposely kept random, but you're likely to catch somebody in the midst of a feast; seals, sea lions, sea otters, and aviary birds are all fed publicly. Keiko's lunch time is less visible because he eats topside.

The aquarium goes out of its way to accommodate patrons with special needs, families included. All the restrooms are equipped with changing facilities. Rental strollers are available ($4/single; $6/double), as are wheelchairs ($4), and the gift shop carries disposable diapers and one-size-fits-all rain ponchos ($1.95).

whale was moved from his confining Mexican quarters to five-star accommodations at the aquarium in January 1996. The intention is to rehabilitate Keiko, and eventually to return him to the wild. His caretakers continue to work to improve his cardiovascular conditioning and general health. (Keiko has gained nearly 1,000 pounds since arriving in Oregon, and his skin lesions have cleared up.) He doesn't perform in a show, but Keiko is nonetheless a big draw. He is on view to the public through three large, underwater observation windows.

Hours: Winter, 10 am-5 pm daily (closed Christmas Day); summer, 9 am-6 pm daily
Fees: $8.50/adult; $7.50/senior; $4.25/child 4-13 years; free/child under 4 years

There's more than enough to do in Newport to fill a day, even without factoring in the requisite hours at Keiko's place. Stroll along the historic bayfront to get a feel for the industry that built this town. Inspect the fishing boats, crab traps, and shellfish steamers, but beware of the trio of attractions just up the street at

Mariner's Square. No self-respecting kid will leave before seeing them all.

Operated in concert, **Ripley's Believe It or Not!, The Wax Works**, and **Undersea Gardens** (250 SW Bay Blvd., 541-265-2206) provide frivolous entertainment. They're fun for adults who are in the right mood and for kids who aren't either too old to know the difference or too young to be truly frightened.

Of the three attractions, only one offers any redeeming value. Housed in a floating exhibit hall that's sunk into the bay, **Undersea Gardens** is no competition for the big aquarium, but its underwater view of native marine creatures is fittingly complementary. Don't miss the "show," in which a scuba diver, wired for communication with the audience and announcer, tours the tank and hunts down crabs, eels, octopus, and other special guests for up-close viewing.
Hours: Winter, 10 am-5 pm daily; summer, 9 am-8 pm daily
Fees: $5.75-$14.50/adult; $3.50-$8.50/child 5-11 years; free/child under 5 years

Though the aquarium cafeteria is adequate for a quick bite, the menu is predictable, and the small indoor space gets noisy and crowded at lunch time. Opened 40 years ago, the original **Mo's Restaurant** (622 SW Bay Blvd., 541-265-2979) may be just as crazy at noon, but the clattering and chattering here is part of the charm. Order the famous clam chowder with garlic cheese bread or grandiose onion rings to fulfill your grease quota for the year. Children will probably opt for fish and chips, hot dogs, and grilled cheese sandwiches.

The Pacific Ocean roils, boils, and explodes along the rugged coastline just north of Newport. For a scenic detour, take U.S. 101 to **Otter Crest Loop Drive** at Cape Foulweather. Bring binoculars and a generous dose of patience in winter and spring to help you spot migrating gray whales.

During Whale Watch Weeks, in late December and again during spring break, 29 sites along the coast are manned by volunteers who are trained to help novices spy whales. To receive *Whale Watch Spoken Here*, a booklet with site map, contact Mike Rivers, program coordinator: 541-563-2002.

Yaquina Head Outstanding Natural Area (541-265-2863), operated by the Bureau of Land Management, boasts some of the coast's best tidepools. A popular attraction staffed by interpreters year-round, dawn to dusk, the park is on Agate Beach, just off U.S. 101 at the north end of Newport. Concrete pathways and manmade pools are accessible to wheelchairs (and toddlers). But the beach also features plenty of natural tidepools.

Tides are at their lowest daytime levels in spring, though any day with a tide below +2 feet uncovers a multitude of marine treasures: sea urchins, sea stars, anemones, chitons, sculpins, shore crabs, and lots of kelp.

Bring rain gear and wear sturdy tennis or running shoes to help you maintain your footing on the slippery rocks, and keep a close watch on your children at all times. Collecting is not allowed, so leave buckets in the car. And plan to lunch elsewhere. Picnicking is prohibited at Yaquina Head, but the neighboring buffet-style Izzy's Restaurant welcomes children (sand, sea salt, and all).

Other less-developed tidepool areas include **Otter Rock Marine Gardens** in Otter Rock State Park (541-265-4560), 7 miles north of Newport; and **Seal Rock State Park** (541-867-7451), 5 miles south of Newport.

Drive south on U.S. 101 to Yaquina Bay State Park, just west of the Yaquina Bay Bridge. There you'll find the historic **Yaquina Bay Lighthouse** (541-265-5679). Built in 1871, the refurbished lighthouse, Newport's oldest existing structure, was recently relit following 122 years of darkness.

Children are invited to imagine what life was like for a lighthouse keeper in the old days, and to climb as high as the watch room, where the keeper spent the night. With its view of the open ocean, this is a great spot for whale-watching. *Hours:* Winter, noon-4 pm daily; summer, 11 am-5 pm daily ■

Chapter 9

SEASON BY SEASON

Mother Nature's clock is as accurate as a Swiss watch, yet local families need not rely on her precise timing to anticipate seasonal changes. Instead they can coordinate their annual rhythms to the region's cycle of traditional festivals and performances and favorite celebrations. The Ringling Bros. & Barnum & Bailey circus is in town? It must be fall. A towering evergreen commands its place of honor in Pioneer Courthouse Square? It must be winter. Packy the elephant digs into his birthday cake? It must be spring. The Willamette River teems with dragon boats? It must be summer.

This month-by-month listing of metro-area family events is designed to ensure your calendar is never blank.

WINTER

JANUARY

All-Breed Dog Show
Expo Center
248-5144

Dogs and their owners compete in confirmation, obedience, and agility events. The junior showmanship competition is open to youngsters and their pets.

Wrangler Pro Rodeo Classic
Rose Garden
235-8771

Real cowboys spend three days in the dust competing in roping, bucking, and riding events.

Youth Outdoor Sports Fair
Oregon Convention Center
800-545-6100

Kids learn about fishing, boating, ecology, and animal habitats at this event, part of the International Sportsmen's Exposition.

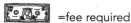 =fee required

FEBRUARY

Doll & Teddy Bear Show
Expo Center
284-4062

From antique to new, from handmade to factory-made, this show and sale highlight anything and everything to do with dolls and teddy bears. (The show returns in August and November.)

Oregon Cat Fanciers' Show
Memorial Coliseum
503-824-6116

Hundreds of felines representing 35 species are judged on standards of "purr-fection." Information booths and vendors offer tips to pet owners.

Original Rare Animal Expo
Washington County Fair Complex, Hillsboro
503-738-6996

Children are invited to ride llamas, visit the petting zoo, and meet miniature donkeys, emus, hedgehogs, snakes, and iguanas.

Pacific Northwest Sportsmen's Show
Expo Center
285-7756

The largest and oldest show of its kind in the region, the Sportsmen's Show spotlights hundreds of new recreational products and services. Free seminars and demonstrations cover everything from fly-fishing to hunting. Kids can fish for trout in the on-site pond.

Tree & Trail Day
World Forestry Center
228-1367

Help plant trees and spruce up the trails at the World Forestry Center's Magness Memorial Tree Farm. Bring work gloves and shovels.

Walt Disney's World on Ice
Rose Garden
321-3211

Starring former competitive skaters, each four-day ice show extravaganza is based on a recent hit Disney movie.

MARCH

Annual Winter Games of Oregon
Mount Hood
520-1319

Skiers and snowboarders of all ages are eligible to compete in Olympic-style events at Timberline and Mt. Hood SkiBowl.

Kid Safe
Two Portland-area schools (locations vary)
221-7161

Sponsored by the Northwest Osteopathic Medical Foundation in cooperation with Eastmoreland Hospital, this free, all-day health and safe-

ty event for children features a dozen workshops in fire safety, stranger danger, emergency preparedness, etc.

Lewis & Clark International Fair
Lewis & Clark College
768-7305

The foreign students at Lewis & Clark showcase their cultures and customs with a multiethnic buffet lunch, followed by music and dance performances.

Petco Pet Fair
Expo Center
285-7756

Gather tips on pet care, watch demonstrations, and see professionally trained animals do their tricks.

St. Patrick's Irish Festival
Kells Irish Restaurant & Pub
227-4057

The region's largest St. Patrick's event, this authentic festival features live Irish music and a street fair with a petting zoo and craft activities for kids. Proceeds benefit Providence Children's Center.

Shamrock Run
Waterfront Park
226-5080

A benefit for the Doernbecher Children's Hospital Foundation, this fitness event consists of the Leprechaun Lap (a 1K run, walk, or jog), the Shamrock Stride (a 4-mile walk), and an 8K race.

Shrine Circus

Rose Garden

682-4420

This is a good-time, old-fashioned, three-ring circus with acrobats, big cats, and clowns.

EASTER EVENTS

■ **Alpenrose Dairy Easter Egg Hunt**

Alpenrose Dairy

244-1133

Youngsters are invited to search for eggs, gifts, and prizes.

■ **Oaks Park Eggstravaganza**

Oaks Amusement Park

233-5777

Sponsored by KUFO radio, this annual Easter event features a free continental breakfast, a performance by Ladybug Theater, and an egg hunt for children aged 6 and under. Discounted ride packages are available.

■ **Rabbit Romp**

Metro Washington Park Zoo

226-1561

This event features egg hunts, games, crafts, and a petting zoo. The Oregon Humane Society sponsors an exhibit of adoptable pets.

■ **RiverPlace Tulip Festival**

RiverPlace Esplanade

228-5108

A flower sale to benefit Easter Seals, this colorful event features hundreds of tulips as well as egg hunts, entertainment, and children's activity centers.

SPRING

APRIL

Camp Fair

Clackamas Town Center & Lloyd Center

244-0111

Representatives from day camps, overnight camps, sports, theater, and academic camps answer questions and provide information about their summer programs.

Children's Tree Trail

World Forestry Center

228-1367 ext. 108

One of the nation's biggest Arbor Day celebrations, Children's Tree Trail features a guided walk through Hoyt Arboretum, special hands-on activities, a picnic with Smokey Bear, and free admission to the World Forestry Center.

Earth Day

Locations vary

823-2223, 823-5120

This Earth Day event showcases interactive exhibits from environmental agencies, as well as environmental projects designed by local students. Sponsored by Portland Parks & Recreation.

March of Dimes WalkAmerica
Rose Quarter
222-9434

Enter a 3K, 10K, or 20K walk and help raise money for the March of Dimes Campaign for Healthier Children.

Packy's Birthday Party
Metro Washington Park Zoo
226-1561

Watch Portland's popular pachyderm feast on his special wholewheat cake with peanut butter frosting. Kids' games and people food are also provided.

Portland Juggling Festival
Reed College
282-1429

This is the largest regional juggling festival in America. Be a spectator, or participate and have a ball at any of 30 different workshops.

Trillium Festival
Tryon Creek State Park
636-4398
Hands-on crafts and activities center on horticulture and gardening. Purchase plants, trees, and shrubs to support Tryon Creek State Park educational programs.

Woodburn Tulip Festival
Various locations in Woodburn
800-711-2006
Tour the tulip fields at their peak, in early April. Entertainment and activities are offered at various locations.

MAY

Children's Day
Japanese Garden
223-1321

In honor of the Japanese Boys' and Girls' Day celebrations, this one-day event showcases a variety of Japanese cultural activities, from origami to martial arts and traditional dances.

Cinco de Mayo
Waterfront Park
222-9807
This Hispanic celebration features ethnic foods, entertainment, dancing, and arts and crafts booths.

Doggie Dash
Waterfront Park
222-5103

Sponsored by K103 radio, this 5K fun run/walk is for canines and their owners. Entry fee includes T-shirt and doggie treats.

St. Johns Parade

St. Johns neighborhood
286-1550

A 34-year tradition, this down-home, neighborhood parade includes marching bands, floats, clowns, and horses.

SUMMER

JUNE

Cruisin' Sherwood

Old Town, Sherwood
625-6873

A display of more than 300 souped-up show cars, from old to new, Cruisin' Sherwood also features crafts, food, and games for children.

Festival of Flowers

Pioneer Courthouse Square
223-1613, 295-8084

This celebration of flowers showcases a showstopping, artist-designed floral display.

Lake Oswego Festival of Arts

George Rogers Park, Lake Oswego
636-1060

An art show and sale with more than 1,000 works by regional artists, this festival also spotlights craft activities and performances for chil-

dren. The Teddy Bear Parade is an annual favorite.

Pioneer Living & Trail Tales

End of the Oregon Trail Interpretive Center, Oregon City
657-9336

Watch demonstrations of pioneer chores and crafts, listen to special stories, and enjoy traditional entertainment.

Rose Festival

227-2681

Consistently ranked among the world's top 10 festivals, the Rose Festival dates to 1907, when Portland's first floral parade was accompanied by two days of activities celebrating the rose. Today, more than 80 events span three weeks and dozens of area venues. Below is a chronological sampling of some of the festival's family events.

■ **Fireworks Spectacular**
Waterfront Park

This gala display marks the official opening of the Rose Festival.

■ **Festival Center**
Waterfront Park

Carnival rides, games, around-the-clock entertainment, and food booths take over Waterfront Park for 10 days.

■ **Starlight Parade**
Downtown Portland

The first of three festival parades, this nighttime event features clowns, marching bands, and eccentric floats.

■ **Li'l Briches Rodeo**
Alpenrose Dairy

Children ages 3-12 compete in silly, rodeo-style events (there is no riding, however): calf-flagging, pig scramble, cowhide race, three-legged race, and ring-a-ribbon.

■ **Alpenrose Milk Carton Boat Races**
Westmoreland Park
Participants vie to keep afloat in their creations.

■ **Rose Festival Fleet**
Waterfront Park
More than 20 ships arrive, dock, and are open for tours.

■ **Junior Parade**
Hollywood district
With more than 10,000 child participants, this is the largest parade of its kind in the world.

■ **Grand Floral Parade**
Downtown Portland
The highlight of the Rose Festival, this event is the country's second largest all-floral parade. Dozens of floats, meticulously decorated with live, natural materials, are joined by equestrian teams, marching bands, and celebrity guests.

■ **Showcase of Floats**
Rose Quarter

 donation
Here's your opportunity to view the parade floats up close.

■ **Dragon Boat Races**
Waterfront Park
Teams of paddlers race in heats in traditional, colorful shells.

■ **Air Show**
Hillsboro Airport

Bring earplugs to this airborne spectacle. Watch flying and sky-diving exhibitions and jet races.

■ **Budweiser/G.I. Joe's 200**
Portland International Raceway

World-class race-car drivers compete for prize money and points in this National Championship Auto Racing Team contest.

Taste of Beaverton
Griffith Park, Beaverton
644-0123
This arts and crafts fair features children's events, entertainment, and food.

Tigard Festival of Balloons
Cook Park, Tigard
245-5220
Colorful hot-air balloons ascend at dawn, then "park" on the lawn, festooned by lights, at night. Carnival rides plus food and craft booths are also on-site.

Tryon Creek Moonlight Walk
Tryon Creek State Park
636-4398
Follow the leader on a nighttime hike (flashlights allowed).

JULY

Da Vinci Days
Downtown Corvallis
757-6363

This three-day celebration concentrates on the arts, sciences, and technology, with interactive games; human- and electric-powered vehicle races; and music, theater, and storytelling performances. "The Village" showcases special activities for children ages 3-13.

Fort Vancouver Brigade Encampment
Fort Vancouver
800-832-3599, 360-696-7655

Witness a re-enactment of the annual return of fur-trapping brigades.

Molalla Buckeroo
Molalla Buckeroo Grounds, Molalla
503-829-8388

Sure, there are bucking broncos, but kids also like the train rides, parades, and carnival that come to town.

Multnomah County Fair
Oaks Amusement Park
289-6623

Displays of livestock are interspersed with carnival rides and craft and food booths.

Oaks Park Fireworks
Oaks Amusement Park
233-5777

Visitors are encouraged to come early to enjoy the amusement-park rides and to picnic. No alcohol or personal fireworks allowed.

Oregon Trail Pageant
End of the Oregon Trail Interpretive Center, Oregon City
657-0988

A new, historical musical drama is scheduled to premiere in 1998.

Riverfest
Clackamette Park, Oregon City
650-5219

This three-day festival features waterski and boat shows in addition to carnival rides, entertainment, and food booths.

St. Paul Rodeo
St. Paul Rodeo Arena
633-2151

Now in its 62nd year, this smaller-scale rodeo is ideal for families. Carnival rides and games, a parade, and fireworks displays are other featured activities.

Sherwood Robin Hood Festival
Stella Olsen Park, Sherwood
625-7537

Friday's festivities feature a "knighting" ceremony of community leaders. Saturday begins with a parade; games, crafts, and entertainment continue all day. The annual archery tournament takes place at Hopkins Elementary School.

Turkey-Rama
McMinnville
472-6196

This event got its name way back when McMinnville was home to many turkey farms. Now the town features sidewalk art shows, a carnival, children's fair, and "The Biggest Turkey" talent contest.

Vancouver Fireworks
Fort Vancouver Parade Grounds
360-693-5481

Considered the largest display west of the Mississippi, this extravaganza is preceded by an all-day festival.

Washington County Fair & Rodeo
Washington County Fair Complex, Hillsboro
648-1416

Visit with livestock, watch a rodeo or 4x4 truck pull, then stay for live entertainment.

Waterfront Blues Festival
Waterfront Park
282-0555

 (donation)

Four days of live, outdoor performances by local and international blues artists, plus a July 4th fireworks display. Proceeds benefit the Oregon Food Bank.

AUGUST

Antique Airplane Fly-In
Evergreen Field, Vancouver
360-892-5028

More than 300 aircraft that pre-date 1940 arrive from around the country for this weekend event. Model kits, toy airplanes, and other related merchandise are on sale.

The Bite
Waterfront Park
248-0600

 (donation)

"Grazing" takes on new meaning at this annual feast, where noshers nibble their way through a la carte samples from dozens of area restaurants. Family activities include "moon bouncers," an inflatable slide, clowns, and face painting. Continuous entertainment is featured on multiple stages. Proceeds benefit Oregon Special Olympics.

Bridge Pedal
281-9198

This noncompetitive, 35-mile bike ride takes in all 10 Willamette bridges. Families may opt to try the shorter, 12-mile route from the Fremont to the Marquam bridge. Proceeds benefit the Oregon Safe Kids Coalition and the Bicycle Transportation Alliance.

Clackamas County Fair

Clackamas County Fairgrounds,
Canby
266-1136

Livestock displays and rodeos are joined by a carnival and food and craft booths.

Clark County Fair

Clark County Fairgrounds,
Ridgefield, Wash.
360-573-1921

This fair features 4-H exhibits and a carnival, plus a special kids' park complete with pony rides, a petting zoo, and live entertainment.

Festa Italiana

Pioneer Courthouse Square
223-1613

An outdoor street festival complete with live music and dance entertainment, this event nonetheless focuses on Italian food. Kids like the pasta, pizza, and gelato.

Fiesta Mexicana

Legion Park, Woodburn
503-591-3365

This celebration spotlights the traditional folk dances, music, foods, and arts and crafts of Mexico.

Hawthorne Street Festival

Hawthorne Blvd.
774-2832

This funky neighborhood festival complements its funky surroundings. There's an art-car parade, side-walk art event for children, plus food, crafts, and entertainment.

Homowa Festival for African Arts

Cathedral Park
288-3025

An outdoor festival, this cultural event features traditional African music, dance, and storytelling performances.

India Festival

Pioneer Courthouse Square
223-1613

Indian dancing, music, crafts, and food take over the heart of downtown.

Kids' Biathlon

Location to be announced
641-3345 ext. 170

Child athletes (ages 6-14) compete in a kid-size biking/running race. Competitors receive T-shirts, finishers' ribbons, and refreshments.

KidsFair

Location to be announced
797-3430

Hosted by Fred Meyer, this event features interactive activities and demonstrations, plus stage entertainment for children throughout the day.

Laura Ingalls Wilder Weekend

Pomeroy Living History Farm,
Yacolt, Wash.
360-686-3537

Visit with a blacksmith, feed

chickens, and grind corn. Then watch a one-woman show starring everyone's favorite *Little House* character.

OBT Exposed!
South Park blocks
227-0977

Oregon Ballet Theatre rehearses publicly under tents outdoors for two weeks in preparation for the new season.

Obonfest
Oregon Buddhist Temple
234-9456

This Japanese-American Buddhist festival features ethnic foods, dancing, and crafts.

Oregon State Fair
Oregon State Fairgrounds, Salem
378-3247

With its big-name entertainers, cultural arts, 4-H exhibits, livestock displays, carnival, and special line-up of kids' activities, this is the mother of all fairs.

Tualatin Crawfish Festival
Tualatin Community Park
692-0780

A Tualatin tradition for more than 46 years, this annual celebration features live music, craft and food booths, and a crawfish-eating (shells and all!) contest.

AUTUMN

SEPTEMBER

Bones & Brew
Holladay Park
225-5555

An invitational cook-off showcasing tongue-tickling tidbits prepared by some of the nation's top barbecue chefs, this event also features hands-on kids' activities and entertainment.

Celebration of Cultures Festival
Downtown Gresham
667-0180

Hosted by the Gresham Sister City Association to honor its three sister cities, this open-air festival features multiethnic food, entertainment, and special activities.

Horst Mager's Rheinlander Oktoberfest
Oaks Amusement Park
232-3000

Bavarian food and music share space with the Kinderplatz's puppet shows, games, and craft activities.

Mount Angel Oktoberfest
Mount Angel
845-9440

Bavarian delicacies, music, dance, sporting events, and traditional arts and crafts entice the entire family, while the free Kindergarten, with its rides and entertainment, is a big hit with the kids.

One Stop Kids' Health Fair
Legacy Mt. Hood Medical Center, Gresham
335-3500

The hands-on activities here help promote safety and good health.

Ringling Bros. & Barnum & Bailey Circus
Rose Garden
321-3211

The nation's premier three-ring circus brings on the lions, tigers, and bears—plus clowns, acrobats, and a whole lot more.

Wintering-in Harvest Festival
Bybee House, Sauvie Island
222-1741

Watch demonstrations of candle-making and rope-making. Then sample fresh, pressed apple cider and tour the historic house.

OCTOBER

American Girls Fashion Show
Governor Hotel
228-4294 ext. 328

Bring your favorite doll to a dress-up tea party. Proceeds benefit the Oregon Symphony Music for Youth Program.

Fort Vancouver Candlelight Tour
Fort Vancouver
800-832-3599, 360-696-7655

Visit the historic fort when it's illuminated by candles.

Halloween Stable Spooktacular
Jenkins Estate, Aloha
642-3855

This Halloween event, with its carnival, crafts, and contests, is recommended for children age 8 and under.

Harvest Festival
Oregon Convention Center
800-321-1213

A celebration of American arts and crafts, with booth after booth of holiday gift ideas, this festival is more than a shopping spree, it's also a lot of fun: There's live entertainment, strolling musicians and jugglers, and artisan demonstrations.

Hood River Valley Harvest Festival
Hood River Expo Center
800-366-3530

The bounty of the fertile Hood River Valley—its produce and crafts—is showcased at this annual event.

Jenkins Estate Autumn Festival
Jenkins Estate, Aloha
642-3855

An annual fall event, this festival features hay rides, arts and crafts booths, music, and dancing.

Monster Manor
Northwest Childrens Theater & School
222-2190

Visit Monster Manor and meet Dracula, King Kong, the Mummy, and Wolfman. Fearless souls end up at Winnie-the-Pooh's Pumpkin Patch. Proceeds benefit Northwest Childrens Theater & School.

Portland Greek Festival
Holy Trinity Greek Orthodox Church
234-0468

Come to fill up on souvlaki, baklava, and other Greek specialties, and to enjoy Greek music and dancing.

Portland Marathon
Downtown Portland
226-1111

Kids are invited to join in the 2-mile Kids' Run. Other events include a 5-mile run, Mayor's Walk, and sports medicine and fitness fair.

Pumpkin Festival
Pomeroy Living History Farm, Yacolt, Wash.
360-686-3537

Feed chickens and goats, make scarecrows, wind through the hay maze, then take a hay ride to the pumpkin patch for a prize squash.

Salmon Festival
Oxbow Regional Park
797-1846

Celebrate the annual return of the migrating salmon with guided salmon-viewing walks, hands-on nature activities, cultural performances, music, and food.

Sauerkraut Festival
Downtown Scappoose
503-543-6895

A weekend family event with more than 100 food and craft booths, the Sauerkraut Festival also features pig races, mule rides, a petting zoo, fun run, and tours of the Steinfeld's sauerkraut plant.

WonderWalk
Locations vary
222-9434

Sponsored by the March of

Dimes, this mall pledge-walk includes activity stations for kids.

ZooBoo
Metro Washington Park Zoo
226-1561

This popular, two-week Halloween event centers on a haunted train ride. Games, crafts, and food entertain kids who are too young to enjoy getting spooked.

NOVEMBER

Christmas at Pittock Mansion
Pittock Mansion
823-3623

Pittock Mansion is all dolled up for the holidays in accordance with a different theme each year, some especially appropriate for children.

Christmas Tree Lighting
Pioneer Courthouse Square
223-1613
Join a chorus of carolers at the official lighting of Portland's Christmas tree.

Clackamette Gem & Rock Show
Oregon City High School
656-9959, 654-9584
This two-day gem and mineral show features specimens, finished jewelry, demonstrations, a fluorescent exhibit, and a kids' corner with a dig site, special activities, and crafts.

Columbia Gorge Model Railroad Show
2505 N. Vancouver
288-7246

Examine one of the nation's largest model railroad layouts—and hobnob with other hobbyists. As many as 30 different trains run each day during the railroad club's month-long open house.

Festival of Lights
The Grotto
254-7371

The largest choral festival in the Pacific Northwest, Festival of Lights showcases singers from 130 school, church, and civic choral groups. Performances are held in the Grotto's 600-seat chapel, which is known for its cathedral-quality acoustics. Outdoors, a walk-through lighting display depicts the story of the birth of Christ, and there are puppet shows and a petting zoo for young children.

Meier & Frank Holiday Parade
Downtown Portland
203-9166
Welcome the season with a post-Thanksgiving parade of floats, bands, celebrities, and—the guest of honor—Santa Claus.

Oregon Air Fair
Oregon Convention Center
800-547-6922
View military and coast guard

aircraft, plus helicopters, seaplanes, and hot-air balloons at this aviation event. Hands-on activities run the gamut from creating paper airplanes to operating flight simulators.

Portland Winter Ski & Snowboard Show
Expo Center
541-387-3700

Dozens of ski and snowboard vendors and resort representatives provide information about their goods and services. The accompanying swap meet is a great place to purchase used winter gear.

ScanFair
Portland State University
227-5004

Sponsored by the Scandinavian Heritage Foundation, this traditional holiday festival features all-day entertainment, craft activities for children, art demonstrations, food, and handcrafted items.

Singing Christmas Tree
Portland Civic Auditorium
557-TREE

Sixty children and 200 adult performers are joined by a live orchestra in this popular, annual holiday program.

Verboort Kraut & Sausage Feed Bazaar
Visitation Church, Verboort
357-3860

This weekend fund-raiser for the parish school features a sit-down dinner of homemade sausage, sauerkraut, and applesauce. Crafts, candy, and quilts are displayed for sale.

Wild Arts Festival Show and Sale
Montgomery Park
292-6855

Sponsored by Portland Audubon Society to benefit its educational programs, this showcase features the nature-related arts and crafts of various Northwest artisans. Activities for children include face-painting, hands-on crafts, and visits with kids' authors.

Wooden Toy Show
World Forestry Center
228-1367

Talented wooden-toy makers from throughout the Northwest display and sell their wares.

WINTER

DECEMBER

Alpenrose Storybook Lane
Alpenrose Dairy
244-1133

Visit the flocked, indoor fantasy forest and its baby farm animals. Meet Santa Claus, and stay to watch cartoons in the old opera house.

Best Christmas Pageant Ever
Lakewood Center for the Arts,
Lake Oswego
635-3901

This traditional holiday comedy tells the story of a band of brats who participate in a small-town Christmas pageant.

Christmas at Fort Vancouver
Fort Vancouver
800-832-3599, 360-696-7655

Enjoy traditional Scottish and Irish holiday music in a historic setting.

Festival of Lights Hanukkah Gift Fair
Mittleman Jewish Community Center
244-0111

There's lots to choose from here: books, fine art, jewelry, toys, children's clothing, and special Hanukkah supplies.

Festival of Trees
Oregon Convention Center
215-6070

This four-day show features 50 8-foot trees thematically decorated by sponsoring companies, groups, and individuals, plus gingerbread creations. Holiday entertainment is provided by area choirs and dance groups, and children can visit Santa.

Great American Train Show
Expo Center
285-7756

Hundreds of tables laden with hobby materials and gear attract train fanatics to this annual show and sale. Kids flock to the layout that's set up especially for their use.

Hanukkah Celebration
Mittleman Jewish Community Center
244-0111

This one-day fair features Klezmer music, dancing, food, and crafts. Join in the singing, and stay for the candle-lighting ceremony.

Hanukkah Menorah Lighting
Pioneer Courthouse Square
977-9947

In an annual tradition, a large menorah is erected in Pioneer Courthouse Square and Hanukkah candles are lit at public gatherings.

Holiday Cheer & Authors' Party
Oregon History Center
306-5200

One of the oldest and largest book signings in the nation, this event spotlights many of the region's finest authors and illustrators.

Holiday Toy Show
Children's Museum
823-2227

Come see this exhibit—a survey of the year's best and worst toys— before doing your holiday shopping.

International Christmas Tree Festival
World Forestry Center
228-1367

Seven Christmas trees, decorated by diverse cultural groups in keeping with their traditions, are on display at this holiday event. Music, singing, folk dancing, and demonstrations are other featured activities.

Kids' Holiday Concert
Arlene Schnitzer Concert Hall
228-4294

Join the Oregon Symphony in its annual celebration of the holiday season with music from around the world. Bring a bell to help Santa Claus find his way to town.

The Nutcracker
Civic Auditorium
227-0977

The Oregon Ballet Theatre's elegant production of *The Nutcracker* runs for three weeks with 22 performances.

Peacock Lane
SE Stark St. & Peacock Lane
234-4653

Plan to meet with a mob of gawkers on this street, where every house is done up in lights.

Portland Parade of Ships
Willamette & Columbia rivers
222-2223

Festively lit vessels ply the waters of the Columbia and Willamette rivers on select nights in season.

Queen Anne Victorian Mansion
1441 N. McClellan
283-3224

Over 1 million white lights are ablaze on the grounds of this 6,300-square-foot house.

Santa Land
Downtown Meier & Frank
203-9166

The 10th floor of the downtown Meier & Frank department store is transformed into a winter wonderland. Kids under 51 inches tall can ride the monorail for a bird's-eye view of Santa.

Shilo Inn Lighting Display
Shilo Inn Headquarters, Beaverton
641-6565

More than 95,000 lights, plus a 15-foot Santa Claus and Frosty the Snowman, turn this office building into a holiday spectacle.

Winter Wunderland
Portland International Raceway
232-3000

The racetrack is converted into a drive-by lighting display with animated characters and broadcast holiday music.

Woodcarvers' Show
World Forestry Center
228-1367

The Western Woodcarvers' Association displays its unique wooden creations, leads demonstrations, and offers useful tips.

Zoo Lights
Metro Washington Park Zoo
226-1561

This month-long display of thousands of lights and animated animal silhouettes delights visitors of all ages. Come for a train ride, entertainment, and refreshments. ■

Chapter 10
BASICS

Unless your child is a sleepy infant or gourmand teen-ager, you probably don't take him to restaurants expecting a relaxing four-course meal. In truth, the places that focus on families have found that the recipe for success features a heaping dollop of noisy commotion. It's high-energy, giddy, good-time activity—which thankfully masks poor table manners—but it's commotion nonetheless, and it precludes serious conversation and good digestion. So you don't go out to eat with the kids for the food or the ambience. You go out to have fun.

Each of the restaurants sampled below offers added value to families in particular—special playrooms, kids' menu as well as varied selections for parents, reasonable prices, and friendly, attentive service. Some up the ante with take-home treats, free meals, or fully equipped changing facilities. But beyond the crayons, finger foods, and high chairs, these restaurants have proven they know children. For parents it's most reassuring to realize your kids can't create any chaos these folks haven't seen before—and mopped up with a smile.

Aztec Willie & Joey Rose Taqueria
1501 NE Broadway, Portland 97232
280-8900
Lunch & dinner daily
Prices: $2-$9/adult meal;
$2-$4/child meal

Sister to two other local taquerias (Santa Fe and Mayas), Aztec Willie & Joey Rose is named for the owners' two young sons, who specified that "their" restaurant should feature a playroom. And so it does. A glassed-in area along the far wall is equipped with a child-size table and chairs, wooden toddler play kitchen, and a small, well-worn collection of toys.

Really, though, there's better entertainment elsewhere—at the cafeteria line. Hoist the little ones up so they can see the array of choices and watch the nimble-fingered chefs roll up hefty burritos. Adventurous kids should try the tamale plate. Picky eaters can stick to the safer quesadillas.

A popular neighborhood hangout, the restaurant is busiest on Friday nights after 6 pm. Even then the wait lasts only 20 minutes at most, and with the kids cavorting in the playroom, the time passes quickly.

One warning: The dining room's small, round glass tables and delicate, tippy metal chairs are more aesthetic than functional. Hold out for the largest table you can, then suggest to the children that they use their very best "restaurant" manners to avoid disaster.

Chevys
Five area locations, including
8400 SW Nimbus Ave.,
Beaverton 97008
(plus four other area locations)
626-7667
Lunch & dinner daily
Prices: $6-$13/adult meal;
$3.95/child meal

In a city where there are numerous successful restaurant chains that cater to families by offering satisfying meals at affordable prices (Red Robin, Stanford's, Chili's, Tony Roma's, and Olive Garden come to mind), Chevys is the big enchilada. The Mexican food here is good (the restaurant prides itself on using strictly fresh ingredients), and the festive south-of-the-border, anything-goes atmosphere particularly suits parents and their unpredictable tablemates. Yet, while other eateries also offer helium balloons and kids' placemat menus with games and take-home crayons, Chevys has something more: a tortilla machine. *(See also Active Play: Indoor Fun, Behind the Scenes.)*

Adults are just as fascinated as kids to watch it work, and have even been known to sneak a pinch or two from Junior's wad of dough to play with while awaiting dinner. If your little ones are too young for chips, request a basket of warm tortillas instead. But beware: You'll be hard pressed to refrain from spoiling your own appetite. Tortillas turn up yet again as the crispy cones of the free kiddie ice cream treats. And yet again, grown-ups wish they weren't.

The Beaverton Chevys—the region's largest, with a seating

capacity of 320—may be the best bet for families. Because it serves as a training facility for managers, its service is especially consistent and efficient. Perhaps even more important, it accepts reservations.

Chez José

2200 NE Broadway, Portland 97232
280-9888
8502 SW Terwilliger Blvd.,
Portland 97219
244-0007
Lunch & dinner daily
Prices: $4-$10/adult meal;
$2.50/child meal

Hip, healthful Mexican food is the specialty at Portland's two Chez José cafes, and the choices for refined palates are considerable: from fish tacos and chipotle-honey camarones to lime chicken enchiladas and squash enchiladas with peanut sauce.

Yet these trendy twin eateries have also made a conscious effort to appeal to tots' conservative tastebuds—with cheese quesadillas, bean burritos, and chimidogs—and have developed a loyal following among neighborhood families. For good reason: At Chez José, children under age 7 eat free from the kids' menu daily, 5-7 pm (That amounts to a savings of $2.50 per child.) Arrive during these hours, and your kids will likely make new friends among the tot dining set.

On weekdays the wait is brief, about 10 minutes; weekends are quite busy. Children like the zany, colorful decor and the noisy hustle-bustle. They're given crayons to

color with, and if you're in luck, the waiter will be able to scare up an Etch-a-Sketch or Magnadoodle. (The managers replace such toys with regularity, but they tend to disappear just as quickly.)

Cucina! Cucina! Italian Cafe

130 Center Ct., Portland 97227
238-9800
10205 SW Washington Square Rd.,
Tigard 97223
968-2000
Lunch & dinner daily
Prices: $6-$15/adult meal;
$3-$4/child meal

This fast-growing, Seattle-based chain of yuppie Italian eateries attracts families with more than its menu. Sure, kids (and many adults) favor pizza and pasta, but when you're greeted with a helium balloon and take-home toy, allowed to scribble on the menu and tablecloth, and invited to play with pizza dough, you're bound to look forward to a return visit. (Babies receive a special bag with bib, oyster crackers, and packaged wipe.)

Even at its slowest, Cucina! Cucina! seems to buzz with activity. Perhaps it's the colorful decor, the bicycles suspended from the ceiling (can you find the tricycle?), or the television sets tuned to sports games (Portland only). There's nothing staid about Cucina! Cucina! And should a child begin to squirm, a server may offer her a trip to visit the pizza chef and his two wood-burning ovens. Would she like to bake her doughy creation?

The only problem with the

Cucina! Cucina! formula is that it works so well. In Tigard, expect to wait 45 minutes for a table on weekdays, longer on weekends. If you can plan ahead, take advantage of the Telephone for a Table program. Call as you leave for the restaurant, and the hostess will add your name to the waiting list in advance.

Located adjacent to the Rose Garden, the Portland outlet is a zoo on event nights, but is relatively calm at other times. (Reservations are accepted for all groups on non-event nights.)

It's best to call ahead to inquire about the Rose Garden schedule; even if you don't mind a crowded restaurant, you might feel differently on confronting a crowded parking lot. Ask for a validation stamp when paying your restaurant tab, which entitles you to 2 1/2 hours of free parking in arena garages. On nights when the Trail Blazers play at home, the fee structure changes dramatically: You'll be charged $12.50 with validation to park in arena garages.

The Ivy House
1605 SE Bybee Blvd.,
Portland 97202
231-9528
Lunch & dinner daily, brunch on weekends
Prices: $5-$16/adult meal; $1/child meal

Open just a year, The Ivy House is the inspired creation of Brian and Lisa Quinn, two chefs who met at the California Culinary Institute and now have two young children. What the Quinns have created is what

they longed for as parents who enjoy fine dining: a charming restaurant that serves ambitious gourmet meals to discerning adults, and simple, conventional favorites to kids.

Located in a quaint, older house festooned with vines, the two-story restaurant has a main-floor dining room with a working fireplace and sun porch. Families have the upstairs to themselves. Four tables are set with white tablecloths and linen napkins, and a plastic, tot-size table commands one wall. The adjacent alcove is given over to top-quality toys: a Brio train set, dollhouse, play kitchen, and storybooks. If you're the only family upstairs, or you can reach agreement with neighboring diners, a television set with videocassette recorder is also available (it's hidden behind curtains when not in use).

Just outside the restroom, a counter-top outfitted as a changing table is stocked with disposable diapers and wipes, and a comfortable settee serves as a private nursing station. A smaller, downstairs playroom accommodates overflow families.

The children's menu is short but sweet: hot dog, hamburger, and noodles with butter. Older kids can order double portions or consult with the chef regarding other options, such as a grilled chicken breast with pasta. At brunch there's French toast, waffles, and scrambled eggs. Far more interesting are the seasonal adult selections, and even parents whose children are well-behaved may find themselves planning to return without the brood to give full attention to the food.

Jamie's Great Hamburgers

838 NW 23rd Ave., Portland 97210
248-6784
1337 NE Broadway, Portland 97232
335-0809
11900 SW Beaverton-Hillsdale Hwy.,
Beaverton 97005
643-1771
Breakfast, lunch, & dinner daily
Prices: $4-$7/adult meal (less for
breakfast); $1-$4/child meal

Once you've been to Jamie's you'll be soured on McDonald's forever. The Happy Meal and its sterile, plastic surroundings are no competition for these "Happy Days" retro soda fountains with their black-and-white linoleum, red bar stools and banquettes, and wholesome American food.

Drop a quarter in the jukebox and introduce your children to Elvis Presley. Then slip into a booth and order burgers all around. Vegetarians can opt for a Gardenburger or one of the entree salads. Kids' meals come stuffed into colorful cardboard cars with big fins, for which imaginative diners find numerous uses at home.

The service may not have that fast-food finesse, but the teen-agers on the wait staff are personable and accommodating: Want a milk shake instead of the small sundae? Sure. Need more root beer in your float? No problem. Their friendly, laid-back attitudes seem to go with the '50s-era surroundings.

Old Spaghetti Factory

0715 SW Bancroft St.,
Portland 97201
222-5375
Lunch & dinner daily
Prices: $5-$8/adult meal;
$3-$3.75/child meal

"Factory" is not a word usually associated with fine dining, which goes far in explaining this restaurant's success with families. The Old Spaghetti Factory has hit on a winning formula: simple, good food at reasonable prices; fanciful antique decor; and friendly, efficient service.

The flagship of a 30-restaurant chain, Portland's outlet on the Willamette seats 450 at capacity, and patrons regularly wait upwards of 45 minutes for a table at dinner time. Weekend evenings are especially busy. To avoid the crowds, families are encouraged to arrive before 6 pm, to visit for lunch, or to call ahead to assess the estimated wait. If you do get stuck in a long line, send your children upstairs where, in view of the lobby, they can watch G-rated videos and play video games.

Children choose from three pasta entrees at dinner. Kids under age 7 eat from colorful dinosaur plates and are treated to take-home plastic cups. If they're not won over by the view of the river or the authentic Council Crest trolley car (good luck getting a table inside!), they'll likely be impressed by the miniature loaf of bread that arrives on its own wooden board to be sliced by hand.

Old Wives' Tales

1300 E. Burnside, Portland 97214
238-0470
Breakfast, lunch, & dinner daily
Prices: $4-$12.50/adult meal (less
for breakfast); $1-$3/child meal

Your first inkling that Old Wives'
Tales emphasizes nutritious, alterna-
tive foods comes when you notice
the candy jar at the cash register by
the front door. It's full of sugar-free
lollipops. Of course, most kids don't
notice the difference, as long as
they can choose for themselves.
Which is precisely why this restaurant works for families: The choices
are innumerable. And then there's
the legendary playroom . . .

A brightly painted circus-train
climbing structure equipped with
navigational controls, peek-a-boo
windows, stairs, and a tunnel occupies a carpeted corner room. At first
glance the playroom appears best
suited to preschoolers, but when the
restaurant's busy, it's a free-for-all,
and parents are encouraged to
supervise the chaos lest a toddler
end up at the bottom of the heap.
Families are virtually guaranteed a
table near the playroom; the far half
of the main dining room, as well as
a more private room at the rear, are
reserved for others.

When the kids are ready to
break for some food, they may have
difficulty making up their minds—so
will you. The menus at each meal
fill two pages, with the options for
children ranging from sandwiches
and natural turkey franks to burritos
and noodles in parmesan cream
sauce. The best selection for picky

eaters is the salad bar, which features daily ethnic specialty preparations plus fresh rolls, wheat crackers, and rice cakes.

Lunch time, when many local
business people come to dine, and
brunch, a meal favored by families,
are hectic at Old Wives' Tales. Come
virtually any evening to avoid a
noisy crowd.

The Original Pancake House

SW Barbur Blvd. & 24th Ave.,
Portland 97219
246-9007
Hours: Wed-Sun, 7 am-3 pm
Prices: $5-$9/adult meal;
$4.50/child meal

Founded in 1953 in a cozy little
house on Barbur Blvd., The Original
Pancake House hasn't changed much
in the ensuing 40 years (though 75
franchises now dot the nation), and
the owners—and die-hard regulars—
like it that way. The intimate, homey
quarters seat just 72 patrons, almost
as many as are often found waiting
patiently in the adjoining sun porch
for as long as an hour.

That's the major drawback
here—the wait. Plan your visit to
follow the lunch rush, but don't
count on outfoxing the early-morning crowd either. Eager diners fill
the porch even at dawn. Best to
come armed and ready, with books
and lap games. The hostess is likewise prepared; ask her to unearth
the coloring books and crayons she
keeps tucked in her desk.

The dining room, with its fireplace and country-style wood furnishings, puts one in mind of

Grandma's house. And then the food arrives to complete the impression. "Generous" may not go far enough in describing the portions. The house specialty, a fluffy 2.5-inch-thick apple pancake, commands an entire dinner plate.

Entrees this big are meant to be shared, and the Pancake House almost encourages family-style dining by offering only one menu item especially for children: three buttermilk pancakes with sausage or an egg. (Be aware, however, that servers levy a charge of $1.50 on each person over age 6 who splits an entree.)

The Original Portland Ice Cream Parlour & Restaurant
1613 NE Weidler St.,
Portland 97232
281-1271
Lunch & dinner daily
Prices: $4-$9/adult meal;
$2.50-$4/child meal;
$2-$6/ice cream treats

Even if you're not part of a party at The Original Portland Ice Cream Parlour, you might as well be. Patterned after the Farrell's restaurants many parents remember from their childhoods, the old-fashioned Gay '90s decor; enormous, gooey ice cream confections; and birthday-party fanfares will leave a sticky chocolate smile on your face.

Eat a light entree to concentrate on the sundaes and shakes, or come just for dessert. The kids won't care what they're eating; they'll be too busy enjoying all the hubbub. Sirens, bells, and drums announce each birthday celebrant while the

teen-age waiters and waitresses race with great tubs of ice cream to the table, then tease and taunt the honoree for all to hear. Ask your server to sprinkle your kiddie sundaes with plastic zoo animals, and your children will feel special, too.

Birthday parties have to reserve months ahead for weekend evenings, when the place is hopping. Families may prefer to come on a weekend afternoon or in the early evening when the atmosphere isn't quite so frenzied.

Worse than a supermarket checkout aisle is the candy-store display adjacent to the waiting area. Choose your poison: Kids who won't be diverted by a sucker can play video games until your table's ready.

A Place to Eat
15230 SW Sequoia Parkway,
Tigard 97224
968-6900
Lunch & dinner daily, brunch on Sunday
Prices: $5.95-$8.75/adult meal;
$3-$4.95/child meal; discounts
for seniors

Tucked into a corner of a Tigard industrial park, it's a good thing A Place to Eat is off the beaten path. Closer to home, and one's waistline would disclose the effects. Based on a smorgasbord approach to dining, A Place to Eat spotlights a nutritious spread of fresh produce, hot entrees, and home-baked goods reminiscent of the groaning buffet tables aboard cruise ships.

Teach your children about the haywire connection between eyes and stomach, or they'll pile their plates with more than they can manage (you'll be tempted to do likewise). Your kids will want to take charge, and you really can't complain—at least they're eating. For the most part, the choices are healthful: salad bar with 43 toppings, focaccia (tell the kids it's pizza), two pasta dishes, a baked potato bar, and rotisserie meats, plus hot muffins, chocolate mousse, brownies, apple crisp, and serve-yourself soft ice cream for dessert. Choose from made-to-order omelets and Belgian waffles at brunch, then waddle home.

The attractive, newish restaurant, which seats about 200 (add 100 in summer on the outdoor patio), is spacious and airy. Avoid the noon hour on Sundays, when churchgoers mob the place after services and the wait approaches 30 minutes, or weekdays, when local office workers lunch here. Come for an early dinner most nights, and have A Place to Eat to yourselves.

Almost as fun as a return trip to the buffet is a trip to the space-age restrooms, where doors, faucets, hand dryers—even toilets—operate automatically. Another unusual (and useful) accessory is the special infant high chair. Made of metal mesh, the stand cradles a car-seat carrier at chair level, so Baby isn't left to grovel under the table or rock-and-roll on top. ■

I f you think we're lucky to be parents in a region that's overflowing with specialty stores that cater to kids' needs, whims, and dreams, think how lucky our children are! Here are some of the best places to find quality kids' clothing, toys, books, and furniture:

DOWNTOWN PORTLAND

CLOTHING

Gap Kids
Pioneer Place, Portland 97204
228-8115

Gymboree Store
Pioneer Place, Portland 97204
224-2075

Scooter & Beanbag
Pioneer Place, Portland 97204
226-7951

TOYS

Finnegan's Toys & Gifts
922 SW Yamhill St., Portland 97205
221-0306

BOOKS

Borders Books & Music
708 SW 3rd Ave., Portland 97204
220-5911

The Looking Glass Bookstore
318 SW Taylor St., Portland 97204
227-4760

Portland State Bookstore
1880 SW 6th Ave., Portland 97201
226-2631

Powell's City of Books
1005 W. Burnside, Portland 97209
228-4651

RiverPlace Book Merchants
0315 SW Montgomery, Suite 340,
Portland 97201
248-5674

MATERNITY

Mimi Maternity
Pioneer Place, Portland 97204
241-1536

NORTHWEST PORTLAND

CLOTHING

Daisy Kingdom
207 NW Park Ave., Portland 97209
222-4281

Hanna Andersson
327 NW 10th Ave., Portland 97209
321-5275

Mako
732 NW 23rd Ave., Portland 97210
274-9081

Ragazzi
Montgomery Park,
2701 NW Vaughn, Portland 97210
274-9681 (by appointment)

TOYS

Child's Play
907 NW 23rd Ave., Portland 97210
224-5586

Christmas at the Zoo
118 NW 23rd Ave., Portland 97210
223-4048

BOOKS

Catalyst Booksellers
2332 NW Irving St., Portland 97210
221-4224 (by appointment)

New Renaissance Book Shop
1338 NW 23rd Ave., Portland 97210
224-4929

NORTHEAST PORTLAND

CLOTHING

Gymboree Store
Lloyd Center, Portland 97232
281-6892

Mako
1425 NE Broadway, Portland 97232
331-0446

Old Navy Clothing Co.
Jantzen Beach Center,
Portland 97217
289-9086

RESALE/CONSIGNMENT CLOTHING

A-2-Z Kidz, Inc.
1590 NE 172nd Ave., Portland 97230
408-8648

Gingerbread Express
4410 NE Tillamook St.,
Portland 97212
284-2908

Granny's Baby Booty
5916 N. Greely Ave., Portland 97217
285-8447

Just 4 Kids
1925 NE 42nd Avd., Portland 97213
249-7556

Zanzibar
740 N. Killingsworth, Portland 97217
283-7797

TOYS

The Disney Store
Lloyd Center, Portland 97232
249-8311

Kay-Bee Toy & Hobby Shop
Lloyd Center, Portland 97232
284-2997

Teddy Bears Picnic & Paper Place
1724 NE Broadway, Portland 97232
281-6729

Toys R Us
Jantzen Beach Center,
Portland 97217
289-4691
Lloyd Center, Portland 97232
335-5955

BOOKS

A Children's Place
1631 NE Broadway, Portland 97232
284-8294

Barnes & Noble Booksellers
1231 NE Broadway, Portland 97232
335-0201
Jantzen Beach Center,
Portland 97217
283-2800

Broadway Books
1714 NE Broadway, Portland 97232
284-1726

Powell's at PDX
Portland International Airport,
Portland 97218
249-1950

Tower Books
1307 NE 102nd Ave.,
Portland 97220
253-3116

FURNITURE

A. Jay's Baby Shoppe
12435 NE Glisan St.,
Portland 97230
254-0991

MATERNITY

Motherhood Maternity
Lloyd Center, Portland 97232
249-0373

PARTY SUPPLIES

Michaels
4401 NE 122nd Ave.,
Portland 97216
257-0704

The Paper Tree
2916 NE Broadway, Portland 97232
284-4741

SOUTHWEST PORTLAND

TOYS

Thinker Toys
7882 SW Capitol Hwy.,
Portland 97219
245-3936

The Big Mouse
The Water Tower at Johns Landing,
5331 SW Macadam Ave.,
Portland 97201
241-8399

BOOKS

Annie Bloom's
7834 SW Capitol Hwy.,
Portland 97219
246-0053

Water Tower Books
The Water Tower at Johns Landing,
5331 SW Macadam Ave.,
Portland 97201
228-0290

RESALE/CONSIGNMENT CLOTHING

Kids House
7780 SW Capitol Hwy.,
Portland 97219
246-1663

Second to None
6308 SW Capitol Hwy.,
Portland 97201
244-0071

PARTY SUPPLIES
The Party Place
8904 SW Canyon Rd.,
Portland 97225
292-8875

SOUTHEAST PORTLAND/ CLACKAMAS

CLOTHING
Gap Kids
Clackamas Town Center,
Portland 97266
654-3661

Gymboree Store
Clackamas Town Center,
Portland 97266
654-0927

Water Babies
8085 SE 13th Ave., Portland 97202
232-6039

RESALE/CONSIGNMENT CLOTHING

2-Cute
12441 SE Powell Blvd.,
Portland 97236
761-1518

Kid's Closet
10572 SE Washington St.,
Portland 97216
254-0610

The Mulberry Bush
16144 SE 82nd Ave.,
Clackamas 97015
557-3557

Oogla*Plentium
3437 SE Belmont St.,
Portland 97214
234-7933

The Stork Club
7817 SE Stark St., Portland 97215
257-1316

SHOES
Stride Rite
Clackamas Town Center,
Portland 97266
653-7970

TOYS
The Disney Store
Clackamas Town Center,
Portland 97266
786-4020

Imaginarium
Clackamas Town Center,
Portland 97266
786-9640

Kay-Bee Toy & Hobby Shop
Clackamas Town Center,
Portland 97266
652-1472
Mall 205, Portland 97206
253-7092

Kids at Heart
3435 SE Hawthorne Blvd.,
Portland 97214
231-2954

Learning Palace
Mall 205, Portland 97216
251-1833

The OPB Store of Knowledge
Clackamas Town Center,
Portland 97266
654-6960

Toys R Us
12535 SE 82nd Ave.,
Clackamas 97015
659-5163

BOOKS

Barnes & Noble Booksellers
9078 SE Sunnyside Rd.,
Clackamas 97015
794-9262

Powell's on Hawthorne
3747 SE Hawthorne Blvd.,
Portland 97214
238-1668

FURNITURE

American the Beautiful Dreamer for Kids
Clackamas Town Center,
Portland 97266
786-4661

Burlington Coat Factory
10506 SE 82nd Ave., Portland 97226
774-8955

Tidee-Didee Infant Department
6011 SE 92nd Ave., Portland 97266
775-4729

MATERNITY

Generations
4029 SE Hawthorne Blvd.,
Portland 97214
233-8130

Motherhood Maternity
Clackamas Town Center,
Portland 97266
652-2450

PARTY SUPPLIES

Current Factory Outlet
11364 SE 82nd Ave.,
Portland 97266
653-4023

Decorette Shop
5338 SE Foster Rd., Portland 97206
774-3760

Lippman Co.
2727 SE Grand Ave., Portland 97202
239-7007

Party City
8664 SE Sunnyside Rd.,
Clackamas 97015
653-3500

Party Depot
10540 SE Washington,
Portland 97216
252-6032

The Party Place
10101 SE Stark St., Portland 97216
252-3455

BEAVERTON/ HILLSBORO/ ALOHA

CLOTHING

Lads & Lassies Frocks & Britches
11651 SW Beaverton-Hillsdale Hwy.,
Beaverton 97005
626-6578

RESALE/CONSIGNMENT CLOTHING

Kuddly Kids
18280 SW Tualatin Valley Hwy.,
Aloha 97006
848-6046

Wee Three
14330 SW Allen Blvd.,
Beaverton 97005
644-5953

TOYS

Learning Palace
3861 SW 117th Ave.,
Beaverton 97005
644-9301

Learning World
3275 SW Cedar Hills Blvd.,
Beaverton 97005
643-6538

Ludeman's Inner Kingdom
12675 SW Canyon Rd.,
Beaverton 97006
646-6409

Small World Surprise
3075 SW Cedar Hills Blvd.,
Beaverton 97006
646-3202

Teddy Bears Picnic & Paper Place
11677 SW Beaverton-Hillsdale Hwy.,
Beaverton 97005
643-9255

BOOKS

Barnes & Noble Booksellers
18300 NW Evergreen Pkwy.,
Beaverton 97006
645-3046

Borders Books & Music
2605 SW Cedar Hills Blvd.,
Beaverton 97005
644-6164

Powell's Books
8725 SW Cascade Ave.,
Beaverton 97008
643-3131

FURNITURE

Segal's for Children
14356 SW Allen Blvd.,
Beaverton 97005
626-1010

PARTY SUPPLIES

Current Factory Outlet
2770 SW Cedar Hills Blvd.,
Beaverton 97005
646-2822

Michaels
2151 SE Tualatin Valley Hwy.,
Hillsboro 97123
640-8216

Michaels
4955 SW Western Ave.,
Beaverton 97005
646-8385

Party Depot
8620 SW Hall Blvd.,
Beaverton 97005
646-3145

Snead's Party Time
14105 SW Tualatin Valley Hwy.,
Beaverton 97005
641-6778

OREGON CITY/ MILWAUKIE

RESALE/CONSIGNMENT CLOTHING

Kids Collection
10613 SE Main St., Milwaukie 97222
654-7556

Kids Stuff
10527 SE 42nd Ave.,
Milwaukie 97222
653-0354

Kids Zone
17419 SE McLoughlin Blvd.,
Milwaukie 97267
653-5158

We Love Kids
11200 SE Fuller Rd.,
Milwaukie 97222
775-9946

BOOKS

Oregon Book Co.
1900 SE McLoughlin Blvd.,
Oregon City 97045
657-0706

MATERNITY

Pickles 'n Ice Cream
15717 SE McLoughlin Blvd.,
Milwaukie 97267
659-1003

PARTY SUPPLIES

Michaels
1990 SE McLoughlin Blvd.,
Oregon City 97045
655-3488

GRESHAM

CLOTHING

Kids Mart
610 NW Eastman Pkwy.,
Gresham 97030
669-0252

Lil' Britches
325 N. Main Ave., Gresham 97030
492-9378

RESALE/CONSIGNMENT CLOTHING

Child of Mine
40 NW 2nd St., Gresham 97030
667-2245

Kids Count Two
64 NE Division St., Gresham 97030
667-3416

TOYS

Learning Palace
818 NW Eastman Pkwy.,
Gresham 97030
661-0865

Replay Toys
29 E. Powell Blvd., Gresham 97030
667-6686

Toy Bear Ltd.
130 N. Main Ave., Gresham 97030
661-5310

BOOKS

Childrens Books
331 N. Main Ave., Gresham 97030
661-5887

FURNITURE

The Stork's Nest Baby Boutique
227 N. Main Ave., Gresham 97030
666-6289

PARTY SUPPLIES

Current Factory Outlet
2587 SE Burnside, Gresham 97030
661-5031

Michaels
2101 E. Burnside, Gresham 97030
661-1469

LAKE OSWEGO

CLOTHING

Bambini's Children's Boutique
16353 Bryant Rd.,
Lake Oswego 97034
635-7661

Hanna Andersson Outlet Store
7 Monroe Pkwy.,
Lake Oswego 97035
697-1953

Kids for Sure
140 "A" Ave., Lake Oswego 97035
636-9043

TOYS

Bridges a Toy & Book Store
218 "A" Ave., Lake Oswego 97035
699-1322

Red Door Cottage
425 2nd St., Lake Oswego 97035
635-3520

FURNITURE

Baby Bridges Boutique
204 "A" Ave., Lake Oswego 97035
699-0550

Skip to My Room
14990 SW Bangy Rd.,
Lake Oswego 97035
624-3686

PARTY SUPPLIES

Michaels
17880 SW Lower Boones Ferry Rd.,
Lake Oswego 97035
684-8255

Paper Caper
16829 SW 65th Dr.,
Lake Oswego 97035
620-9460

TIGARD/ TUALATIN/ SHERWOOD

CLOTHING

Gap Kids
Washington Square, Tigard 97223
620-3965

Gymboree Store
Washington Square, Tigard 97223
620-2898

RESALE/CONSIGNMENT CLOTHING

Frocks-N-Britches
12955 SW Pacific Hwy.,
Tigard 97223
624-7782

Karen's Kreations
11945 SW Pacific Hwy.,
Tigard 97223
639-7643

Kids Choice
14255 SW 114th Ave.,
Tigard 97224
684-9841

The Mulberry Bush
19279 SW Martinazzi Ave.,
Tualatin 97062
691-1119

SHOES

Stride Rite
Washington Square, Tigard 97223
639-3399

TOYS

The Disney Store
Washington Square, Tigard 97223
624-1305

Imaginarium
Washington Square, Tigard 97223
624-8255

The OMSI Science Store
Washington Square, Tigard 97223
684-5202

Toys R Us
10065 SW Cascade Blvd.,
Tigard 97223
620-9779

Warner Bros. Studio Store
Washington Square, Tigard 97223
620-0405

BOOKS

B. Dalton
Washington Square, Tigard 97223
620-3007

Barnes & Noble Booksellers
10206 SW Washington Square Rd.,
Tigard 97223
598-9455

Borders Books & Music
16920 SW 72nd Ave., Tigard 97223
968-7576

The Dinkey-Bird Bookstore
250 NW Railroad St.,
Sherwood 97140
625-1655

MATERNITY

Motherhood Maternity
Washington Square, Tigard 97223
639-0400

PARTY SUPPLIES

Decorette Shop
11945 SW Pacific Hwy.,
Tigard 97223
620-5100

Party City
9160-A Hall Blvd., Tigard 97223
684-5400

Party Mart
16200 SW Pacific Hwy.,
Tigard 97224
639-9414

COSTUMES

Judy's Costumes
12705 SW Pacific Hwy., Tigard
97223
620-6488

VANCOUVER, WASH.

RESALE/CONSIGNMENT CLOTHING

Children's Trading Co.
703 "E" St., Washougal, WA 98671
360-835-8683

Once Upon a Child
11505 NE 4th Plain Rd.,
Vancouver, WA 98662
360-253-7742

Spanky's
812 Main St., Vancouver, WA 98660
360-693-5115

Taylor's Closet
6204 E. Hwy. 99,
Vancouver, WA 98665
360-695-2828

TOYS

Learning World
13503 SE Mill Plain Blvd.,
Vancouver, WA 98684
360-896-8961

BOOKS

Peaceable Kingdom
204 W. Evergreen Blvd.,
Vancouver, WA 98660
360-694-5508

The Story Station
14415 SE Mill Plain Blvd.,
Vancouver, WA 98661
360-896-6784

PARTY SUPPLIES

Michaels
7701 NE Vancouver Plaza Dr.,
Vancouver, WA 98662
360-892-3155

Party Factory
10512 E. Mill Plain Blvd.,
Vancouver, WA 98684
360-253-3838

SHOPPING MALLS

Beaverton Mall
3205 SW Cedar Hills Blvd.,
Beaverton
643-6563

Single-level mall with 80 stores and small food court. Restrooms equipped with changing facilities. Hands-on activities for children scheduled monthly. Anchor stores include: Emporium, G.I. Joe's, PayLess Drugs, Ross Dress for Less, and Tower Records. Children's stores include: Game Trader, Learning World, Magic Fest, and Small World Surprise.

Clackamas Town Center
12000 SE 82nd Ave.,
Portland 97266
653-6913

Most-visited mall in Oregon features 185 specialty shops and services, five-theater cinema complex, food court with 22 eateries, and an ice-skating center. New soft-sculpture play area called the Lunch Box opens in spring 1997. Double and infant rental strollers available. Anchor stores include: J.C. Penney, Meier & Frank, Montgomery Ward, Nordstrom, and Sears. Children's stores include: America the Beautiful Dreamer for Kids, The Disney Store, Gap Kids, Gymboree, Kay-Bee Toys & Hobby Shop, OPB Store of Knowledge, and Stride Rite.

Jantzen Beach Supercenter
1405 Jantzen Beach Center,
Portland 97217
286-9103

Site of amusement park until 1970; original, hand-carved wooden carousel (fee: $1/ride) in enclosed mall, plus 25-30 specialty stores. Sixteen superstores on grounds, including: Barnes & Noble Booksellers, Computer City, Copeland's Sports, Home Depot, Linens 'N Things, Old Navy Clothing Co., REI, Ross Dress for Less, Sleep Country USA, Staples, and Toys R Us.

Lloyd Center
2201 Lloyd Center, Portland 97232
282-2511

Three-story mall with more than 200 specialty stores, a food court with 16 eateries, eight-theater cinema complex, and an ice-skating rink. Children ages 2-10 enrolled in Kid's Club receive free newsletter, gifts, and coupons. Anchor stores include: J.C. Penney, Marshalls, Meier & Frank, Nordstrom, and Toys R Us. Children's stores include: The Disney Store, Gymboree, Kay-Bee Toys & Hobby Shop, and Toys R Us.

Mall 205
9900 SE Washington,
Portland 97216
255-5805

Single-level mall with 80 specialty stores and a five-theater cinema complex. Anchor stores include: Emporium, Montgomery Ward, and PayLess Drug. Especially for kids: The Learning Palace and Aladdin's Castle, a video arcade.

Pioneer Place
700 SW Fifth Ave., Portland 97204
228-5800

Four-story, glass-enclosed mall
with more than 70 specialty stores
and the Northwest's only Saks Fifth
Avenue department store. Food
court with 17 eateries features cascading fountain/wishing well.
Restrooms equipped with changing
facilities. Children's stores include:
Gap Kids, Gymboree, and Scooter &
Beanbag.

Washington Square
9585 SW Washington Square Rd.,
Tigard 97281
639-8860

Popular mall with 140 specialty
stores and five anchor stores: J.C.
Penney, Meier & Frank, Mervyn's,
Nordstom, and Sears. Food court
with 10 eateries, plus 15 other food
services throughout. Single and dou-
ble rental strollers available.
Children's stores include: The
Disney Store, Gap Kids, Gymboree,
Imaginarium, The OMSI Science
Store, Stride Rite, and Warner Bros.
Studio Store.

Vancouver Mall
8700 NE Vancouver Mall Dr.,
Vancouver, WA 98662
360-892-6255

Food court hosts region's largest
mall kids' club every Tuesday,
10:30-11:15 am. Free entertainment
by theater troupes, magicians, puppeteers, clowns, jugglers, and storytellers. Mall houses more than 140
specialty stores, plus public library.
Anchor stores include: J.C. Penney,

Meier & Frank, Mervyn's,
Nordstrom, and Sears. Especially for
kids: Kay-Bee Toy & Hobby Shop
and The Tilt, a video arcade. ■

Portland Parent

P.O. Box 80040, Portland 97280
638-1049

Portland Parent, a monthly newsmagazine, is the metro area's most comprehensive source of information about what to do and where to go with children.

Published since 1991 by award-winning Northwest Parent Publishing, and available by subscription or for free at many family-oriented businesses (e.g., Toys R Us and Target stores), *Portland Parent* offers a half-dozen regular features: a monthly pull-out calendar of local events for children; detailed activity listings; and local news and resource bulletins for families. Articles address a wide range of issues that affect parents and children in the Northwest.

Special supplements are highlighted throughout the year, including A New Arrival (February and August); the Family Phone Book (March); Education Directory (November); and the A to Z Holiday Buying Guide (December).

A committed and knowledgeable staff of editors, advertising sales representatives, and subscription and distribution coordinators is available to address your needs and concerns. Feel free to call anytime with questions and suggestions.

Community Service Numbers

- **Emergency:** 911
- **Poison Center:** 494-8968
- **Child Abuse Hotline:** 731-3100
- **Metro Child Care Resource & Referral:** 253-5000
- **Multnomah County Health Crisis Line:** 215-7082
- **Oregon SafeNet for Women, Children & Teens:** 800-723-3638
- **Portland Women's Crisis Line:** 235-5333 (hotline); 232-9751 (office)

Boys & Girls Aid Society of Oregon

- **Clackamas County:** 654-0025
- **Multnomah County:** 222-9661
- **Washington County:** 641-7820

Services to Children & Families

- **Clackamas County:** 657-2112
- **Multnomah County:** 238-7555 (hotline)
- **Washington County:** 648-8951

QUICK INDEX

Birthday Party Specials

Camping Facilities

Classes/Workshops

Field Trips

QUICK INDEX

■ Tours of Local Businesses
(see Active Play: Indoor Fun, Behind the Scenes)
■ View from Atwater's Restaurant
■ Vintage Trolleys
■ Wading Pools
(select Portland parks)
■ Whale Watching, Newport

Great for Preteens & Teen-agers

■ American Advertising Museum
■ Bicycling
■ Boating & Rafting
■ Bonneville Lock & Dam
■ The Children's Course
■ City Paintball
■ Clackamas County Museum of History
■ Dive-in Movies, Portland Pools
■ Essential Forces Fountain, Rose Garden Arena
■ Family Fun Center
■ Fishing
■ Glow-in-the-Dark Bowling, Tigard Bowl & Brunswick Sunset Lanes
■ Hit & Run Paintball
■ Horseback Riding
■ Hot-Air Balloon Ride, Vista Balloon Adventures
■ Imago Theatre
■ Laserport
■ Little League Softball World Series, Alpenrose Dairy
■ Magic Mile Sky Super Express Chairlift, Timberline
■ Malibu Grand Prix
■ Miniature Golf *(outdoor & indoor)*
■ Miracle Theatre Group
■ Mount Hood SkiBowl Action Park

■ Mount St. Helens Cinedome Theater
■ The Musical Theatre Co.
■ Oregon History Center
■ Oregon Maritime Center & Museum
■ Oregon Museum of Science & Industry
■ OMSI's Laser Light Shows
■ Portland Art Museum
■ Portland's Broadway Theater Season
■ Portland Forest Dragons
■ Portland Opera
■ Portland Pride
■ Portland Power
■ Portland Rock Gym
■ Portland Rockies
■ Portland Trail Blazers
■ Portland Winter Hawks
■ Quarter-Midget Racing, Alpenrose Dairy
■ Quest Nightclub
■ Ripley's Believe It or Not!, Newport
■ Saturday Flight, Hillsboro Aviation
■ Shakespeare in the Parks
■ Skate Night at the Coliseum
■ Skateboard Parks *(various locations)*
■ Snow Skiing/Snowboarding
■ State of Oregon Sports Hall of Fame
■ Stoneworks Inc. Climbing Gym
■ Thrill-Ville USA
■ Teen Night, North Clackamas Aquatic Park
■ Tualatin Island Greens
■ Tygres Heart Shakespeare Co.
■ Ultrazone
■ U.S. Bank Broadway Series

- Portland Audubon Society
- Silver Falls State Park

- Tryon Creek State Park

- Tualatin Hills Nature Park
- Willamette Greenway Trail

Parks with Picnic Facilities

- Blue Lake Regional Park
- Champoeg State Heritage Area
- Columbia Park
- Cook Park
- Hoyt Arboretum
- Ibach Park
- Mount Tabor Park
- Oxbow Regional Park
- Rose Garden Children's Park
- Silver Falls State Park

Restaurants

- Aztec Willie & Joey Rose Taqueria
- Chevys
- Chez José
- Cucina! Cucina! Italian Cafe
- The Ivy House
- Jamie's Great Hamburgers
- Old Spaghetti Factory
- Old Wives' Tales
- The Original Pancake House
- The Original Portland Ice Cream Parlour & Restaurant
- A Place to Eat

INDEX

INDEX

G

H

I

N

O

P

INDEX

INDEX

FUNDRAISING

Raise money for your school or organization with books from Northwest Parent Publishing.

Schools, clubs, employee groups, and other organizations can raise funds by selling the books published by Northwest Parent Publishing.

Call (503) 638-1049 in Portland for information about fundraising opportunities, or write to:

Northwest Parent Publishing
2107 Elliott Ave., Suite 303
Seattle, WA 98121

OUT AND ABOUT PORTLAND WITH KIDS FEEDBACK

We are interested in your comments on using this guide. Did we give you the information you needed? Did you have a terrific experience at one of the places we suggested? Or a disaster? Also, tell us about any places we left out. Give us the details!!!!

_____

_____

_____

_____

_____

_____

_____

_____

_____

_____

_____

_____

_____

Your name _____

Address _____

City/State/Zip _____

Phone ( ) _____

Mail to: Northwest Parent Publishing, Inc.
2107 Elliott Ave., Suite 303, Seattle, WA 98121

Outstanding Resources for Parents
From Northwest Parent Publishing

BOOKS

Going Places: Family Getaways in the Pacific Northwest
The award-winning travel guide for families, covering Washington, Oregon, British Columbia, and Northern Idaho. Describes the hotels, dude ranches, resorts, and B&B's that are best for parents and children, as well as roadside attractions, family-friendly places to eat, and what to see and do once you arrive at your destination. 374 pages $14.95   _____

Out and About Seattle with Kids
The award-winning guide that tells where to go and what to see and do with kids around the Puget Sound region. An invaluable resource for Seattle-area residents as well as out-of-town visitors. 213 pages. $12.95   _____

NEWSMAGAZINES

Northwest Parent publishes five award-winning regional news-magazines for parents. Each publication includes a comprehensive calendar of events, information about local resources and services, and articles about local issues of interest to parents and others concerned about children. Subscription includes special annual supplements: *The Education Directory, A Guide to Private and Public Schools*, Birthdays! *A Guide to Birthday Fun*, and *The Activity Guide: Information about After-school and Weekend Classes.* A one-year subscription costs $9
(special offer with this coupon–regular price $15).   _____

Yes, send me one year (12 issues) of:
Portland Parent   _____
Puget Sound Parent   _____
Seattle's Child   _____
Eastside Parent   _____
Snohomish County Parent   _____
                                              Subtotal   _____
        Washington state residents add sales tax (sub-total x .086)   _____
                                              TOTAL   _____

Your Name _____

Address _____

City/State/Zip _____

Phone _____

Mail coupon to: Northwest Parent Publishing, Inc.
                2107 Elliott Ave., Suite 303
                Seattle, WA 98121

Or call (206) 441-0191 in Seattle or (503) 638-1049 in Portland

Prices include shipping and handling. Allow 3 weeks for delivery.
Satisfaction guaranteed or your money back.